Tender Maps

*Travels
in Search
of the
Emotions
of Place*

Tender Maps

Alice Maddicott

1 3 5 7 9 10 8 6 4 2

First published in 2023 by September Publishing

Copyright © Alice Maddicott 2023

The right of Alice Maddicott to be identified as the author of this work has been asserted by her in accordance with the Copyright Designs and Patents Act 1988.

Typeset by RefineCatch Limited, www.refinecatch.com
Printed in Poland on paper from responsibly managed, sustainable sources by Hussar Books

ISBN 9781914613326
Ebook ISBN 9781914613333

September Publishing
www.septemberpublishing.org

Contents

To Hannah Little, kindest of people

'Delight is a secret. And the secret is this: to grow quiet and listen; to stop thinking, stop moving, almost to stop breathing; to create an inner stillness in which, like mice in a deserted house, capacities and awareness too wayward and too fugitive for everyday use may delicately emerge. Oh, welcome them home! For these are the long-lost children of the human mind. Give them close and loving attention, for they are weakened by centuries of neglect. In return they will open your eyes to a new world within the known world, they will take your hand, as children do, and bring you where life is always nascent, day always dawning. Suddenly and miraculously, as you walk home in the dark, you are aware of the insubstantial shimmering essence that lies within appearances; the air is filled with expectancy, alive with meaning; the stranger, gliding by in the lamp-lit street, carries silently past you in the night the whole mystery of his life . . .

Delight is a mystery. And the mystery is this: to plunge boldly into the brilliance and immediacy of living, at the same time as utterly surrendering to that which lies beyond space and time; to see life translucently . . .'

Alan McGlashan, *The Savage and Beautiful Country*

'No one, wise Kublai, knows better than you that the city must never be confused with the words that describe it.'

Italo Calvino, *Invisible Cities*

Prologue

THE MAYPOOL

The water moved yet was still – a contained rippling, dark yet reflecting, a temperamental mirror choosing to show the sky rather than its inner workings deep below.

I sat alone in the rowing boat on the lake-sized pool and magic was everywhere, despite my leggings and nasty orange sweatshirt, whose colour clashed all wrong with the dark greens and deep water of sky. Hair high ponytailed, with an inappropriate large royal blue net bow that caught dandelion seeds in the wind perched on my head against my mother's wishes.

The world began to divide around me. Gossamer veils cut through the view, spider-silk lines to break up the real world of this holiday in deep Devon, and where I was in that moment. It was a realm within a realm. I was close to somewhere else – nearly touching a different place – a place that filled my body with feelings so strange and strong that it was as if I had travelled there. That I was both there and no longer there.

The sun was cool, glinting stars of light that pulsed and made me squint as they fractured the view. Dragonflies were not just dragonflies, but flying jewels. Pond skaters whispered to me the secrets of walking on water, left feet ripples – miniature hints of something profound. I could not move. I was in a kaleidoscope. It held me both out of body and more alive in my awkward, chubby nine-year-old flesh than I'd ever been before. I did not want to go back to shore and the old stone cottage we had hired as a family, not all that far from our home in the once-upon-a-county that was Avon. I did not want my parents or siblings – I wanted to be with these creatures who, it was suddenly clear to me, knew something my family didn't. The smell of water – the light and colour and shapes I could hear as if they were birdsong. The landscape was alive. The natural world was alive with a different force – one that I had missed till this new moment.

I whispered hello, cautiously, waited motionless in the boat, let the anticipation drift around me.

The fields and hills nearby shuddered, rounded tummy rumblings, shivering grass fur.

At this young age I had discovered something: a quest that would follow me through my life. A thirst for this feeling, this travelling within my world to somewhere new; this communication, connection; an awareness of something different; an invisible realm that was not separate to, but part of our visible realm.

I was convinced from that moment that places have feelings too. This feeling was too strong, too mutual a chemistry, to belong to me alone, to not be a communication. As I let this knowledge flow over my skin, as I closed my eyes to the red glow of the sun through lid-blood, then opened them to the seeds that floated and made the breeze visible, I let them cast their magic and it thrilled me.

Part
One

Thresholds, Kingdoms and Borderlands

The Walk

Press pause on the world.

What would you miss? The sounds, the beauty of movement? The world does not work as a stage set. It needs to breathe, to talk, to live like one of us. When we think it is still or silent it is not really – it is just about to show us something different: this is its chance to show what is really there.

There was no bustle. Traffic noise was taken over with the gentler ambience of birdsong. In the spring of 2020, when the whole world seemed to be falling apart, places that we knew transformed in feeling.

I lived in a village in Somerset, but in the cities the streets were also empty. We could not be indoors together, yet outdoors was still distanced – even in my village there were queues outside the local shop, people nervous to stand too near to each other. Driving to buy essential supplies, I felt suspicion. People perceived a threat in the air. There was an invisible enemy that could catch any of us. My friend got told off by the police for going for a walk too far from her house, even though the place she had gone to was only a ten-minute drive away and more remote than her street, so she would be less likely to catch or spread germs.

We were scared, yet the landscape was not. With people gone the animals came out more and the air was cleaner. Ironically for such a terrible time, it was the most glorious spring. The places changed physically through lack of people, but also atmospherically. We suddenly and unexpectedly, in good and bad ways, experienced the feeling of the world differently. There was a change in how we felt around people through this invisible threat of germs; how our lives and routines, purposes, jobs had all been upended, the horrific news with growing graphs cataloguing deaths – but this was the fear of our human reality, a reality of human contact, projected onto the places where we lived our lives. The places themselves, made remote, emptied, changed in a different way, were more noticeable without the human distractions.

During a spring where my world had fallen apart, as so many others' had, job gone, family in crisis, I was more alone than I had ever been in my life. And as I navigated this strange existence, it was the world that kept me company. The feeling I had been so affected by as a child rose in my local bubble of West Country landscape with a different strength – and it was transformational.

I had walked in my local forest nearly every week for years. I knew the paths and different trees, the changing seasons, bluebells and first green leaves, foxgloves, deep winter mud, evergreens and bare branches, the deer and birds of prey, the baby frogs, the evil flies that bite near the pond. It had always made me feel better, and if you'd asked, I would have said I was aware of its atmosphere and cherished this. But now it felt different. I walked and felt the breeze stroke my skin as if alive; the trees threw the breezes between high branches like a Mexican wave of fake traffic noise; the deer didn't run away so fast; and as for the light . . . It was the same place yet my experience of being in it was not the same; it was transcendental and it was company. The memory of that pool in Devon came back to me – the sense that there was something else going on, that I had somehow travelled within my real world – and this time, as an adult in a place I thought I knew well. No distortion of childhood and holidays, the unreliability of memory – the forest was feeling like this here and now.

What was this place I was responding to? What had happened? Atmosphere as travelling . . . I had never really thought of it in these terms before. I looked around and the forest was the same, yet I felt totally and utterly different. It climbed up me and got inside. My mind was lifted almost as if drugged by the sheer scale of it – the feeling of the forest. I grew up in the Church of England, but do not consider myself particularly religious in my adult life, yet if I were to try to describe this new feeling, I would say that a religious experience, a sense of something else – a divine presence in every part of this place, a spirit in each plant and tree – is as close as I could get.

And when I left the forest after the first walk when this happened, the feeling did not go away. The immediacy of the atmosphere was no longer there, but a trace of it seemed to have latched on and come home with me. I was aware of something. I went back and each time I expected the intense feeling to have gone, but the way I felt in this forest could never disappear. Something had been awakened in my body and mind when I was in this place – as if it recognised my visits and how I had unlocked its secrets, and now it was open to me. I was no longer there alone – I was walking in but also *with* the place. This experience felt like something we were feeling together.

This is how a place can feel . . . I said to myself. I thought back to past intense experiences; usually when travelling in my twenties and a place was exciting and new, I was hyper-aware of the intensity – its contrast, but this felt different. It was not literal travelling to access an atmosphere that would obviously be new and therefore striking. I had opened myself up, or rather it had opened me, and now this strange symbiosis was done, every tiny bit of wonder was flooding into me, into my familiar world. Each subtle change as I walked, metre by metre, path by path, noise by noise, the smell of pine rising or bluebells – hot earthy air . . . The world slowed and the miniature world danced, seeds and lichen, moss worlds and discarded feathers. I felt like I was on a different plane of existence, yet more deeply embedded in the real world.

It seemed impossible that it was so transcendental yet anchored, but like the difference between earth and sky, the elements of the natural world, it also felt unequivocally true. I had found some *thing* – it was not merely in my head. And another truth was that it changed me, was a complete joy at a time of despair. And that in my fumbling cage of language, whatever a spiritual interpretation might be to each individual, the word that kept falling into my thoughts was 'atmosphere'. For the first time, I had truly, deeply felt the atmosphere of these woods. And rather than the word simply being a description of somewhere feeling cosy or creepy or sad, atmosphere was far more complex and profound than I had ever imagined. It was key. It was the heart, the essence – yet fluid, alive and changing; it is the true evolving individual personality of place, and it is there for us if we want it. The world can speak to us, but obviously its language is different. Atmosphere as earth words . . .

I took the atmosphere of being in the forest home, glowing like a secret pocket of pulsing light in my heart, comforting yet strangely, awesomely powerful. I felt like I'd discovered a secret of the world that my childhood self, back on that magical pond in Devon, knew and lost. I could not lose it again. And so my quest to understand it began.

But how can we ever understand something as elusive yet present as atmosphere?

When I began to research online the scientific reasons behind the atmosphere of a place, the combination of things that create it, I could find nothing; no matter how I phrased it in the search engine, there weren't any mentions of atmosphere other than the kind that encases planets. The gaseous sort that enables us to live, makes somewhere habitable or not. Yet when I think of atmosphere in those terms, habitable, life-sustaining, the other kind is not so different – it might be what attracts or repulses us about a place, makes somewhere *feel* like home (we always say 'feel' when it comes to home – an emotional rather than a rational response to a place), terrify or inspire us with awe.

My guesses were all I had and they were obvious – geology and architecture; but that is how somewhere looks, not feels, and as any descriptive writer knows, ignoring all the senses other than sight leads to a poor portrait of a place. And beautiful places can feel sinister in one location and in another – a similar landscape or building – cosy. So is it the associations we bring to a place? Perhaps in part, but my inkling was that it lay deeper than this, seemingly intangible but somehow physically there, invisible to the eye – a beast of instinct, ancient, stealthy rather than subtle, it can hit you in the gut or soothe the greatest pain. It is a presence. It is a very real ghost.

Atmosphere is intrinsic to place. Even though we may not always be consciously aware of it, we would not experience a sense of place without it, but rather, a disjointed combination of experiences that don't define where we are. Places would blur into each other, become a series of images, with smells and sounds and other sensory experiences; and that sense of where we are, where we truly inhabit in any given moment, would be confused or watered down and no more powerful than a reproduction. Atmosphere is what gives a place its identity. It might change for each of us, yet that is no bad thing – it doesn't need to be consistent, but to communicate with us as to where we are, as to who this place is. Atmosphere is the voice of place.

We all have moments in our life when we are more alert to our surroundings than others. My particular circumstances during lockdown were strange and would set me off on a weird life I had not planned; a search for a new home at a time when I hadn't been looking for one. My walks made me more in tune with the landscape I loved and comforted me like an invisible blanket. However, this solace-in-place wasn't a fresh need, but a quest that had been alongside me the whole time. With the enforced introspection of lockdown, I realised I had been strangely dedicated to my craving to *feel* the world around me for years; to feel alive in a place; to sense its atmosphere; to feel at home within small corners of the world.

Even as a child I was in thrall to atmosphere. As a teenager too. Then in my twenties I took flight and travelled. Relentlessly. Peculiarly so: at a time when my friends were settling down, moving in with boyfriends, building careers, I was either ill at home or saving up through working in not-so-great jobs, to fly, to be in the world, to feel free and excited and open to everything. I did not realise it at the time, but I think now that I was in thrall to the same impulse

I'd had on the Maypool, the same quest to experience places, to inhabit places in a heightened state of feeling, to experience the world emotionally; not to collect, but to *feel* as many places, as many atmospheres, as I could. The woods in lockdown reminded me that atmosphere is not mere background, but all around: it made itself known.

As I looked back at my own travels and realised how urgent but unexplained this search for atmosphere was, I wanted to understand better what atmosphere actually *is*. It was both the most unknowable yet most powerful thing I had experienced, and it influences everyone. I wanted to explore how others responded to it – to search through history, writing and art; to see how people have tried to show it, to illustrate, understand and explain it. I wanted to search through my travels and other people's travels and the places that linger as an atmosphere in our heads. I wanted to know if – when something is so alive and in constant movement – it can ever be caught, fleetingly embraced in a net of words.

As I started this journey, I had a single conviction: that being open to atmosphere was key to the creativity of being in our world. A place's personality is mapped through our feelings. We create it, tenderly, together.

Maps of Tenderness

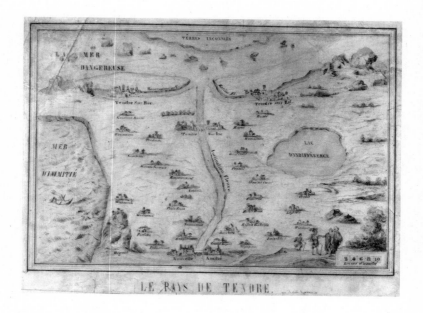

A group of women sits in a Parisian drawing room. It is the seventeenth century. There are no men present. Refreshments are brought in by a discreet servant, but the main focus is the talk – is each other. They are discussing an idea. It is a private though animated setting. Let us imagine a room painted soft green-grey, pictures on the walls, a small ornate sofa, ornaments from across the newly discovered world, books. There is a large table and on it a large piece of paper – a blank luxury not to be lightly filled.

The women are standing around, leaning forward, only marginally hampered by the stiff garments of the day – corsets under stomachers, petticoats peeping through the heavy skirts of pastel silk held in shape by padded rolls; ruffs have given way to wider collars now. They have ink, they are mark making. They are mapping. They are creating a *Carte de Tendre* – a Map of Tenderness.

Because of their class, and because this is Paris in the seventeenth century, there is a freedom, for these particular women, in this space. Intellectually, Paris has always been experimental, hungry for ideas: over a hundred years before the revolution, the French salon was already going strong. But these women, here, are free to talk about how they feel. They are free to create.

Picture the ink flowing as if quills are but extensions of their fingers and the ink a strange product of their veins. Picture the feelings taking form, quivering out, sniffing like small creatures before forming shapes on their chosen bit of the large sheet. They need homes, and the shapes they have chosen resemble places. Houses, mountains, rivers and sea. There is something for everyone in a landscape.

Maps of tenderness. Emotion. Stories located in feelings on a map. These were real physical things, published and celebrated, discussed in salons, a realm of creativity that was the terrain of women before fashionable men caught on. They were linked to literary publications; part of experimental fiction. Yet they were not physical guides of imaginary worlds, such as a Tolkien map of Middle Earth, but depictions of the emotional journey of the protagonist in the form of a map. This was a new way of mapping the world through how they felt – landscape becoming feeling, emotion as location, rather than location as a physical place on a map we could follow. Topography as vessel, co-conspirator, keepsake box.

The woman who most notably brought this genre to the literary world was Madeleine de Scudéry. Her 1654 novel *Clélie* shows a map of the land of Tenderness, but rather than a real place this map is a narrative voyage. Created by the main character, it tracks the location of her emotional journey: *Lac d'Indifférence, La Mer Dangereuse*, small settlements, little clumps of houses and trees like small humps holding the feelings of *Oubli, Tendresse, Exactitude, Perfidie* . . . The dangerous sea spans the top, calm yet full of rocks, and above it the edge of an unknown land, *Terres Inconnues* . . . Undiscovered. Where desire might lie, just out of sight. There are no borders as such – drawings of towns and feelings as written words, acknowledged. There is no set route; like old maps of the earth, depicted as if it were flat, we could wander off the edge. The sea pierces the land made up of little humps below, tears a vein with its river, a strange tentacle named *Inclination Fleuve* that, if dwelled on, starts to look like a tube, a birth canal, a map of the interior of a woman's body.

Intimate. Female desire laid out for the literary world to see – a map of the unspoken, the undercurrent of the female point of view of love and relationships. We take our bodies with us, they are how we experience place, they are key to atmosphere, not dislocated from it. Intimacy is integral – it is our relationship with place. At this point in history – long before the eighteenth century with its Romantic male writers and painters striding the hills, the twentieth with the largely male Situationist movement, and the twenty-first with its hipsters exploring urban ruins, voyeuristic, conquering – psychogeography, emotion, was a uniquely female approach to place; a way that place could make visible the female experience. Yet psychogeography as a discipline is concerned with places that exist in the physical world, or at least could. Before the golden age of intrepid early women's travel writing in the nineteenth century, still in a time when most did not stray far from their homes, women created their own imaginative lands of exploration, and they called for place to be seen differently. To show their experience through the veil of allegory and fiction. A necessary filter that was seeking to reveal safely in plain sight, rather than conceal women's lives and loves. It was searching for the truth, and the way to do this was to work with the idea of place – metaphorical, not tagged and literal, locations.

None of which means these places don't exist – they are just not places as we think of them normally. The place is in the moment. The room, the map, the collaboration, the feeling. It is there: your physical surroundings may not be treacherous seas and little villages, but your mental surroundings can be . . .

Look at Scudéry's map on page 9. The Lake of Indifference

stands alone, marooned and strangely pale, a crater to the east, a place of entrapment. To the west, the Sea of Enmity is choppy and rough, with traces of lost boats in danger of sinking, the shipwrecks of emotion gone wrong, a sea that falls off the map. We too could fall off the map ... Women often fell off the map if love went wrong. This is a treacherous land, but one that is open to women, a site of exploration, emotional freedom outside the confines of society, a narrative, the route and layout of which could be simple or not. There are choices in how to navigate this space, but if you strayed just a little you could be sucked into an emotional place of no return.

To discover Scudéry's *Carte de Tendre*, this map, to know that it was created by a woman and published all the way back in 1654, seems radical. Yet Madeleine de Scudéry was a well-connected and respected woman of letters: she wrote extensively, not just novels but essays and correspondence. The salon she hosted at her home in Paris was a collaborative intellectual and creative space for women, and her Map of Tenderness triggered a fashion for both men and women to create such maps. It is clear that her idea spoke to something missing in how people saw both emotion and place represented: it was emphatically emotional yet there was something deeply logical about seeking to represent place through feelings, and feelings through the creation of a map, a containing document, a place. As these maps became fashionable it is inevitable that some would have not had true emotional depth, but there is an openness to Scudéry's original. Where most others were of islands or had borders, hers spills over, leaves land undiscovered ... It leaves room for subjectivity, as true experience of place does. And hers was collaborative – created in a salon where women poured in their experiences, discussing it together, creating this place together, mapping their bodies and experiences in this collective realm.

By locating feeling and story in a map, Scudéry shows how place and feeling are interconnected. This mapping is an acknowledgement of a multisensory experience not only going beyond sight, but beyond the idea of the five senses to locate our connection with our bodies in space somewhere else: a corporeal mapping of place, tied up with memory and emotion, personal and collective experience.

It is both subtle and political, active and simmering gently. Maps, songs, love letters – a peculiarly female communication – a way in to the secrets, the undercurrent, the hidden conversation that atmosphere understands.

Are we all living maps? Not in the sense of the physical analogy, the scars on our bodies that mark our experiences, the wrinkles that show our age. I don't mean even the slightly stranger analogy palm readers believe in, the idea that there are other lines mapping our futures, holding our life experience, its inevitabilities quite literally in the palm of our hands: skin roads. Perhaps a better term is map makers, or map vessels, with which as we move through places, rather than our lives being detached from place, we absorb something. That our experience is not disconnected, that it inhabits the places we walk through, and those places contribute to it. We are connected to our landscapes; we take them with us as we keep moving. We are always moving.

Entropy: the second law of thermodynamics. We leak energy, and emotion is energy. Even sitting here at my computer at a little table in this cottage, which has become my home this last year, I am not static. I am moving onwards. This small house, which has existed for a couple of hundred years, the surrounding chalky downland and the nearby forest are moving with me. Changing, ageing, layering up all that has happened here.

It is part of something large, multisensory, faceted, fluid.

We are interactive.

I have often felt as I walk that I am mapping a place inside myself. That as my feet move one in front of the other, the ground is imprinting itself in me. That the thoughts triggered in each moment become part of my own personal map of the place. And the urge to record what this feeling gives me is sometimes the urge to draw lines and landscape, what we would recognise as a map, but equally the urge to write – a story, a memory, a poem. It is the urge to play a song in my head that feels like the soundtrack to this landscape. This moment in this place.

When I think of that pond in Devon, I know it has both a physical location which is still there, and another which is part of me. I know that the cottage and the pool are still there, but in another way I am not convinced they are. It seems surreal that the pond could go on existing, and also that the place as I knew it – that moment of atmospheric thrall – has travelled. It belongs to its place, but it is also mine, within me. I take it with me as I travel onwards.

If places are like this, then how can we map them? Maps in their traditional guise are pieces of paper, or these days, interactive layouts on screen, which give us the information we need to get around. But their creation is something else, a measuring of place yet also an extraction; an attempt at distilling the moving, the changing, the impossible. Mapping a place is about collecting data, yes, but it is interactive, collaborative. It is our attempt to both capture place and to understand it. It is a personal act, a creative act. I am not even thinking of the wealth of artists' maps. Mapping goes beyond maps. It is a quest to pin down that which will always be fluid. It is an open quest: moments caught on paper that are out of date – like all present time – the second they have happened. But still we keep trying, searching, travelling to try to make sense of the world and show that, in some way, we know it.

The seventeenth century was a time of great world exploration, which was not available to women. Nearly two hundred years after Columbus, whose expedition was based on the misreading of an old map (he sailed west thinking he would reach China, not the then-unknown-to-Europe Americas, and died still thinking he had been in the Far East), post-Raleigh and his 'discoveries', this was a golden age of world mapping.

The Mercator projection, the origin of the most common world map today, was made in 1569. We can presume someone as educated as Scudéry would have seen it. As an intellectual woman of means, she would perhaps even have owned a globe, giving her a better sense of the layout of countries on the earth. So her approach to maps was not in ignorance of world mapping as done by scientific cartographers. It was a conscious branching out. A way of taking a form men used to contain the world – to represent the travels that women would be prevented from going on, and the scientific capturing and tagging of adventure – and claiming a representation of the world for the personal, for women's lived experience. They chose to do this not by mapping the domestic sphere, but the emotional and creative. Something that no physical limitations can bind. The creative emotional sphere is within the power of each of us – it can be shared with creative output, but not invaded, not 'discovered' in a colonial sense. It is personal. And by locating it in place, we are claiming a bit of the world for the unseen.

For many years I have taught creative writing to children. When I teach with a therapeutic angle I often use the idea of world building as the creation of a safe space, escapism as healing, and the importance of an imaginative space of one's own to retreat to. I have drawn maps with children to build ownership of their imaginative worlds, to make their ideas more concrete. These could be seen as maps of tenderness – places carefully chosen to chart the world of their minds, to make them feel safe. There is arguably a human need to locate our feelings, to put them into place.

This is echoed in the history of maps. In medieval maps the unknown places in the world are often labelled with emotion, with fear, full of monsters, with walls of fire to stop those regions that Christians thought the Word of God had not reached from seeping in. The known world is calmer. Catalogued. Even though it may have been full of war or famine, on the map it is not depicted with the language of emotion in the way the unknown world was. Monsters keep their distance.

Yet we still use the language of emotion when mapping. Especially when we reach for the unknown.

Quests for the North and South Poles are the stuff of exploration legend. Poles are remote, unreachable: fixed locations for the purpose of cartography that also move as the earth does;

that remain unobtainable for most, a strange conceptual frontier. 'Accurate' globes rotate on points that could be technically wrong. As if acknowledging this, their frustration of mapping, their elusive yet essential quality, the Antarctic – container of poles, the last great unexplored landmass – is described in a language that would seem more at home on Scudéry's Map of Tenderness than in a modern scientific atlas.

The Pole of Inaccessibility. The Pole of Ignorance. These are real places, the least known places in the known world. When faced with a lack of knowledge, even in modern science and cartography, we linguistically return to our emotions.

I could see the Poles of Inaccessibility and Ignorance as metaphorical top and tail to Scudéry's map. The outer reaches of what goes emotionally wrong; causes of romantic pain. It seems that to map what we cannot explain is the geographer's or cartographer's primal urge – secret feelings, held at a safe distance.

In a way, a map of emotion could be seen as a method worth trying in the impossible task of recording that most elusive feeling, the personality of place.

It seems to me that if we really want to know a place, we should abandon attempts to contain, to name, to stamp our identity on it. We should listen to its identity. Communicate. Abandon control.

For places to open up – for us to truly travel not *to*, but *in* them – we need to think of our places as companions, not destinations.

We need to travel in a different way. To hold place dear.

Dear beautiful, strange, dangerous, glorious, dark, wonderful, brutal, gentle wide world.

You are my one true romance.

And this book is my map of tenderness.

Prince Edward Island

'Willows whiten, aspens quiver ...'
Alfred, Lord Tennyson, 'The Lady of Shalott'

I stand on the seashore and look out. Rolling sand and crispy ice. Back in town, low generic ranch-style houses, wooden walkway, a smell of salt and water and a sense of fishing ever there. Souvenir shops – surreal somehow. Diners sell lobster. I eat pancakes drenched in maple syrup. Another day, grass and the odd tree, no hills really, low down. Pretty, but I can't distinctly remember this landscape. I sit in the car and I can't remember the roads. But the sea, I can always sense the sea.

Yet if I close my eyes I see orchards, blossom blooming, gentle valleys and old wooden houses by babbling brooks and secret streams – lakes shining like happy bloated ribbons round gabled farmsteads, cows and chickens, little birds. I wander down paths framed with birch trees, tiptoe through gently haunted woods. The sun star-pulses the air. Temporary gold-blinded, I look at my feet and see buttoned boots. My dress long, puffed sleeved and gently flowered. My hair is once again the henna red I dyed it in my teenage years. I stop and make a crown of flowers. Softness and warmth. This place is pure comfort, yet looking back there's a poignancy, the suggestion of a life that could have been in how I imagined my future when I was a child.

In 1997, when I was eighteen, I made my one and only literary pilgrimage, though to call it that is perhaps false. I was not so much visiting the setting of a book as a fan, as searching for a place that lived inside me in a way that has formed who I am today: Prince Edward Island as it exists in the books of L. M. Montgomery.

When I was a child, *Anne of Green Gables* was my favourite book. The intensity of this was fed by the 1980s television version made by Kevin Sullivan and starring Megan Follows and Jonathan Crombie as Anne Shirley and Gilbert Blythe. When something happened that my childhood brain found hard to cope with, I disappeared into this fictional version of Prince Edward Island, where I deeply felt I would be happy and understood. Before I met Anne, I had never met a character who I knew would understand me – who would get how I thought, who would be my friend – but it was the place she inhabited too, the atmosphere of which the TV show made so vivid to me. Even now, in my forties, I save the DVD for when I truly can't cope with something; I retreat into its atmosphere as the one consistent imaginary sanctuary in my life. I cannot bring myself to watch Netflix's *Anne with an E*, even though I'm told it is good, as I can't bear the thought that the later TV series may somehow pollute the earlier version for me.

While it may not inhabit my imaginary life in quite the same way now as when I was little (I remember dragging a dinghy into the middle of a pond in order to play the 'lily maid' as Anne refers to Tennyson's 'The Lady of Shalott' in one of the most famous scenes from the book), it retains an atmosphere part visual, part memory, part literary that is so entwined in my life and key experiences that it is part of me now, in a way no other place created by another is.

I was travelling on a gap year before moving to Edinburgh for university. My trip was part adventure, part work experience on the children's show *Sesame Street* in New York and then at another children's television company in Montreal. I caught the train from Toronto to Vancouver – itself a strange experience of changing atmospheres, as each day I woke to a new landscape: forests and lakes, prairies, mountains … But I knew where this trip was to end. I'd saved up from my pub waitressing job so that I could spend the last ten days in a B & B just outside Charlottetown, on Prince Edward Island.

People in the Montreal company were bemused. Why go there? You're in the best city in Canada (true – I really love Montreal). The countryside is kind of boring. There's nothing to do there. I kept my secret safe – that this was an *Anne of Green Gables* pilgrimage – knowing they would belittle it and it would feel too personal to have this dream dismissed. Like Anne hating the grown-ups laughing at her when she was being serious, I wanted this secret, this imaginary realm, not to be spoiled by those who were not, in Anne's words, 'kindred spirits'.

Leaving Montreal, I boarded a plane to Halifax, Nova Scotia, then another for the short hop to Charlottetown. The B & B owners kindly came to pick me up (all organised by phone and letter in those pre-internet days) and drove me to their beautiful old wooden house. I climbed up to my room and grinned – it was just like Anne's, iron bedstead and patchwork quilt in a room high up in pointed gables. It was an instant haven.

Yet the reality of Prince Edward Island, or PEI as locals call it, was slightly different to what I had in mind. I didn't have enough experience to know people rarely walk outside the cities in Canada, and the house was a few miles out of town, with only a main road and no pavement to get me there. There was also no public transport to speak of, and the tourist house they say is Green Gables was closed for refurbishment. But I was not going to let this deter me.

The lovely people I was staying with gave me lifts into Charlottetown so I could potter round its streets. They even drove me to 'Green Gables' and to Summerside, another town where *Anne of Windy Willows* is set, to get a sense of the island and then the sand dunes round Cavendish, much closer to where Avonlea was supposed to be.

I had a wonderful time. Just by chatting to her in a shop, I made a friend who I am still close to twenty-five years later. But the atmosphere I craved – I didn't find it. I started to wonder where this atmosphere existed. Was it through the filter of Lucy Maud Montgomery's mind? Was it through my own childhood experiences? Was it simply that conjured in a TV show back in the eighties? I began to think more about atmosphere as an act of creation – as human as much as natural phenomenon of the world; how we can take a place and change its atmosphere through our own creative acts, both as writers and artists, or through the creative power of the reader or viewer.

The Kevin Sullivan TV production starts with Anne walking through some woods while reading Tennyson's 'The Lady of Shalott'. The trees are thin. Music plays in the background as Anne whispers the words, 'Willows whiten, aspens quiver, little breezes dusk and shiver.' At this point we are not even in PEI but on the Canadian mainland, yet all blurs into the same atmosphere. The combination of image, music and words brings me instantly to tears in a way that is gently primal: I have no control, it is a soft mourning for a childhood self and a world I am not in. Yet rather than upsetting, this grief is comforting, a welcome home, a refuge which this atmosphere never deadens for me; for it is always, reliably, still there.

It is not located in a real place, but a place of the imagination. It is both inside me and accessible in the outside world. It is one of the only atmospheres that it is in my power to trigger, and consequently I use it sparingly; save it so it does not dull.

As Anne moves from the mainland to Prince Edward Island after hearing she will be adopted, the atmosphere is still a lasso isolating the intense feeling of the film, but the light changes. Gone are the muted woods, the darkened room of the orphanage where Anne talks to her imaginary 'window friend' Katie Maurice – her reflection in a glass pane – and we arrive in a rich springtime full of blue sky and blossom.

Anne is met at the station by Matthew Cuthbert, who hasn't the heart to tell her there's been a mistake and he and his sister Marilla wanted to adopt a boy. It is as if Anne, transformed by her arrival in this beautiful place, has cast a spell on him. As their horse and buggy make their way to Green Gables, we pass along the strange red roads so characteristic of the island. But there is a particular moment that truly feels like our crossing over into Prince Edward Island as a magical place: when they begin to drive down a grassy lane through an orchard of blossom (in the book, it is more of an arch – a sloping blossom tree tunnel), and something significant happens. Anne asks what the place is called and Matthew says, 'The Avenue – pretty, ain't it?' But Anne responds that pretty isn't the right word for it – it is *wonderful*, so from this moment on it becomes 'The White Way of Delight', its rightful name. This renaming continues throughout the journey like a strange awakening of the landscape – Barry's Pond becomes 'The Lake of Shining Waters'. Other places throughout the book have new names – Idlewild, Lovers' Lane, the Dryad's Bubble – but there is something in the combination of arrival and journey and spring and renaming on that first journey which pulls back a veil on a gentle, hidden depth of atmosphere; it speaks to Anne so strongly that it invites us into her interior world. The renaming shows the landscape's potential for imaginative inspiration. We each have the power to rename the ordinary (renaming or the knowing of true names has always held power in folklore and magic, a famous example being Rumpelstiltskin) and by connecting with it in a creative way, to transform our experience of it and perhaps how it exists in the minds of others – how it feels to them. We can make our own places within places, imaginative sanctuaries for ourselves, yet we can pass them on creatively.

L. M. Montgomery was very aware of her own internal world. For her, it was built in childhood, and as she grew up and her life wasn't quite what she expected (in her early thirties and, after a time spent at university and working on a newspaper in Halifax, Nova Scotia, living with her austere grandmother, who needed her care in Cavendish), she retreated into her childhood world, her own world, where her creativity could, and did, flourish. In her memoir, *The Alpine Path*, she talks of how when young she inhabited 'a world of fancy and imagination very different indeed from the world in which I lived, moved and had my outward being ... Well, I grew up out of that strange, dreamy childhood of mine and went into the world of reality I met with experiences that bruised my spirit – but they never harmed my ideal world. That was always mine to retreat into at will.' On having to move back home she said: 'I did so less unwillingly because I knew I could possess my ideal world here as well as elsewhere – that no matter what was missing outwardly I could find all in my own peculiar kingdom.'

I for one am glad she could, as it was in these years that she wrote *Anne of Green Gables* and created the world, her own peculiar kingdom, which I still retreat into as an adult. But this idea of her imagination as a kingdom, as a place where she could live differently, is an interesting one. It is not an abstract thing, but a location; an inner world. It interacts with the external world, takes her experiences and through her creativity produces a concrete thing for the outside world. This then, in the form of the book and its later incarnation on film, creates another space whereby it can live in our imaginations and become part of our world too.

I strongly believe reading is a creative act, and in being so it occupies a special space, our place of creativity and play, the potential space where I believe we may experience atmosphere. Therefore, something that should be a place devoid of atmosphere due to lack of sensory experience, becomes another form of it. However, this is different to virtual reality. The place within a book is not trying to compete with the physical world, but is rather comfortable in its own parallel world. It is not a simulacrum but a different realm, a collaboration with the author's mind, just as atmosphere is a collaboration with a physical place.

So there can be two Prince Edward Islands, both rich in atmosphere, subjective for each visitor. There is the place I visited as an eighteen-year-old; the island that I returned to for a friend's wedding in 2008; the sliver of land hovering in the Gulf of St Lawrence. Then there is the place that is the 'reality' of the atmosphere of L. M. Montgomery's mind – the creative power of atmosphere made tangible through her writing, her pulling back of the veil to reveal her inner essence of Prince Edward Island, both contained in the book and lost to time in how it is the creation of another age. Imagination as a place.

I think L. M. Montgomery would have understood this idea. She said in her memoir, '[A]mid all the commonplaces of life I was very near to a kingdom of ideal beauty. Between it and me hung only a thin veil. I could never draw it quite aside, but sometimes a wind fluttered it and I caught a glimpse of an enchanting realm beyond – only a glimpse – but those glimpses have always made life worthwhile.' She uses this concept with another of her characters, the lesser known but I think equally wonderful Emily in *Emily of New Moon*, who regularly experiences something she calls 'the flash'. The flash is a moment when Emily's experience of place changes; it hits her suddenly, atmosphere supercharged and world-changing:

> And then for one glorious, supreme moment, came 'the flash'. Emily called it that, although she felt that the name didn't exactly describe it. It couldn't be described – not even to Father, who always seemed a little puzzled by it. Emily never spoke of it to anyone else.
>
> It had always seemed to Emily, ever since she could remember, that she was very, very near to a world of

wonderful beauty. Between it and herself hung only a thin curtain; she could never draw the curtain aside – but sometimes, just for a moment, a wind fluttered it and then it was as if she caught a glimpse of the enchanting realm beyond – only a glimpse – and heard a note of unearthly music.

This moment came rarely – went swiftly, leaving her breathless with the inexpressible delight of it. She could never recall it – never summon it – never pretend it; but the wonder of it stayed with her for days. It never came twice with the same thing. Tonight the dark boughs against that far-off sky had given it. It had come with a high, wild note of wind in the night, with a shadow wave over a ripe field, with a grey bird lighting on her windowsill in a storm, with the singing of 'Holy, holy, holy' in church, with a glimpse of the kitchen fire when she had come home on a dark autumn night, with a felicitous new word when she was writing down a 'description' of something. And always when the flash came to her Emily felt that life was a wonderful, mysterious thing of persistent beauty.

It is fleeting but the feeling it gives her, this momentary crossing into what feels like another world, leaves her 'breathless with the inexplicable delight of it'. She cannot explain or control it, but it is there in the natural world for her to experience. It reminds me of the transcendent feeling I get walking in the woods or up on the downs, and of the trance-like pleasure when writing is flowing. Both are inherently feelings that are deeply connected to atmosphere. They are also intrinsically moments of hope; and 'the flash' is a truly hopeful thing: if it comes, Emily is suddenly content, transformed if feeling down; it supersedes everything as the most powerful of atmospheres can, but it is active, not passive – it takes over, is key to life moving forward without despair, as hope is.

The real PEI, as opposed to the fictional world of Avonlea and its surrounds, feels extraordinarily of the sea. I was aware of the sea in *Anne of Green Gables* – Anne and Diana take walks on the sand dunes, and there is a great poetry reading given by Anne at the seaside White Sands Hotel. On rereading the novel with this in mind, I was surprised to discover that from Green Gables you can see the sea too. All the same, the idea of PEI being an island and therefore surrounded by sea, rather than an island in order to contain the imaginary space, had never really reached me in the atmosphere of the book or filmed version.

Charlottetown smells of the ocean. I almost expected locals to dress as fishermen, bright yellow waterproofs licked with salt; and in the salty air, my hair immediately frizzed. (In fact, I'd met my dear friend by wandering into the local branch of The Body Shop for emergency curly hair products.)

Cavendish is the village where L. M. Montgomery lived much of her life and where Avonlea is thought to have been based, and it is an area of beautiful expansive sand dunes. I wandered. I saw a lighthouse that I felt I had seen before, where Anne and Diana walked, but still the atmosphere I was looking for was not there. This island is a comforting, lovely place. But I'd expected blossom-filled valleys ... That first visit in 1997 took place in May, deep spring in England, yet it was the first time I'd seen frozen sea ...

Chunks of ice crenellated the surface like cracked, glistening icing. This whole area of Canada is called the Maritimes. The accents sing softer than elsewhere – feel cosier somehow, comforting. It is a lovely place. However, the Avonlea of my imagination it is not. The closest I have found to the Maritimes in the Anne books is in the fifth story in the series *Anne's House of Dreams*, when she is first married to Gilbert and they live in a little cottage near the fictional village of Glen St Mary in the wilds of the more remote north shore. The sea is everywhere in that book; it feels like a different island, yet atmospherically it rings true.

Part of the difference in atmosphere today has to be down to the obvious changes since the 1900s ... cars, modern houses, drive-through Tim Horton's and fast food restaurants ... But one of the things I really hadn't thought about was the Anne tourist industry – I just didn't think it would exist. Literary tourism does a little in the UK; I'm from Bath and there's a Jane Austen museum and festival, even though she didn't like the city. Up on the Yorkshire Dales, they are rightly proud of the Brontës. In the Quantocks, the National Trust owns Coleridge's cottage, but it is easy to avoid it. To experience the place without noticing any of it. However, on Prince Edward Island *Anne of Green Gables* is possibly the most famous thing its tourism industry capitalises on. Locals have a love–hate relationship with the book; there is a frustration caused by the way in which visitors try to redefine the residents because of it. Souvenir shops were full of Anne pens and key rings and mugs. Cafes were themed.

When I stood outside the closed Green Gables, historic home, the lady I was with told me that it wasn't the 'real' Green Gables. A suitable house had been found and no one could tell me what, if any, connection it had to the book or L. M. Montgomery. Looking through pictures now, it seems to be where her aunt and uncle lived, so there is a connection. But truly the inspiration for Green Gables? It was a lovely old wooden house with its window frames, not gables, and roof painted green. But to me it wasn't as convincing as the one in the eighties TV series. It had less character. As I stood in front of it, a teenage pilgrim from across the Atlantic, the atmosphere was wrong. Just like L. M. Montgomery herself felt when visiting the Trossachs as a fan of Walter Scott's novels, my PEI was a lost domain of the imagination.

As a child, I lived for moments spent intensely in my imagination. I found them wandering the woods, playing in the river, sitting in that boat on the Maypool, but I found them too in the made-up worlds of the books I read, the imaginary friends in their kingdoms that spoke to me. I found them with Anne. I travelled in my mind, and, as I grew up and travelled in the real world, I still held these places within me.

I think back to Anne's island. How alive it is. The trees are sentient. The brook talks. She names and befriends her pot plants (a geranium named Bonny, a detail taken from L. M. Montgomery's own childhood). Can a place only be this alive if we know it intimately? Does it have something to do with the strength of our having been a child there? Of our imaginations developing in it? And can we ever regain these places or are they lost to our pasts – somewhere we can only reach again in a poignant but wonderful flash . . .

The Woods Between Our Worlds

It is the 1790s and two young girls at different ends of the country have come into possession of an exciting new belonging that will enable them to travel in their minds.

One of the girls is a farmer's daughter, Ann, who lives in the North West, Lancashire or perhaps further north, into Cumbria. Picture her walking down a familiar country lane when a pedlar approaches; she knows this one, she has been warned to be careful of strangers but her mother has bought things from this man and they have always been of serviceable quality. She waves at her father out in the fields to let him know she is there, as she chats and discovers that the pedlar has an exciting new product – perfect for a girl her age.

Picture another girl. West Country now – deepest Devon, perhaps the South Hams, an area that is rural and gentle and wild, not taken over by rich tourists yet, just valleys and farms and sea. She sees the front door open and the pedlar stands there. He talks to the female servant and she seems happy; he has something that will be perfect for young Dinah's birthday. The maid hands over money and hurries inside before Dinah can see what she has bought – the mistress will be pleased!

Days later and the two girls hold their treasure. It is the latest thing! A piece of fabric, marked out and ready. A piece of fabric holding a template of the whole country, and with their gentle stitches they will mark it as their own.

In the Wells & Mendip Museum in the heart of Somerset, there is a wonderful collection of embroidery samplers created by girls, sometimes as young as seven, hundreds of years ago. Among the samplers of biblical scenes and passages of text, of Gardens of Eden, prayers, houses, animals and alphabets, there are a few that are different: for these samplers are embroidered maps of Great Britain. They show a flutter of nearby borders, France, the still unified Ireland, but the focus is on England and Wales and their counties; Scotland is there in outline but less known, less detailed.

We don't know much about these maps, beyond that they were probably bought from pedlars (maybe later sold in shops) and therefore created, as many samplers were, by ordinary girls across the class divide, practising their needlework skills. There are some examples that we know were created as a school-leaving task, which while beautiful, with a high standard of stitching, follow the templates set out. But the ones bought from pedlars are different; they include a degree of personalisation. Over two hundred years ago, a young woman couldn't set off alone and travel the world. Their places were familiar locations that they could reach and see; or imaginary, where they could travel, like I did as a child, in their minds. This was not a task to be assessed by a teacher, but a way for these young girls to make their mark on their country; to follow the lines on the map, but also to claim it, to add places they knew or were interested in. Maybe to mark their own homes, to mark their presence in a country they were unlikely to travel. Like initials carved in a wall or tree, these girls let us know they were here.

The map embroidered by Ann Mercer, possibly in 1794, is unfinished, but compared to the 'text book' embroidered maps by other young girls, this farmer's daughter's is tantalisingly individual. She outlines the main map, partly delineates the counties as is required from the template, practises her lettering by stitching letters, yet then she adds her own marks which were not on the template. It is the mountains, hills and rivers that she chooses to make visible. The dramatic markers, the lifeblood waterways, the natural borders that no county line abstractly stitched can show. If we are correct and she was from the North West, then the Peak District or the higher Lake District might have been known to her. But the Mendips, Exmoor, the peaks of Wales are marked too. Dark brown, stronger in stitch and colour than the county boundaries, they hold more power – seem to show her defiance of how the land is conceptually divided, revealing her interest in the bold, the landscape of adventure. Her young working-class girl's nod to the contemporary obsession, far from her world, with the sublime. They curve and scar and make no pretence to be contained, to dampen their impact.

Ann also marks the rivers – the Thames, Severn, Exe, Tamar and more are there – strange black veins pushing out from the surface. Again, these are true boundaries of land, true markers of place, key to its spirit, its feeling, more than any arbitrary county delineation. They are boundaries, but also landscapes that are definers of place. Places with hills and rivers are consumed by the identity these features bring – the creatures, the smells, the beauty and dangers. While perhaps her father travelled or she had cousins who visited the family, it is unlikely that Ann went to any of the locations beyond her local area; yet we can imagine her at home in the farmhouse, dreaming of what those other places were like, choosing to add them to her map, to change its feel, to show the landscapes that emotionally spoke to her. On her map, counties have but initials. The seas are written in full.

Dinah Cartwright's map is more conventional in terms of following the template of counties, but just as unique as Ann's for all that. Finished in 1796, her sampler is dated down to its completion day, August 15th. Naming, dating, claiming this map as her very own, even mentioning the place it was finished, Burgh. But what is particularly fascinating here is the places which are named that are not on any template. We can surmise from looking at these that Dinah was a West Country girl. The presence of Lundy Island off the north coast of Devon, a Cornish lighthouse, the Barbican in Plymouth all suggest this, and maybe 'Burgh' refers to Burgh Island off the coast of South Devon. Lundy is tiny, unlikely to be known to someone from another area. She was delineating her country but also the places that meant something to her, changing the atmosphere of the southwestern tip of her map. Making it more than an abstract outline of place, but rather one containing emotion, a tender mapping of her life, her home.

These girls' maps show the coast of France hovering. A wriggling line, with the Channel Islands clearly marked and named nearby. The politics of the time would have made France both distant and near, a potential threat rather than the neighbour we see it as today. Indeed, one possibility is the map templates were sold as nationalistic souvenirs, to encourage unity and pride when dramatic events unfurled on the continent. But as I stare at these maps created by ordinary English girls, I think of France and the French society women who created maps of tenderness. I think of that conscious mapping of emotion, of being adult and educated and wanting to make a map to validate women's emotions. To tell a story and to show their story. Then I picture a young working rural girl, aged ten or twelve, stitching at home, mapping tenderly without realising what she is doing, without knowing about the salons of one hundred and fifty years previously. Not collaborating and empowering, challenging the mapping norms, but simply claiming her world by herself. A place for her, within her childhood places. A place between her interior world of imagination and the exterior world of the area that she knew.

When I was seven we went on holiday to France – near Autun in the Morvan region of Burgundy. It was the first time I had been abroad. But in terms of atmosphere, the foreignness isn't what stands out. It has no more exotic a memory atmosphere for me than holidays in Devon or Cornwall, where we usually went, or visiting cousins in Kent. There are moments that I remember strongly – seeing a chateau with a brightly patterned tiled roof, learning to swim in Lac des Settons – but what really sticks out is the day when we went to a forest; a forest with a frisson of wild boar and a special heart: a boulder known as the Fairy Rock, the *Roche des Fées*, nestled deep among the magical Morvan trees.

My family blur into the background. When I think back I remember an overwhelming feeling of being by myself in terms of human company, but not alone. The rock was large, though with memory and childhood scale I have no idea how big it really was. I think there was one main rock with lots of others scattered around it like satellite fairy rock towns. I solemnly climbed up it and stared out. And as I did, it was as if the real world froze and I was in a kind of paused world; that the people were frozen, but I, and the rest of this world which now crept in, were not. The space around me was filled not only with air but with miniscule beings, feathered and light. They drifted in slow motion as if in some kind of amniotic fluid; the light seems hazy, the trees there like sentinels, but a little distant. Even the feeling of the actual forest was slightly distant to that of the place I had somehow accessed, as if I had travelled somewhere else.

I knew it was called Fairy Rock and obviously was keen to see fairies. In those floating objects I thought I did. And when the image of the memory fills my mind, I do see them. My logical mind might say they were midges or floating seeds, but what I see are tiny fairies, delicate, translucent, not quite what I thought they would be, which convinced me of their reality even more. I did not hallucinate Cicely Mary Barker's flower fairies, which I was very keen on at the time and would have been very keen to befriend. Nor did I try to befriend these fairies, as I did virtually every other creature I met (I think my parents were quite relieved we didn't meet any wild boar that day). I simply absorbed their feel. I didn't merely look at them. My shy, serious, seven-year-old self stood still and willed the world around me into being – the strange air as it slowly flowed, the forest smells that heightened, the sounds that seemed to stop. I was not passive in this atmosphere but somehow contributory to it. It was there outside of me, but I also willed it into existence with my desire to see a fairy and my hyperactive imagination and openness to the moment. The atmosphere was real. The experience was real. But pure sensory scientific explanations make no sense – it went beyond a normal experience of place in a way that may only be possible for a child. I had travelled in a way that I'm not sure adults do. If I had embroidered a map of France, this would be the most prominent place on it.

I mention this moment now, because in my memories it is not so much about a strong atmosphere, as it was on the pond in Devon, as a strangely significant moment when I felt I crossed over into another realm, where the 'normal' world of everyone else stopped; and my gateway there was atmosphere and my child's imaginative power to get closer to a deeper feeling of place. I was collaborating with the world, yet in thrall to it when it revealed itself and I entered it. That moment stands alone as a self-encased memory realm. I have no idea what happened when it stopped and we drove back to the holiday cottage. The two moments are almost disconnected. I was somewhere else. I had crossed the threshold in those woods and I was between worlds.

Borders are theoretically a human construct. They may have a logical geographical element – a dramatic change in landscape or a large river or sea (did Ann Mercer feel this when she embroidered these more vividly than the county borders on her template?); they might be where one language changes to another ... But my instinct is that it is not so simple. That there is something very distinct in the feeling of crossing a border and that a border has a different kind of atmosphere, is a threshold to somewhere else; yet in being a threshold it is a unique atmospheric location in itself.

As a child, I was fascinated by C. S. Lewis's Narnia. An imaginary world accessible from one's house! It might appear at any time through a wardrobe or an old picture! I spent many a day sat in various cupboards in hope, closing my eyes and pushing the back, wondering if I felt even a little give. Surely an imaginary world would know that I was a good person to find it, surely ... Part of this was the result of a very active imagination, while with adult hindsight I'm sure another part was an attempt to escape from a childhood of school bullies and not many friends. In Narnia, one could go from ordinary to being the queen of a magical realm! And even more appealingly, the animals spoke – always a huge plus in my creature-obsessed brain of fairies disguised as slugs and pet woodlice ... But looking back at it now, at my time sat in wardrobes, I think I was seeking an atmosphere, too – that of intense childhood play, yes, but also one in connection with my house, which felt like my friend, my ally – whereby the ordinary could be genuinely transformed into the threshold to another world, the place where the veil between this world and the magical/spiritual was more thin.

I was sure the world was full of secret ways to cross over. I was fairly certain there might even be a genuine borderland – a threshold land – where the crossing over was less likely to be a complete case of chance involving household objects. This belief was augmented when I read, a while after *The Lion, the Witch and the Wardrobe*, C. S. Lewis's *The Magician's Nephew*. In the novel, the frightening Uncle Andrew discovers a box full of dust, fairy dust he feels, from which he forges yellow and green rings. He has already disappeared a guinea pig with them, so when his nephew Digory and Digory's friend Polly stumble on Uncle Andrew's secret study, itself a strange in-between world within their house, he tricks Polly into disappearing too, thereby forcing Digory to follow suit to rescue her. So far so good magical children's adventure plot. But where it gets really interesting is where they go; the logical thing in terms of the tropes of children's fiction would be to travel straight to a different world, and in the later Narnia books this is what happens. But in *The Magician's Nephew* things work differently and Digory finds himself in a strange forest full of pools of water. It is clear from the start that, unusually, this is not a world but a different kind of place – a contained place with its own green light and no sounds, yet this wood is very much alive. It is as if Digory has entered into an atmosphere – a place that is more like being inside a mind or a body, a woodland that functions as an interior. However, this interior is the gateway to potentially as many worlds as there are pools. It is a threshold. A place that holds many other places. As Digory would later say, 'It was a rich place: as rich as plum cake.'

'Rich' is a good word to describe threshold places, borderlands. They may be small and deeply contained. They may lack certain things, such as the sounds of wildlife in 'the Wood between the Worlds', yet these things aren't absences so much as signs that this place is 'other', that it functions differently. They contribute to a distinct atmosphere that in itself signifies this otherness. What works for C. S. Lewis's imaginary border world also works for the borders in our own atmospheric worlds – cities and countryside. It works for our interior borderlands, too – our bedrooms where we fall asleep and cross the atmospheric threshold into our dreams. It works for the strange knowledge that we have crossed county boundaries, real borders that remain invisible and unmarked by an official crossing. It works when we think of particular thresholds within our own experience of place – the sense that we are near the edge of a magical or spiritual realm in our own worlds. Thresholds are places in themselves, not blank nothingness between two places. More than that, although physically they may take up virtually no space, psychologically, atmospherically, they are vast. Whether the doorway to a house, an invisible border in our real world or a portal in an imaginary one, thresholds are places of transformation. They are the calling cards of atmosphere; they are 'the woods between the worlds'.

When we are children, these woods can be easier to access, are more visible, are simply there in our day-to-day way of looking at the world. We are constantly moving through thresholds. We are on the cusp.

Childhood is a layer, a feeling of place, past yet present within us. It is somehow different to memory or our imaginations. We have layers of atmosphere that are not so much our memories as the feelings imprinted within us – they are both subtler and more visceral than the memory of an event, and they cannot be pinned down.

Childhood is realm of its own that lives separately to what we would call memory; that has its own set of intuitive memory atmospheres; that functions as an autonomous atmosphere within each of us which we carry throughout our lives. Perhaps it can make us respond differently as adults to certain atmospheres of place, but it is not just the memory of a childhood event, but childhood as a place that causes these things. It is a place we can visit in our day and night dreams. It is a realm with buildings and countryside and holidays and events good and bad, but a realm it is. It is not abstract. It is an indescribable place. A contributor to all our atmospheres. A place we can crossover to.

Childhood stays with us like a wood between our worlds.

Another place, a threshold place, a different space. Why do we develop these places within ourselves that become so vivid a filter for the external world when we are children? If this kind of experience in childhood can be a place, childhood is also where we develop our relationship to both places and the subtly different spaces: our interior spaces, the space that is our connection to those who are raising us, our relationship to the external world. The psychologist D. W. Winnicott in his 1971 book *Playing and Reality* talks about the idea of a third space, where play and then cultural experience lie.

The third space is not so much a way of seeing the world differently, though it results in this, as a way of being that functions more as a conceptual location – the threshold through which we move from our inner world towards the external world of our reality, which as we grow up and develop we inhabit more frequently. It is different to the two spaces psychologists often talk of: it is not our inner psychic space nor is it the external world, but rather a third space that is somehow in-between, a transitional place, a space where a creative way of living happens.

As a Freudian psychologist working in the field of transitional objects, Winnicott views this as a space that emerges when the child begins to separate from the mother and discovers the world. When children begin to play they are in a creative way of living, but they are not quite playing in their inner world, no matter how internally created the play might seem, as this third space which they occupy is a place based on experiences, but also not quite of the external world. It is an intermediate state where we develop creatively between our inability and ability to accept reality. It is the place of play for children, but Winnicott believes that for adults it is the place of cultural experience, of imagination, of religious belief. It is the place for that which we know to be real but cannot explain in terms of rational external reality. Yet it is no less real for that. We are not trying to make sense of external reality so much as creatively approach external phenomena. If atmosphere is intrinsically creative, then this is the kind of place that we can inhabit alongside it; where we can interact with the experience of the world around us that we cannot rationally explain away. Atmosphere can sit there. We can join it.

Childhood is an atmosphere we all hold inside ourselves. If I were to describe it, I would say that it is a filter we all have, or rather the creative kindling for how all the atmospheres we encounter later in life will present to us – how places make us feel. Childhood is also a time of intuitive creativity and an internal place where the border to daydreaming is always closer to us – where we can step over, create epic games in the playground where experience of place is transformed. I wonder if this is what it means to exist more in Winnicott's third space. That we lose it as we leave it, as we grow up. When the external becomes less internalised, or the internal can no longer break free, make itself known in the external world. I can remember inventing a game with a friend about an imaginary tunnel network. During our lunch break, we were not on the concrete playground but climbing through these tunnels, which were real in our minds. It was just that no one but me and my friend could see them. The atmosphere of that game – of being in that imaginary world made present but invisible in the real one – stays with me to this day, far more than the atmosphere of my classroom or the playground itself. I can remember classroom and playground – the often traumatic feelings of being bullied at school – but the atmosphere that endures is of the realms that I and my one good friend created. In terms of memory and atmosphere, they are more real to me.

I think back to Ann Mercer's map and the places she crossed over to in her mind as she created them in thread, ignoring the template, making her third space real.

We play, we create through the places in which we move through our lives, we gather them in us from outside and re-gift them imaginatively. The tender embroidery, layered memories on cloth of life, stitch by stitch ... I wonder if these places were more real to those eighteenth-century girls too. I wonder where as adults we leave them – mind or world. They do not want to be extinguished. Our lost domains of tender sparks are spluttering, softly.

The Lost Domain

'But he kept wearily to his course. At a corner of the wood he came upon two white posts marking the entrance to an avenue. He turned into it and had not gone far when he was brought to a halt in surprise and stood there, stirred by an emotion he could not have defined. Then he pushed on with the same dragging steps. His lips were cracked by the wind which at moments almost took his breath away. And yet he was now sustained by an extraordinary sense of wellbeing, an almost intoxicating serenity, by the certitude that the goal was in sight, that he had nothing but happiness to look forward to.'

Alain-Fournier, Le Grand Meaulnes

When I think back on my life and the places I have lived it, some of my most vivid moments were not as an adult or a child, but during the in-between stage. Teenage years were lived in the places I had known as a child, but in a different atmosphere, body and mind – with changing emotions which in turn changed how I communicated with, and related to, the world around me.

There is a difference to how we experience the world at this time which affects both its atmosphere for us and the atmosphere we project – our charisma, how we come across, anxious and unsure or gloriously full of life. When our perspective is so different, so on the cusp, the world and its feelings offer themselves up in different possibilities – they are not our shelter or, as in childhood, all we know; they are not where we have settled or made complex adult decisions; they are just what they are, what they always are, but we have a different way into experiencing them. They are in the moment, yet open to the vast possibilities of our future. And they are arguably where we are freest to discover, to open ourselves up to them, and become. To build the atmosphere of ourselves, to cherish the places that found us.

Picture your life as a timeline. It could be a dry task, like a history exercise in the classroom, but this timeline is different, it is pulsing. The rigid lines marking events can be there, but there is another line, thicker and fluid, which moves, appears unexpectedly, with the rainbow transparent skin of bubbles, flexing its surface, solid yet breakable, magic yet there. This line encases our adolescence like a strange evolving chrysalis. We move through its challenging soapy sparkles. We emerge the other side, its magic popped, yet transformed, new in feeling, the world all different, our adult lives waiting for us – that moment of how we felt in the world evaporated, remaining in small droplets, hanging in the air.

I spent my youth in love with the indie underground, another layer in our curated human world, the cultural one – subculture. Days spent rifling through record shops, discovering new bands as if treasure, dancing the night away from the age of fourteen – an age that seems rather tender to be gigging and clubbing in today's slightly more ID-obsessed world . . . Before I discovered travel, my adolescent atmospheres were geographically small – my village, Bath, the odd trip to Bristol – but musically vast. Moments held in music. Gigs in literal underground caverns of clubs. The moment of sitting on a park bench in the early hours with a boy, talking and just feeling the chemistry in the air. But always linked by music. Music as illustrating the room, life, the world. Clothes linked to music – charity shop dresses, attic finds, homemade strangeness that acted as a signifier to others; a kind of code, a contribution to the atmosphere of self, surface maybe, but there as a sign nonetheless. Fashion as communication, curation of self, of personal atmosphere. Charisma is atmosphere . . .

I say 'surface' because it was an interesting time compared to the world today. As a teenager in the early nineties, I was part of the last generation to grow up without the internet. The music we listened to and what we wore revealed our identity at a deeper level in some ways than if we had just been able to Google something, stream a band . . . If you met someone at a gig of an obscure band you liked, wearing a certain thing, hair a certain way, chances were you'd have stuff in common. There was no instant gratification. It took time and effort to find out about things, to research deep into a world you wanted to be part of . . . It meant something. Yet it was, of course, not entirely reliable – complete idiots sometimes liked good bands; cool clothes and music taste doesn't equal clever and fascinating or kind, but it did signify something: like a password to a secret realm, it was a knowledge that let you in, and for a teenager, that this knowledge was not the mainstream had great appeal. It was a world within the world, a more secret world within popular culture that one could visit and become part of.

And if one entered this realm – became part of this subculture – there was no social media, no phones. Cameras were a rare thing, usually disposable, brought out for a special night such as a birthday . . . When we watched something we usually watched it with our eyes, no screen filtering the experience. When we found a special object in a charity shop we just bought it and told our friends. When a new band was discovered it was held as a thrilling secret, shared with those closest, but no stranger could know what we'd found. We felt no need to tell the world; we were building our own.

When I think back to this time in my life, the bands I loved, their music brings an intense feeling. Madder Rose, Mazzy Star, The Sundays, Suede, My Bloody Valentine, Jon Spencer Blues Explosion, Tindersticks ... their names an incantation of a moment. Sonic Youth. Driving along, if I put on an old CD my car is transformed with this layer of memory, changing the atmosphere of the landscape I am driving through. Music has that power. I have taught creative writing workshops for teenagers where we play different music as we write and it filters through, affects the tone of writing. It is an atmosphere influencer in a way few manmade things have the power to be. But if I think back to adolescence, was that way of feeling in itself an atmosphere? That way of being – of experiencing the world, all exciting and new, no filter, with undercurrents of delight and discovery – was a very particular, unrepeatable relationship with the world. A collaboration with our surroundings. It is not pure memory or looking back to suggest this. Adolescence is a period dominated by feeling – an intensity that builds a realm.

I wonder if, as we grow up, we shed these different bubbles, these gentle casings of atmosphere, fragile, translucent, soapy points of tenderness, and enter new ones. Atmosphere is our relationship with the world, and we travel through different ways of being in that relationship. The feelings can be hard to get back. We can have wonderful new ones, but the way in, the secret password to that particular world, is time limited. Atmospheric travel, like time, is a one-way street. Our memories are where the fragments, the dust on this road, hold on.

I first read *Le Grand Meaulnes* by Alain-Fournier on holiday in France. I was eighteen and had just finished my A-levels, and in a moment of abandon my parents had hired an old falling-down house in rural France – our third foreign holiday and the first in seven years – as if they sensed we four kids were growing up and with my older brother already having left home, this might be the last chance for us to holiday all together. It was a time of transformation, a time where part of me was aware that life, for the first time, had got to a stage where I was about to make a change from which there would be no true return – leaving home, leaving adolescence for early adulthood away, alone, at university.

Perhaps it was because I was on the cusp of leaving this adolescent domain that the book spoke so strongly to me (plus a teenage propensity for doomed love that doesn't have quite the same pull on me in my forties). Perhaps the knowledge of the true heartbreaking story of how the author Alain-Fournier died at the tender age of twenty-eight at the front in 1914, just after the outbreak of World War I. Perhaps it was the heat and dry rural roads, the crumbling stone of this old French house, which itself stood alone like a strange temporary domain for my family. Rereading the book now, it is not the love story that I mourn for – it is heartbreaking, that is true – but rather it's that the magic of the lost domain is glaringly only real in terms of atmosphere. This makes it more beautiful to me, more powerful and understandable in how it intoxicated Meaulnes, but I can also see the inbuilt tragedy from the start. Atmospheres should be treasured, but if we let the quest for the exact same one consume us we are doomed. We cannot recreate the exact same moment; they would be but photocopies, frustrating holograms our hands push through. And in trying to do so perhaps we miss the joy of the memory and the joy of the new atmospheres we discover every day. Here the desire for the lost atmosphere has gone dystopian – it is the vital force that is atmosphere kept in a cage. Unable to flow and change and just *be*, it becomes toxic.

Worlds in fiction can hold us close, fictional worlds within our real one can hold us back, a dangerous intoxication of bliss, an atmospheric withdrawal we might never stop craving. Yet in the novel, as well as the literal lost domain of Meaulnes's quest, there is another: the metaphorical lost domain of adolescence – a time when existence and feeling are heightened. When, like Meaulnes, we can invent who we want to be, begin to experiment with our curated atmosphere of self, and leave our birth lot behind.

The quote from *Le Grand Meaulnes* at the start of this chapter describes the moment when Meaulnes, lost and weary, stumbles his way into the place that will change his life forever. The emotion he felt was not one that he didn't or wouldn't describe, but that he could not have, even if he wanted to. It was an atmosphere that defined this place he would later struggle to find again. It was one place in one moment. Anonymous and powerful and strange. A place not described through what he saw, but by the feeling of being there – the only sensory experience referred is to that of a wind that seems alive, that could steal his breath. He had crossed into a mysterious domain that at this point is not a place: he has crossed an invisible barrier into an atmosphere. A place he will fail to capture again, even if physically in the same spot; places don't get lost unless physically destroyed, but atmospheres can be, even if their places look exactly the same.

In the novel, Meaulnes, a charismatic older boy who arrives in a small French village and soon becomes the leader of the 'cool kids', stumbles upon a decaying aristocratic estate during an extraordinary party thrown to celebrate the engagement of two young people. He is lost, having set out without permission, borrowing a neighbour's horse and cart to pick up the narrator's grandparents as a surprise. He is parted from the horse, injures his leg and strays to a smallholding, before wandering again and finding an old chateau. He wants adventure, he wants to escape from rivalry with other boys. But he could never have anticipated how he would become waylaid.

Lost. And not lost in the wilderness of a new place, but in an area that should have been familiar. Roads become unrecognisable. As he approaches, it is more akin to crossing over into a fairy realm, than a place in his ordinary French village life, which, experience would suggest, would not produce anything this extraordinary.

He stays the night before the party. Caught up in the strangeness of the atmosphere, he does not seem to consider leaving. He follows instructions as if in a dream, appearing the next day for the party in fancy dress – a top hat and wide-legged trousers, puff-sleeved black coat and fine shoes, an outfit from a different world to that of a poor adolescent in rural France at the turn of the twentieth century. He goes down to an empty courtyard, the weather is spring-like though it is winter; in fact he has been wafted away into a spring morning

– caught up and transported rather than it feeling like simple unseasonable warmth. Everything is different to how it should be in his life, yet he is still in the real world near the place where he lives.

The domain – always it is referred to as a domain. I have not read the original French, but the conscious choice of this word, loaded with separation, indicating a different place within this one, is significant. It is even physically contained: 'the whole domain was hedged in by woods which concealed it from the low-lying countryside'. He has crossed a threshold.

Fancy dress, strange weather, children without corresponding adults (there are adults at the party, but local labourers, none of whom are named as parents to the many children that frolic freely or strangely group together for night-time stories), everything here is atmospherically geared to suggest *other*. Meaulnes peers at his reflection and sees himself transformed – he can be someone else here, can leave the confines of his life. Everything is geared to ensure nothing would be the same again for Meaulnes.

The atmosphere that night is so rich that it seeps into Meaulnes's whole being and becomes almost a poison. Desperate to recapture that place and that moment and the beautiful young woman, Yvonne de Galais whose home the domain is, Meaulnes's life turns into a hopeless quest to find both the place and her again. The moment in the novel where he is in the place is brief. The story is his quest, the poignant fruitlessness of trying to regain something lost. Even when he eventually finds the place again it is not there in the same way – everything has changed, yet his thirst, his need for it as it was, does not. He meets Yvonne again and she falls in love with him, but he leaves her for another quest – to find the lost fiancée of her brother Franz, as if this will somehow bring that night, the fete, back to him; as if the potential for happiness, the gaining of his goal, is a bittersweet impossibility, that in this case ends tragically. He technically has what he wants, yet he does not feel so and loses it all – loses her – for the sake of the quest.

Atmosphere acts as heart, as protagonist of place made visible only to the initiated. There is a hint that such places could be anywhere, yet are nowhere; are hidden behind a veil in all of our ordinary worlds. And as with fairy worlds, you cannot guarantee entry, they can be lost. Just like our adolescence, with atmosphere, you can never return in quite the same way again. If Alain-Fournier had described the arrival in the lost domain in more objective terms, rather than through a shift in atmosphere, it would not have been so convincing; it would not have become literally and metaphorically elusive – a symbol for the hopeless quest for what we have lost and how, in holding on, we can lose what we have. Atmosphere can steal our hearts and grasp them, just out of reach, pulsing in an unobtainable impression, the past that was fleetingly there, a feeling.

Meaulnes fell into an addictive spiral – his own personal poison. The reality of fiction in our minds can be an atmosphere we carry and grow with, it can inspire, heal and help, but the atmosphere of fiction in reality, refusing to see the truth of where we are, or to be certain what is the truth, is a much more duplicitous companion. Imagining things differently can be good, memory can be good, but if we let a past atmosphere consume us, if it becomes a hope for what can never be, or maybe never was . . . I know that feeling. It is hard to let it go.

There was a Time when our Shadows
Talked to Each Other – Sicily

Iremember a white town blanched in sunlight, where the paint made me feel like I could peel the walls as if artichoke petals, hard yet furry.

I had walked all day, or not, the tiredness is easier to remember than what I had done to deserve it. But the sky, as I sat at the side of a street, the sky was all hazy for the fluffing – light, light, light. All wrapped up, I was, in streets and peeled paint and washing hung across streets as it should be according to old photographs and Mediterranean preconceptions. That was soothing. Wet sheets ribboned the air – empty trousers and socks – blowing out, they floated for the world, each other, invisibly held each other.

I remember a garden, but perhaps that was Sardinia – this trip blurs. Cicada-orchestrated garden of a hundred songs, I was lost, and held, by soft stones and honeycomb wire. Setting fires with found branches below blocked-up chimneys, I wrote his name in the sky, all lava ink and charcoal. It stayed there for a while. Imprinted in the air. Rhythms.

He was always there. The strong root of my bough break.

Warm land of air smote with oranges, dust-caressed tyres, lemon exhausts fumed my hair and skin.

Long-lost trail of mopeds and maze-dripped streets. The cars do not know where to park so just stop – conceptual pavements outline their progress to the centre of the town square.

Beep, beep! Horns hyperventilated, disturbing my utter sense of quiet. Though I didn't lose it entirely. There was a stillness.

A scattering of sparrows.

That night, a midnight explore down by the old fire station; our shadows grew and talked – held hands – we were linked in walls and night light; he understood everything and it broke my heart. But not as much as the feeling that the memory of my connection with him, him and me in that place that felt so true, was perhaps a misunderstanding.

Down the wall that held shadows, the islands of pebbles were moving on. Softly, softly they swirled off in the sea of dust.

A megaphone called through the empty mist. There were no fires or bodies to burn, but ours, yet someone called out.

I wonder if anyone else heard it.

The event happened – but the feeling?

Things that are not true have the power to refuel stars.

Approaching Enna, we climbed up in the car as if making for a town in the sky. It hovered above us as we wound our way up twisting roads as if on a reverse helter-skelter. I had no sense on the approach that this was going to be an atmosphere that would stay with me forever, that had a life of its own that would affect not just me but another.

Enna is my lost domain – my *Le Grand Meaulnes* moment – not a party in a once aristocratic estate that felt unreal, but a stop on a theatre company schools tour with a colleague who was a friend that

I was falling in love with; and I didn't understand right then how it could be so intense, yet not real. Unrequited love, blurry love, blurred with place, is an atmosphere unto its own. Yes, there are pheromones and human chemistry – an atmosphere of people, an atmospheric communication, which can be explained scientifically as well as by a mutual connection, and getting on . . . (In fact, I am starting to think more and more about the reciprocal nature of atmosphere – like true sexual chemistry, I am not sure it can exist unless it's mutual, unless there is a communication, a collaboration open, energy flowing.) But this was something different.

I look back now with twenty years' hindsight and it was not a great love in the adult scale of things – it did not take long to get over, but the feeling of Enna did. The magic of that moment will be with me forever – a hint at a feeling my life could have been richer for having so much more of; the fuel that led to years of wanderlust, travelling to feel, rather than settling in the established role society expects from you as your twenties progress. It set me free to discover places I may never otherwise have travelled, to forget caution, to be an adventurer – yet it also held me back.

It was not just the atmosphere of the town. As for Meaulnes, I suspect that if I ever went back to Enna it would not be the same. It was an atmosphere that was a combination of place, person and moment in time –a night-time walk to be specific – that was so strong it became an unspoken bond between us; that was so intense and strange that looking back twenty years later, I cannot quite believe was real. I know it happened, and he knew: I would get cryptic emails referring to it randomly for years afterwards – just a walk – we didn't even kiss, then. Yet there is part of my logical brain that says it cannot have happened. And it wasn't just that it was dreamlike – in fact, it wasn't, I was supremely awake – it was that it holds more than any other atmosphere moment a strange age-sensitive aspect. I was twenty-three, so not quite adult, not quite adolescent; but as an adult now, I wonder if I would ever be able to feel a place in the same way. I hope I would, but the strange mixture of age and adventure and future as a vast place, somehow made the feeling of being there in that moment more intense. It was fleeting, like Meaulnes's party, and it was out of reach the second it was over. There will be other atmospheres, but to search constantly for this one would drive me insane; it did a little – a blissfully doomed quest that would hold me back rather than propel me forward into the future that in those days was so endless and bright. But somehow I don't regret it at all.

Sicily itself is undeniably a country rich in atmosphere – a country, or at least a kingdom, in itself as it feels so distinct from the Italian mainland. When I was there I explored its rich history – from the ruined temple and amphitheatre at Segesta, to the amazing Roman mosaics at Piazza Armerina (ancient bikini girls!) and the lively markets of Palermo. I watch *Inspector Montalbano* on telly now, the excellent detective drama set in Sicily, and feel nostalgic for the place I spent a month driving around in 2002. Yet I am watching the series as an adult, finding the scenery and comedy of some of the characters comforting. I thrill at the aerial shots of crustacean-like hill towns. The Mediterranean sun on pale stone. The stony landscape and glittering sea. The locations of the TV show trigger memories, yet the places they portray, some of which I visited, have nothing to do with the atmosphere of Enna that night. They are obviously Sicily and that makes me happy – I can link them to the place. But my domain was a different place, an undercurrent, within it.

When I think back to Sicily and its atmosphere, I am struck by how different it is to certain preconceptions. Sicily's history is dark in terms of popular consciousness, as it cannot avoid the Mafia. Organised crime is a powerful subconscious atmosphere influencer. Walking down a dark street in a beautiful medieval town would seem magical in some places, but knowledge of past crimes can change all that to a sinister feeling. Yet if we take away our preconceptions, if we can let go of them, remove that layer that builds an atmosphere and in this case clouds it, then Sicily is quite a different place. Sometimes dark, yes, but for me the atmosphere was one of warmth and freedom and light. It was friendly and a little wild. The Arabic kick it has was more dominant than I had thought it would be. Spice. Rocky heat and endless lemon and orange groves. The most sinister it felt to me was when climbing Etna in thick mist, the tang of volcano in the air promising violence of the earth, not people.

And the buildings and art – glorious mosaics and baroque towns, earlier medieval streets, sunshine and sea and ancient churches. Warm food and red wine. It was full of heart. Steep, steep steps in a lot of towns, hill hugging. I sat and watched old men in the park – I have a photo from the pre-digital age when landscape features were a new thing. The print is twice the length of an old photo and shows a bench with twelve old men, sitting and talking. I found a particularly good stick on a walk and saved it as a staff and the only people who looked at me oddly were my colleagues. They considered a found stick to be an affectation instead of appreciating the genuine pleasure of discovering something beautiful and strange and useful for clambering up hills.

Enna is right in the centre of Sicily. Far from the sea that rings the island, it is sometimes known as its navel. It is a hill-top town, high and looking out across the landscape, buildings like strange crenellations of a castle rock. But that is to understate it – it towers over the landscape. With sheer cliff faces tumbling to the ground, it is worthy of *Lord of the Rings* in terms of being a dramatic natural fortress. And though the landscape is dry there are springs of fresh water, perhaps explaining to me the sense of water I felt despite the barren surrounding rocks. Enna is called the navel, but that central position makes me think of how the centre of a place is often seen as the heart. Yet Enna is largely forgotten, not a big tourist destination, marooned in the landscape of the interior. It is not beating, keeping the blood of Sicily flowing – the sea does that more, as if the country's veins are more an exterior sack, a caul of salt water. Conceptually, though, atmospherically, there is something central to it in its position. Like a heart, it is hidden yet powerful. Our adolescence could be seen as our central heart – the place at our core from which the rest of our lives develop, under our choices rather than the parental directions of our childhoods. This is conceptual speculating, I know, but when I think of Enna as a place this secret heart of atmosphere, this sense of contained feeling, feeling that defines us, seems at one with the town I remember – its old buildings and steep force field of cliffs.

The town had an extraordinary feeling of containment. Virtually impossible to leave on foot and high, as if floating like a strange city in the clouds, it had a natural border that kept its atmosphere inside. I could picture that to leave one would need a magical ladder, a beanstalk, a Magic Faraway Tree. Perhaps if I'd stayed longer it would have changed – a different world at the top of the rocks every day.

I could see the landscape around it, but it did not intrude into the walls and streets. The landscape was barren. The food in a small restaurant we ate in was the best meal I have ever had. Lush ricotta . . .

Contained – yet not an interior. A realm to wander around, like our youth is in our memory. I wonder if there is something in that: that the atmosphere was so powerful, because it functioned as a moment in time as well as place. That it felt like a domain, as our youth is a lost domain. When I left I somehow knew I could never recapture it. But the fortified position on the hill would somehow keep it safe, preserve it as if in a glass bubble, invisible to others, but still there. I am not sure I want to go back in case I cannot find it.

And the man I was with. I wonder now if I was not so much falling in love with him as with the atmosphere of us being together in that time and place and how magical that felt. That this contained atmosphere heightened this – as if anything that happened as we wandered Enna would not count elsewhere but was somehow rarefied by its presence in that place and moment. When it all went wrong the betrayal felt not so much of me, as of our moment together in this little town.

We snuck out for a midnight walk, leaving our other colleague to rest in the hotel. We had had the extraordinary dinner. We had to get up early, but we both agreed there was 'something in the air', not just the cliché, but a real feeling that meant we could not sleep. We had travelled all around the island, but the pull of this Enna night was different, more powerful and calling for us to throw sleep aside and wander.

We followed our instincts, walking slowly, whispering as if words spoke too loud might shatter the night air, disturb something, break this strange feeling to pieces. I felt like I was carrying this feeling, a fragile object, thinnest porcelain or glass made into a delicate sphere or bauble; petal-like, it could disintegrate rather than smash. We hardly dared speak. But softly we did as we whispered our way through the streets. We veered away from the centre, wandered down. I remember a feeling of mist though there might have been none.

There was a surreal moment. Down what felt like steep steps towards a more modern building a tannoy sounded – an Italian voice penetrating the air like a strange horn. We were near the fire station, I think, but there was nothing to suggest a fire. Nothing to suggest these sudden loud words meant any action. I still find it hard to believe that they happened, but then why would I make it up?

We came to a wall and our shadows elongated. We stood and stared at them as if they were on a stage and our hands drifted closer till our shadows were holding hands where our bodies barely touched. Shadow selves, something part of us trickling out and smearing, caressing, soaking, gently staining – the words are all too harsh, too thick and physical to describe the ephemerality of our marking, its temporary quality, which emotionally felt as strong as a dark mist tattoo. I know he felt it, if that alone. *We will always have Enna* . . . Months later he wrote that . . . Months after we'd lost contact . . .

I found my diary from that trip this morning. I searched through its pages – mostly creative writing, poetic prose fragments rather than descriptions of my days, it took a little while to find the entry. The 15th of March 2002, writing in Trapani, Enna the night before: *Had the most amazing explore last night . . . Felt like I was in an Antonioni film . . . Spiralled down old new paths till we found what looked like a distant glowing ghost town, only to realise it was a cemetery not so far away. The mist came down so we could feel the cold and damp and see it moving so quickly. The stars were bright though. Very beautiful. Very lost. Think it's one of these moments I won't be able to find again.*

I had forgotten the magical cemetery. Ghost town seems right, though. Beautiful. Lost. But the strangest thing reading this just now, having already written the preceding lines of this chapter, was that it was clear, twenty years ago, that atmospherically, I knew.

Enna is a town of tradition. At Easter time there is a famous parade through its streets. The white hooded gowns could seem disturbing, eerily reminiscent of attire associated with the Ku Klux Klan, though obviously very different in meaning and symbolism. When the hoods are pointed they are deeply unsettling; when not pointed occasionally more reminiscent of how a child would make a ghost from a sheet. But taking away the Christian context, the procession has an air of the undercurrent, of something waking up, something normally dormant in the town coming forth and for that moment taking over the citizens and streets and making itself known. A different atmosphere of place wanting us to be reminded that it is there, that there are levels of meaning in place which we don't always understand; that have the potential to become even more prominent, to wake from their usual slumber. I don't think it is surprising that All Souls' Day is a bigger festival than Christmas in Sicily, in terms of community celebrations.

I discovered later that Enna is also the site of the story of Persephone and her abduction by Hades to the underworld. There is a cave nearby, apparently once surrounded by a beautiful flower meadow, now barren like the rest of the landscape. This cave was the entrance. It tantalises me; the sense that under this strange contained town of atmosphere was the way into the classical underworld. And the site of the once meadow: as well as the underworld, Persephone is associated with spring and with rebirth when once a year she emerges into the world above ground; has she stopped? Are the flowers barren in protest at her absence? What happened to those flowers, the landscape now so rocky and dry – is this the underworld creeping up?

Sicily, underworlds … Cosa Nostra, the Mafia – it is another underworld that Sicily is famous for, and it was often these smaller, less well-known towns like Corleone that were the places from where the Mafia ruled not just Sicily, but large parts of the political establishment in Italy and criminal goings on further afield – such as the USA … A place of underworlds.

The Mafia is undeniably a part of Sicilian history and dominated its story through the majority of the twentieth century. The killings – I remember reading of one that was named after the yearly tuna fishing event, which turned the sea red with blood … The country was bathed in death – massacres – streets falling silent at night as people stayed indoors. By the time I visited in 2002, they had woken up again; when I walked through Palermo at night, people were around. Evening *passeggiata* in Modica is one of my favourite people-watching memories – men parading and strutting, window-shopping, eyeing themselves up in the glass, scooters lazing and girls with their friends, walking and watching. The smell of coffee and chocolate mixed with fumes.

I feel strongly that the Mafia is a part of Sicily's history that atmospherically is distorting to think about too much. It makes feeling the true sense of the land a bit like trying to read a text that has been redacted with black marker: history has decided that you will always view this ancient place through a few recent decades of human darkness and excess … I found a similar thing in places such as Serbia and Georgia that have had late twentieth-century wars; some were sure these areas were dangerous, alarmed at my visiting. But those connotations fade more quickly, are not propped up by films and myths. Not classical gods and goddesses, but dark reality stumbling into the realm of story fuel; and stories become part of a landscape, where it can be hard to avoid them.

Land of underworlds and myth, what might or might not have happened, but under all of this a layer – an under, not an over layer.

Perhaps the Mafia is an over layer, but Persephone, the feeling in Enna that night, the old not modern criminal underworld – that was what was simmering underneath. I could feel its presence, its wanting to wake up. It didn't obscure the feeling of the place, it revealed it.

I was young. I am clear that affected how I felt at that time in that place. Yet I wonder about that moment of transition from child to adulthood and how a sense of 'under', of darker, different realms is something we have a stronger affinity with, closer access to atmospherically at that age.

My feelings in Enna were not one of a dark underworld, but beneath the surface they were. Love and longing are something we hold inside, can be unspoken, fragile and vulnerable. This emotional state can lead to light or dark, free us or bury us. As we walked round Enna my feelings were present with us – a strange power that I felt could break out, like power released in an earthquake, and ruin everything. This is metaphorical, though the power is real, but I think there is something more explicit in this idea of underworld, or our need to imagine its presence, our ability to feel it is there.

And I believe this feeling is stronger in us when young. It always amazes me when people are shocked that children's imaginations are dark – in my experience, young people both write and enjoy reading things that are a bit scary. The psychology of fairy tales helps children make sense of darker feelings they may be having. When working with young people, an actual underworld or different version of this world comes up again and again. It is not just the fact it is a well-made TV series that makes *Stranger Things*, the hit Netflix show, so popular. Its visual realisation of the Upside Down, a terrifying dark world literally under ours, appeals to adolescents, as well as adults tapping into their adolescence – aided in this case by the perfect eighties set-up. And in the Upside Down there is a monster that is as much a presence as a physical thing, a monster that possesses an adolescent boy. It is the underworld that imaginatively could be everywhere. Light and shade. Our feelings of place aren't all joy, they aren't all one thing. There is a potential darkness everywhere; it simmers, a potent lining for our world in light, ever there, full of intrigue and its own pleasures, its own variety which it brings to the world.

Enna is an atmosphere of pleasure yet heartache. A most treasured memory, yet one laced with the dark. Persephone, after all, was both the queen of the underworld and the goddess of spring. In terms of my age then and its atmosphere, this makes perfect sense.

Travel – memory ... After the Italian months, I let fly. Rootless, searching, I quit my job, unable to be near him, disappeared – Berlin, Rome, Paris ... Months drifting. Then chronic ill health recurred and grounded me. Trapped, I dreamed of travel, held off for a few years then let fly again. Nashville for a long while. Armenia, Georgia, in-between roamings – Venice, Istanbul, Belgrade many times ... Art projects in Romania. I went everywhere that would take me.

Looking back, I can see that what for a while seemed like adventurous fleeing from a life where I was unhappy, was more complex than this. I wasn't running away so much as trying to find a way of living where I was free and not held back by ill health. Where creatively my brain worked, un-bogged down by what should be a reality – home, family. Why was this supposedly more real than when travelling, where I felt more alive? I was again questing for atmosphere, just more internationally than when a child on the Maypool.

It was my twenties, my young adult (not adolescent) life when this happened. I look back at the intensity of those moments and try to picture feeling that way now. I hope I could feel like that, but there is something in middle age that changes the nature of travel. The adventure can be there, but I cannot ignore that, for me, there is no longer a future that feels infinite, nor a period of time that feels liberated in its forward momentum towards a more exciting future; a time ahead where things I thought were bound to change – house, kids, husband. I had no huge craving for these things, yet I felt they were inevitable. Until they arrived, as long as I had the money to get by, I did not worry about the future. All was one glorious present, an atmosphere on whose sheer abundance to get drunk. Places were anything but background, they were new friends, locations to get to know, to reinvent myself, to discover and hold dear. The world was full of feelings for the taking. It was the time of my life when I made friends with the world. I was open to it and, in welcome, it flooded in. My tender map changed by the day and even if there were moments of pain, the pinpoints burst brightly.

*Part
Two*

Sentient Shapeshiftings

Invisible Cities

'The city, however, does not tell its past, but contains it like the lines of a hand, written in the corners of the street . . .'

Italo Calvino, *Invisible Cities*

In my twenties I was an urban traveller. Edinburgh, London, Tokyo, San Francisco, Rome, Paris, Belgrade, Yerevan, Tblisi . . . I got to know places by walking them, endless roaming on a quest for new streets and strange surprises, the joy of peering in lit-up windows at twilight, the discovery of places where I would then imagine living, or where it seemed like I'd stumbled into a different city, realms within realms, atmospherically distinct, alive.

I've always liked the idea of sentient buildings, of places being alive, and as I wandered, I began to think more about this idea of city as collaborator, of place as potential realm of communication that we just don't engage with normally. What stories had happened in these places? (Folktales are by nature rural, from a time when cities as we know them barely existed; urban myths are a different thing – connotations of lies or humour more than true stories of place.) What did they feel about the city around them? As they couldn't literally talk, was there a way to make these thoughts and feelings – which I guessed at – more 'visible'? I engaged on a series of projects to try to find out.

Looking back, I can see a certain naivety or lack of finesse in their execution, but the ideas behind these projects were deeply genuine. In my twenties, I created a number of works under the umbrella *'and the ghosts so silver'* – fixated with a sense of the hidden, the gentle haunting, the ephemeral. I hid homemade miniature books around cities in the cracks of walls. They held but one line to be completed by the finder and sent back to my anonymous address. I wanted the place where they were found to act as a kind of site-specific illustration – as if the place might seep into the words of the finder and come back to me. I made a library of these miniature books, which I displayed at a literature festival as an archive of city word illustrations. But looking back, I think it was the atmosphere of these places I was curious to find – to see if what I felt, what these places communicated to me, were different in the hands of others.

I became obsessed. I left Post-it note trails on walls and lampposts for people to follow – stories and poetry fragmented and responding to each place. I created ephemeral anonymous graffiti out of dust and leaves on the street, swirling words as if the place was talking as an antithesis to the tagging and claiming of normal graffiti. I created soil histories – buried works that might never be found, trying to capture the hidden layers, a kind of ephemeral archaeology of atmosphere; I was digging, I was seeking. I wanted to erase myself. To be anonymous. To let the city speak. And pre-social media, this did not seem strange. I was quite content to just let the works be – to leave them for the city to do with what it would. The city was my collaborator. I wanted to heighten how I felt in it – to seek out its hidden depths, to let it know that I saw it. This had its own creative joy for me. Without realising it at the time, in a different way, I was again in thrall to atmosphere.

Although my heart is in the countryside, the places that my mind creates in dreams are always cities, intensely atmospheric and weirdly consistent from dream to dream. They are not just replicas of cities that I know, but their own thing, recognisable to me, recurring across months and years, different to their namesakes in the 'real' world.

When I arrive in a city in my dreams I know where I am, even if it is an area of this dream city I have not explored before. Bristol, Glasgow, Berlin, Nashville, Montreal ... I am never in any doubt as to where I am in these cities. But I do not know this because I recognise the strange curving flyover that Bristol only has in dreams, or the deep loch that seems to sit in dream Edinburgh, where there is no hint of reality's nearby sea, but rather I know where I am by their atmospheres. It is strange, for example, how I always thought Paris was a city of golden light, but the first time I arrived there in my dreams, it was dark and I had to find a place to stay in a small, curved row of buildings tucked into the city as if they could be tumbled upon and swallowed up at any time.

Sometimes I analyse the recognisability of these places and their consistency – dream London has a certain light. While the buildings can change every time I visit, there is occasional architectural logic: a strange series of glass towers in which I move flat endlessly and that I think are supposed to be in East London; high-up places that are more Hampstead or Highgate ... The city climbs to the northern suburbs and the East End is hotter and low down. The atmosphere varies, but is still distinctly dream, not real, London. For that is the strange thing. The atmospheres of these dream cities are consistent, but when I think of the atmospheres of the real places they are not the same at all.

Dream Manhattan is full of dark water. It curls around, black from the lack of sun, which hovers in the background. I always find a friend here and we go down scruffy alleys full of shops of the coolest clothes and records I can never find again. Sparkles from the dresses shine through the dusty windows. Over the tar-like river, Brooklyn is sunnier. The streets widen to show houses with many families, who hang their bodies or belongings out of high windows.

Our dream versions of real places are not necessarily something we pay attention to. We may remember a dream, the atmosphere may follow us around a little the next day, but when analysing dreams we tend to think of what happens in them or who was in them rather than how they felt in terms of place. Was it an ex-boyfriend or old friend you'd argued with, were there classic anxiety events: teeth falling out, tsunamis, never finding a clean toilet, being late or – a new one for me recently – losing control of a car?

I used to be able to fly over rooftops to escape, but that dream freedom has deserted me the last couple of years.

I think there is a strange power to the atmosphere of night dreams – the subconscious access they give us to a place, that even if in the height of reverie I am not sure we could conjure in our waking hours. The conscious creative power might be in our ability to daydream, the human poetic power, but the deep intense inspiration that exists around our conscious thoughts, itself acting as an atmosphere does, a mist of uncontrollable inspiration, inhabits the night.

I remember how dream Tbilisi appeared ringed with water. And as I arrived the city wove itself around me, more beautiful than any I had seen before – the buildings grew out of the ground in pastel shades, as if so old they were part of the earth they stood on. I got on the monorail that led around this dream city, dripped down to the water and threaded together the parts that made it. The areas were scrunched up like discarded handfuls of paper. Old and accidental, this place had grown to look more natural than any I had ever seen.

I have asked friends and students how they dream places. Some have dream versions such as mine, others anonymous places, others a more logical reproduction, but they all have in common an intensity, a feeling that this place *is* somewhere. Somewhere that is both of itself and ours.

We are no more than surface tour guides for transient visitors when relaying our dreams. A dream atmosphere is hard to get across as we, as the night dreamer, will be living the intensity of being present in the dream that others cannot access. A retelling is but a facsimile, rather than a creation – a case of you had to be there, be the dreamer – whereas a daydream is more communicable in its creative consciousness; its part-awake nature gives us a conscious creative power to tell something others might have a chance to reach. We can tweak it to their needs, while night dreams will stay stubbornly true to what they want to be.

But if retelling our dream places falls short of doing their magic justice, perhaps there is another way that they are uniquely placed for a personal experience of atmosphere. Are dreams where we distil the dominant atmosphere of places? Where when descriptive words fail us, our imaginations can create that most intangible of feelings visually, then layer on our other senses as things happen to us in them? A 3D inner portrait of the true nature of a place as it speaks to us individually? The way a place can communicate its true identity to us and how we relate to it? Our archive, where we keep atmospheres we have experienced safe, able to live again even though we will never experience them again exactly the same in the awake world.

Dream cities are ours alone.

And if we are lucky, we can take this feeling into our day lives – hold it close so we can recognise those strangest moments, when sometimes the atmospheres of our waking and sleeping lives collide.

Venice

'It is encircled with illusory reflections, like mirages in the desert – wavering trees and blurred hillocks, ships without hulls, imaginary marshes: and among these hallucinations the water reclines in a kind of trance.'

Jan Morris, *Venice*

The city with the most pervasive atmosphere of dream space I have visited is Venice. This is not feeling as if in an actual dream, or awake dreaming, but the atmosphere of a dream space transposed to when clearly awake. I have only visited in winter, so it may feel different in summer where tourists potentially make the observance of an atmosphere challenging, but I have an inkling the atmosphere is still there like a deep undercurrent, flowing and twisting the streets, seeping into you, disorientating magic.

I, like many people, had a pre-vision from photographs and films of what Venice would look like, but how it felt was a revelation. The first time I went it was February and dark and damp. I arrived by car and got the train in from a neighbouring town. I was just there for a night, a quick break mid-work tour, but when I look back I hardly remember the city as physical structure, so much as the atmosphere. Unsuspected darkness. Watery, yes, but in a way that was deeper than canals, their damp smell. There was a flow of atmosphere that permeated everything the way damp does a house, but older, less visual, subliminal. I walked and got lost and every time I thought I found my way, a street twisted. Streets that I swore I had been on before mutated like a magical staircase changing direction. Déjà vu hit me at corners. And the darkness – I had not expected the darkness.

My diary of the time has no events, just images from a daydream, awake and seeing something else – dark water and a man who wasn't there.

The second time I went was four years later, in 2006, visiting a friend who was thinking about moving there from Rome. November this time. I arrived by plane and got the boat into town before making my way to my friend's flat on a quiet street that tourists would never find. It's strange, the tourists: in obvious places they swarm like ants, yet in a small city it is still easy to avoid them if you go off the obvious path and don't mind the inevitable mind games of the streets and how they like to lose you.

Labyrinthine city. The streets formed a different pattern to last time. I was here again, yet all the ancient corners were brand new in how I came across them. They had switched memory position.

But, interestingly, on this trip the darkness had lightened. While the undercurrent of darkness was there, the skies had cleared to reveal the light that made Venice so beloved by artists. Sharp blue light, yet not summer blue, watery with a hint of pale grey even in sun. As if clouds were always stroking the sky even when absent. There was a clarity. Light of lakes, not swimming pools. The ground hinted at algae though the cobbles were bare. Smell of water and the loud silence of no cars.

I had very little money so bought a boat bus pass rather than used tourist boats. I would get on one just to see where it went. Get off and wander before catching another. Winding streets of washing lines. Cranes like dinosaurs swaying over the lagoon. It's an age-old travelling with no money trick of mine that started when I was seventeen and exploring Prague with a friend – we would get endless trams to strange suburbs just to see where they went . . . But with the bus boats it could take a day – such a small city yet it was sometimes hours before I realised where I was again. Occasionally, I would take a boat to another island: Burano, Murano with their colourful village feel, but still the watery yet clear light; the cemetery island where I watched lizards run across Diaghilev's tomb.

I was there a week. I did not feel as if I was in a waking dream, but that the whole city had the feel of a dream place – not mine but a universal dream city. This was different to how my dream versions of real places function. There was no consistency here, although I could see how it could speak to everyone – how this atmosphere, the extraordinary visuals, the watery smells would combine and make anyone feel as if they had stumbled into a dream. Yet I could not picture it in my actual dreams. Its atmosphere didn't need that archive, that subconscious way of unpicking its true feeling, uncovering and making it safe. I didn't need to recreate it while asleep. Here, despite the tourist ideas, the undercurrent was on the surface, dark and strange, ready and waiting to be interpreted while awake. The city was its receptacle. It was a living archive of its own dream self. A place that morphed and changed around and benevolently manipulated its visitors and residents alike. A place that felt unique yet imaginatively universal. A place that could be a different version of itself whenever it felt like it.

Invisible Cities by Italo Calvino is a book I came across long before I visited Venice, the city that inspired it; I was intrigued by its title and promise of imagined places inspired by the real. Framed by the narrative of the great explorer Marco Polo, as he talks to the emperor Kublai Khan of all the different cities he has visited, the book takes places into the realm of something that feels plausibly real, yet also impossibly so. We know these cities cannot be: sixty silver domes and a crystal theatre, stilts holding buildings above the clouds, a forest of pipes; we know they are functioning as something else, something within the imagination. '*The city of Leonia refashions itself every day . . .*' It becomes clear the narrative of descriptions of different cities can be seen as versions of Venice, yet where we really are is confusing and strange – we are within a cycle of atmosphere – a place within a place, an Escher staircase city, contained by Kublai and Polo's setting, yet infinite in how it rests in their imagination. Ephemeral yet concrete.

Invisible Cities is full of not so much cities that are invisible, as intangible yet somehow physically present. They are living contradictions. There are so many ways of reading the book, but for me it is one that seeks to or perhaps even draws attention to the fact that it is impossible to seek to paint a portrait of a city, just as atmosphere is almost impossible to describe; to put into words, or show how words fall short of describing all the layers of meaning and experience and feeling that make up a place. How dreams, our inner vision, experience, cannot be replicated.

However, that does not mean that we should not try. It does not mean that it is automatically a failed project, but rather one that should just be approached differently; to not seek the literal but the more subtle; to not seek a concrete portrayal, a photorealist portrait, but something impressionistic. Impressionistic images often give us a deeper insight into the essence of what is being depicted than an attempt to perfectly reproduce a visual record. Think of Monet's water lilies– they are arguably more 'water lily' than any photo of the garden where he painted them would be. He is painting the feeling of what he sees. Atmosphere is impressionistic.

Invisible Cities is not setting itself up as a document of truth. The first line of the book is 'Kublai Khan does not necessarily believe everything that Marco Polo says'. But that does not mean for me that it is not seeking the truth, but rather that the truth is an evolving transient thing that is different for each beholder. There is no one 'truth' to a place. If we let go of the 'truth' of the traditional way of describing a place, then the atmosphere that could be better described within the realm of the imaginary has room to be seen, or rather experienced, as sight is but one perceptive tool in the interpretation of atmosphere. Perhaps we could locate this evolving atmosphere 'truth' in the last line of the first fragment in the book, where, as places change, the 'tracery of a pattern so subtle it could escape the termites' gnawing' can be sensed.

Each city described could be seen as a representation of a different atmosphere of Venice, a different bone in the construction of its atmospheric body, which we can excavate and piece together like palaeontologists of the city, to build the fragile, brittle skeleton that is the intangible feel of Venice and all its incarnations through history. Indeed, Marco Polo says, 'Every time I describe a city I am saying something about Venice.' But what it also does is free Venice from our own preconceptions of it, till it becomes a universal city – both an intimate and all-encompassing portrait of how we experience place and how, when doing so, we also can't always escape home – our sense of interpreting the world through the filter of our own belonging.

Invisible Cities reads more like nonfiction than a traditional novel in terms of its structure and plot, but perhaps Calvino felt this was the only literary space where such freedom of depiction could be had. Literal nonfiction about Venice might not have achieved what he wanted, traditional narrative structure neither. I understand this need to find a different form – to create a space where the subtleties, the complexities of the endeavour of an alternative portrait, a depiction of the multiplicities of a city's identity can breathe. Story, plot, seems a difficult beast for it to survive in – atmosphere is nonlinear, feeling not action, ephemeral and un-pin-down-able in a traditional narrative framework.

I wonder if *Invisible Cities* works collaboratively; that in the creative act of reading we bring our own atmospheres and add them to the layers. In the book Polo says, 'This city does not consist of this (material description) but of relationships between the measurements of its space and the events of its past.' There is a different space that physical description struggles to access, to put into words; as we struggle to enter it physically, absorb its varied memories, there is potentially a dislocation between us and the environment.

Is this why traditional attempts to describe what atmosphere is fail, while at the same time atmosphere is one of the main tools writers seek to use? Can we only describe an atmosphere when it is fictional, rather than recreating an existing one? True atmosphere cannot be held captive – will change in every moment for each person in a place. Language is the tool we humans use to record our expressions, to communicate concretely that which other more subtle forms of communication such as expression or body language can't precisely articulate. Yet it is just a tool. All language is a sign language – a signal of an interior expression, rather than a concrete thing. Some signals delve deeper in terms of communication than others, reach our subconscious – hint at all the varieties of things they could really mean.

The world cannot write. It does not have language as we know it, words and pens and paper. But atmosphere ... Is this the world being creative, the world collaborating with us and leaving its traces in its own part internal, part external space that if we enter we can communicate with it? Atmosphere as a poetic collaboration – that rather than creatures on the surface of a world, we are moving through borderlands, intangible atmosphere lands, together.

Read the signs. Words are not everything.

In one of his cities Polo meets a philosopher who says, 'Signs form a language, but not the one you think you know.' Polo doesn't reply, but in his following description to Kublai Khan says, 'I realised I had to free myself from the images which in the past had announced to me the things I sought.'

Yet the book is divided into chapters where the cities are clearly defined as 'Cities & Signs', 'Cities & Memory', 'Cities & Desire', 'Cities & Eyes', 'Thin Cities', continuous, hidden and trading cities, 'Cities & the Sky', 'Cities & the Dead'. They are categorised but abstractly, in essence. The cities themselves often have the names of women ... There is a refutation of the power of language, then a sense of using signs as a way of categorising, distilling. Describing the signs through the imaginary cities, rather than seeking to describe the 'real' physical place. This is a multi-city of signifiers. And there is a power in their naming, not as Venice, but as women, as exotic words ... A cataloguing and a sense of other within the familiar. A naming to make real something that will forever be elusive.

There is an interesting point in the novel where language in the form of words breaks down and gestures and objects take their place in Polo's descriptions. It is as if language is inadequate. It is not enough, yet it is what we always strive to use first. But when we are trying to describe the indescribable, we are drawn in exasperation to use other means – to show, not tell, to use the primary school descriptive writing cliché, what it is we want to communicate to another – what we want our actions to represent. Is there a better language than the verbal one to describe atmosphere? Will words alone ever be enough?

I collect anonymous old photos and there is one that shows a man standing in wilderness outside an overgrown building. In some ways it is an ordinary image, yet there is something in its atmosphere, even with the distance of photographic reproduction, which is deeply mysterious. I tried to write a piece to accompany it, but words failed me. They were wrong.

I struggled on and eventually got close, but still something was missing in how it related to the photo's atmosphere. I then did something that surprised me. I invented an alphabet and translated the short piece of prose into it. I placed the photo on a piece of paper and wrote the words in my new symbols next to it and suddenly my writing seemed more adequate, more suited to illustrating the atmosphere of the photo, even though no one could read what it said. I had freed myself from the symbols, the letters that formed words, and in doing so had found the literary atmosphere I sought through symbols with no known meaning to others, but power as an image – a series of shapes open to atmospheric interpretation of form.

Imaginary alphabets, or constructed scripts as they are less poetically and technically known, are nothing new. From new alphabets constructed for previously unwritten languages, such as the Korean Hangul, Cherokee and others, to the fictional language alphabets of Tolkien and *Star Trek*, or technical ones such as the International Phonetic Alphabet, people have felt the need to pin language down visually. But while this is obviously for recording and reading purposes, I wonder if we are also forgetting that invented alphabets are a visual choice – that in creating something to represent visually a language that we know, in a synesthetic way we are trying to determine what a letter sound looks like and therefore part of that might be how that abstract shape makes us feel. When I was inventing my new letters I was conscious of the atmosphere of the photo and the piece. The letters I invented are much closer to my favourite swirling Georgian alphabet than the Latin alphabet I write in every day, as those swirls felt right for that image. Atmosphere is therefore perhaps not just about how it feels to be in a place, or how a place makes us feel, but how we feel about the symbols and signs we use to try to capture it.

Can we free ourselves from images, from signs, from preconceptions? I think of Venice and wonder. There can be few cities in the world that can match it for images – photos, paintings, the Rialto Bridge, those beautiful palazzos and the never-endingly surprising strangeness of canals, not roads, sink into the imagination as no other city does. The power lies not in the individual buildings as monuments, as covers for the memory of the city, but rather the whole city is the image – it takes flight so that we can picture a palazzo on a canal that is not an actual street, but which will be, for us, Venice. Yet the atmosphere of the real place was so different to what I had expected that it took over, wiped out what I had expected of the city, showed me how it really was. The lack of cars, that surprising silence I hadn't really thought through, overpowered so much else. It couldn't have been anywhere else, it was not an anonymous city and never could be: it was the Venice of endless images, it just felt different to what I'd expected – its atmosphere confounded all those representations. It made me question if we can ever hope to capture atmosphere at all, if all those millions of photos, the endless beautiful artworks didn't manage it . . .

A city has many lives yet while so many change physically, Venice is strangely preserved. The lagoon, the canals, an island full of historic beauty stands alone, slowly sinking, escaping, pickled, yet alive in its own reality. Changing itself through its atmosphere as humans didn't dare to. With all the water, imaginary water, real water, water smells and sky, it is preternaturally fluid. Everything flows, the streets, the feelings, the light, the public transport, the fashion, the birds and the buildings ... My feelings as I sat on bus boats and soaked myself in winter sun and strangeness flowed around me, seeped out through my pores and fed the watery air, building layers where bricks and new roads cannot. A different type of human contribution to the construction of the atmosphere of place; one taken without our knowing. A creative collaboration, where we are passive; it is the city that is active, it is the atmosphere.

Istanbul – Old Water

It holds an ancient sense of memory, Istanbul. No other place I know so little has stayed with my work so much. The atmosphere was alive, sentient – a creature, its own being wreathing through its streets like a strange mist.

It's a city that exists in the memory of those who've lived there but also in the memory of all its different incarnations. Ottoman Empire to Ataturk, Byzantium, Constantinople to Istanbul. Few cities have seen such vast changes in a worldwide consciousness as this ancient, rambling, living place on the banks of the Bosphorus. It has the feel of an ancient, real place rooted in centuries, but also of being disembodied by all the changes – that somehow in order to survive, its true spirit continued to live not in its buildings, but in its atmosphere.

How memory works in old cities is an interesting thing. Architectural historian Anthony Vidler talks of how the famous old buildings themselves do not function solely as structures, but rather their meaning comes by what they stand for, as tropes of a memory discourse. They represent what has happened to the city throughout history and in this way they can function as centres on a kind of memory map, containing the city's past. For example, when the Renaissance scholar Alberti described Brunelleschi's famous dome of the Duomo in Florence as *covering* the people in the city, Vidler suggests he shows it is inescapable, it is part of the foundations of people's memories within that urban space. The roles of these various monuments are discussed – how did they function and define the place, affect its identity? I think of Istanbul: Hagia Sophia, the Topkapi Palace, the Blue Mosque . . .

Great buildings do have power. Monuments do represent something universal – a collective experience of urban space, though I would argue they are always limited, they don't hold the everyday stories like folktales do: they are too static, devoid of the fluidity of place and story through time. Despite the amazing famous buildings, when in Istanbul, in its atmosphere, I didn't feel it was this monumental human history so much as city itself as lost living entity that was communicating with me. The atmosphere was far closer in how it functioned to folktales wreathing the air as they do on my West Country hills. It seemed more expansive than human history; or perhaps there was something in common with the personal feelings of its people that seeped out and joined together in a strange mist trumping the other feelings of the place that an objective reading of its history and its official architectural representation might conjure. Universal for ignoring the monumental, for letting go of the human, for stirring it all up in a city pot and becoming something new, a new kind of being.

The atmosphere of Istanbul was intuitive – it sometimes ignored its surroundings. But I could not ignore it and consequently all my previous reading about its history, most of which is very old due to historians focusing on its grand ancient past, seemed strangely obsolete. The theory of the famous structures somehow anchoring a memory map seemed wrong: devoid of emotion and personal everyday stories, they were isolated in a different city. There was no emotional topography, no sense of a personal quirky cartography inherent in any literal map of memory that I could picture. Ah yes, there is Hagia Sophia. There is the Topkapi Palace. Here is a new bit of the city. But the atmosphere did not care. The famous places were too abstract — too conscious an idea of what should constitute the memory of a city; and this consciousness felt too constructed, not intuitive enough to contribute meaningfully to the city's atmosphere. Not tender. They were façades rather than containers of atmosphere for me, however undeniable the memories, the events that took place in them over centuries. And they were contained in a very small area — an area full of tourists by day, empty at night. The atmosphere was there, but elsewhere; the atmosphere was its own being, an invisible creature that existed on its own terms.

The only thing that felt like it had true relevance for both past and present in terms of the atmosphere was the water. Old water . . .

My trip there had been strange emotionally, so I tried to think if that could have skewed things. I had gone with a good friend, a relationship that was not romantic but not entirely platonic either, even though nothing physical had ever happened and I was not sure I wanted it to. Sometimes the loveliest thing, it was more of a friendship romance — a sense that this was someone I adored and the fact they were handsome and male was a confusion or annoyance even, rather than relevant to how I felt. But he seemed after years to have concluded that my feelings must be romantic and his were not, and an uncharacteristic arrogance arose and somehow I knew that this long weekend was the end of our friendship, even though we had not fallen out. The blurriness and gossip were something it could not survive.

So we wandered the streets and the rain poured and we drifted and got lost, getting on boats to nowhere, catching the wrong minibus back to the hotel at night, accidentally gatecrashing a party in a guitar shop, being rescued by a Georgian friend who was living there . . . There was a melancholic inevitability to our wanderings. But through all this, the atmosphere was with me. It held my hand and sympathised, though did not soothe. It seemed inevitable to it that this should have happened. My friend disappeared into a mosque I could not enter and the wind from the water caressed my ears. What was happening became irrelevant, I knew that with certainty, as I began to try to rationalise the unexpected feeling of the place. He was not part of this atmosphere. There was a poignant longing, not for him. It was all city. It was alive. It was my true companion on this beautiful, doomed and melancholic trip.

The only book I have read that made sense to me as I thought of this idea of a collective strange atmosphere away from the monumental, one of longing and inevitability, is the novelist Orhan Pamuk's wonderful memoir *Istanbul, Memories of a City*.

Pamuk has spent his whole life living in Istanbul, to this day residing in his family apartment block. The city is a place so inseparable from his sense of self, that its name is the title of his autobiography, their stories intertwined – his memories are memories of a city. I can't help but think he means the sentient city's memories, not just his own.

The book moves between the history of the city and his own childhood, but it is not the famous buildings of tourist collective memory, historical monumental memory, which are the key players here, but the old wooden buildings that have disappeared like living creatures that have died; it is the family apartment blocks; the crumbled palaces dissolved like biscuits into the tea of the old water; the lived-in neighbourhoods. It is the Bosphorus Strait, sentient and full of stories, where, in the words of A. Ş. Hisar quoted by Pamuk, '[w]hen there is not a breath of wind, the waters sometimes shudder as if from inside and take on the finish of washed silk.' But most significant for me was that within its rich pages I discovered the Turkish word which for Pamuk defines the atmosphere of Istanbul, and finally began to make sense of what I had felt there: *hüzün*. *Hüzün* is one of those wonderful things, an untranslatable word. It means a kind of communal melancholy. There is no clarity to it.

It veils reality with a feeling, it brings comfort, softens this sense of acceptance that everything will go wrong – has always gone wrong; *hüzün* is inevitable, but here we are and the feeling is ours. *Hüzün* belongs to us; it is Istanbul.

Hüzün is threaded throughout the whole book, from atmosphere of city to that of the pages themselves. Pamuk dedicates a whole chapter to the topic, fascinating in itself: in the story of his life and the history of a city, while huge events are not mentioned there is an entire chapter about a feeling, an atmosphere. He starts with an attempt at a definition, beginning with the simple statement that it is the Turkish word for melancholy and has an Arabic root, before expanding to show that it is anything but as simple as that. Historically, *hüzün* is a kind of spiritual anguish or feeling of loss, first from partaking too much of worldly pleasures and later via the Sufi tradition of a more compassionate anguish at never being able to get close enough to Allah. But strangely it is the absence rather than the presence of *hüzün* that is upsetting – one should want to feel that we cannot do enough for Allah in this world.

Like many individual's intense spiritual feeling in place, *hüzün* has its roots in a sense of the divine.

But *hüzün* today has become something much less definable, yet a feeling that defines for Pamuk a city and its people. It is a feeling tied to hundreds of years of history and the feelings of its legacy, not just events. It is a state of mind and a state of place; life-affirming and negating; ambiguous and complex; the emotion of a place; an atmosphere. It was even seen as an illness, similar, though different, to how melancholy was viewed in Britain in past centuries. Melancholy is essentially a solitary experience, a turning inward, whereas *hüzün* is communal, making it both internal and external, the latter being key as it means it can *inhabit* somewhere, leave the individual and permeate the collective, the collective that inhabits a city. Set free from the individual, shared, *hüzün* can take root much more easily in the feeling of a place. The city can become the essence of *hüzün*, as much as *hüzün* can be the essence of the city. It could almost be seen as atmosphere *as* place – where the feeling, too fluid to be essential, becomes most physical, tangible – *collaborative*. If this is true, no wonder my short visit followed me home – unaware as I was that I had stumbled on a rare opportunity, a chance to feel an atmosphere at its most physically present, for it to touch and become part of me too.

I might have felt this – that it was in me too – yet Pamuk argues that *hüzün* does not belong to the outsider. It is impossible to explain to someone from elsewhere; the everyday hints and glimpses combined with the vast expanse of history are just too much. It is an atmosphere of both collective and national experience. There is maybe a 'mysterious air' we can access, but he argues this is closer to *tristesse* – a French term, also difficult to translate, for a sense of mysterious sadness – but *hüzün* is never truly accessible to the visitor.

Yet even for the native of Istanbul, *hüzün* is still a complex beast to describe. Despite the documented history of the feeling, the collective knowledge of its presence in the city, even Pamuk struggles to pin it down. Not a flaw of his wonderful writing, but a definition of the challenge of writing about atmosphere. As writers, we create interior atmospheres in our work all the time, but to describe an existing one rather than create our own is a very different thing.

Pamuk does it in an interesting way, taking this chapter on a stylistic route different to all the others. He explains he is about to describe not the melancholy of Istanbul, but *hüzün*. What then follows is one of the longest sentences I have ever read. Five pages long, it lists all the details that combine for him to create *hüzün*. From 'the seagulls perched on rusty barges caked with moss and mussels, unflinching under the pelting rain' to 'the cold reading rooms of libraries' to 'the holy messages spelt out in lights between the minarets of mosques on holidays that are missing letters where the bulbs have burned out', it is the most beautiful list of details you would miss without a lifetime's observation – a list as prose poem, a hymn to a feeling. Yet interestingly for a book that is so personal in tone – it is an autobiography after all – here is where he has had to reach outside to the collective: his personal feelings are not what is essential here. In some ways, he loses his own atmosphere – the atmosphere of his life and his writing – in thrall to the need to pin down; the effectively *hüzün* task of trying, with an inevitable sense of impossibility, to describe *hüzün*. There is a hint of frustration in the list format of this wonderful portrait – words fail when something is an atmosphere; we can try to capture it but the task is never complete; we can pile image upon moment upon image upon memory, but in the end we have but a list – a fascinating and beautiful list – but unless the reader is from Istanbul, it is but a tantalising hint at the depth of *hüzün* – an untranslatable word as deep as old water.

I love untranslatable words. Every language has them. Sometimes they describe behaviour, such as the Georgian *seyri* – meaning going to watch something terrible happening and taking a certain pleasure in it, like when there is a minor car accident and people get out to argue and more stop to watch. Although describing an action, *seyri* is more complex: it is a feeling, a perverse pleasure, not malicious, more detached, which is hard to describe to an outsider. There is an atmosphere in this – if it was truly nasty it would not be *seyri*. One of the more well-known untranslatable words is the Danish *hygge* – that cosy, understated feeling that again is hard to explain if you are not Danish, no matter how hard the media and marketers have recently tried. These untranslatable words have in common that they are hard to describe to outsiders – if you grow up with the feelings you just know what they mean – but what they also nearly all have in common is that they are atmospheres.

Hüzün. Hygge. The Czech *litost* – an infinite feeling, an undefinable longing, a sympathy, a grief. *Toska* in Russian. The German *Heimlich* or *Unheimlich* – the homely or unhomely that Freud was so fond of using when writing on the uncanny. The Arabic *Multaka*, both a literal and conceptual meeting point for sharing. They are all difficult to translate, yet they all describe atmospheres or feelings. They are all different but in a strange way are emotional synonyms – national possessions to capture the atmospheres of places you have to be from to understand. They are often concerned with a sense of longing.

Atmosphere is a quest for something so present, yet something that can never be recaptured the same as before – it is fleeting, we can search but we know that as soon as it floods us, it will pass and we will lose it forever. We might not share the same collective longing specific to our places, but that collective longing for a feeling of place we have lost – for our lost atmospheres – that we all understand.

To quote *Invisible Cities*: 'As this wave from memories flow in, the city soaks it up like a sponge and expands.' We might not understand exactly – but we can add to it nonetheless.

Istanbul. Atmosphere permeating the streets like a strange mist. The breath of the old water, rising up – Bosphorus, Black Sea ... My attempts, anyone's attempts at creative work in these streets is in thrall to this old water. Is but a layer between the dampness, the grey thoughtful sky, the glittering history, the sound of the call to prayer mixed with seagulls – minarets and blocks of flats. Layers that are human and not human.

Belgrade Dream Noir

The streets are made up of many cities. When I first arrived in Belgrade in 2007 I felt as if I wandered from Berlin to Paris by the turn of a corner – that suddenly a place which was slightly ruined and overgrown reminded me of Yerevan. Cities within one city, but not quite any of them. I couldn't describe it – it changed round every corner, an urban shape-shifter forming itself as I walked.

But though I knew Belgrade to be a city of a hundred atmospheres – a city where each corner of the street felt like crossing a border – nothing prepared me for the day of me and my friend Ana's crazy walk and the alternate realm that was a wet September Ada island.

Belgrade is dominated by the Danube to one side. That is a well-known fact. Looking out from the old neighbourhood of

Zemun, it is as wide as a truly exotic river – endless and Amazonian. Yet most of the city river views – looking from the old fortress towards Novi Beograd's tower blocks, for example – are not of the Danube at all.

Ada island lies on this other river that people never realise is different: the River Sava. I wonder how it feels to be a second river. Does the fact that visitors think it is the Danube, that popular imagination has credited it to another, give it a freedom to exist differently – a Narnia-like river only there for those it chooses to find?

That day in 2007, we left Ana's home in Zvesdera along streets that were straight then twisted, through wide boulevards full of tracks and wires and austere buildings that became lower and more village-like; little booths for tickets, sweets and cigarettes; struggling trees and lively bars. One moment it was quiet, then swathes of traffic.

We jumped onto a trolley bus which, despite the humid warmth, had its windows firmly shut. There is an adamant Serbian fear of draughts as the cause of all ailments (the previous night Ana's mother had got up at 4 am to close my bedroom window, as she could not sleep for worrying about the health hazard of it being open), which even the heat could not deter. We changed bus once or twice, running and jumping; not quite sure which one to get, we plaited our way in what we felt was the right direction.

And then huge houses, a divide of urban forest and an old building with a large bay window like a sleepy Cyclops eye. It was a history museum, I seem to recall, but what I remember most is the oldest tree in Serbia, standing there held up by metal posts like robot walking sticks, as we sat and drank thick sweet coffee, ate pancakes drenched with rosehip jam.

It had begun to drizzle and we wandered past endless weddings in large wooden huts by the tramlines, past barking dogs, made multiple crossings of roads. Then an arch made of uneven jagged rocks like the gateway to a dinosaur theme park. We walked through.

There were ferns growing up through the concrete. We climbed steps and before us was an amphitheatre – overgrown and hewn out from the cliffs, crumbled green wooden chairs by a graffitied booth for a non-existent attraction called the Sky Line. It didn't seem outside the realm of possibility that a train or cable car could suddenly appear and that this place would switch; that an invisible trigger would un-decay it all and turn it back to a heyday of I'm not sure what.

We shouted to test our echoes on the natural walls, damp and glistening, spittle of moss. Ghost poetry.

'OK, we go now,' Ana said. 'This day cannot get more strange so I am going to take you to the island which always is.'

Another tram, a confused trek down main roads, past kitsch communist statues wielding phallic spanners and then a bridge – and we were there, on the island.

The rain was getting heavier and we walked towards a cafe that Ana knew. Brightly painted concrete structures grew like psychedelic brutalist mushrooms. There seemed nothing strange about this in the context.

There appeared to be a lake, though I know Ada is an island.

There is a zoo too, not the main city zoo, but somehow we missed that – somehow the things that should have been the strangest were lost in the overall atmosphere, the strangeness of the everyday.

We found the cafe and drank beer while old men had a fishing contest. They were pestered by swans so had to delay, and were mainly smoking and drinking in the rain. One swan was apparently particularly problematic: 'He is psychopath – this very difficult swan.' I looked around at the wood and water and thought what a perfect house this place would make, with a bed on a sleeping platform.

I was not sure this day was reality.

We stood up and went on our way. While forgetting the zoo, Ana was sure there were many houses on stilts and these floating houses were what had caused her to bring me to Ada in the first place. I was already obsessed with the surreal Belgrade tendency to take normal caravans and float them on empty oil drums, so Ana said to see these stilt houses was a must.

But of course these stilt houses were nowhere to be found.

We walked and walked. Past the Red Star yacht club, which was the only place where birds were singing – hundreds in one tree. No people except for one lonely American child roller-skating, no stilt homes. But then we stumbled on a fairy tale.

A hidden village – small wooden houses, some ruined, some not, with perfect front gardens and painted wooden gates; too little for grown-ups, it was like a village for lost children. So many flowers. 'I have never seen this place before,' Ana said. 'We are unlocking deep weirdness.' I smiled. I dared not talk too loud in case I broke the spell. I trailed my fingers on the fences, but no yard dogs jumped up to bark. Apart from a flood of atmosphere and plants, it was empty.

It was another mysterious domain, lost to normal visitors, like Meaulnes and his doomed quest to find his domain despite it being a real place, not too far away. I am convinced that most people do not know the houses are there. Ana had never seen them before. And the scale. Looking back we must have got that wrong, yet it is the clearest memory of that day. A pinpoint blush of tenderness. I close my eyes and I can picture a small wooden cottage – bigger than a model village, smaller than a house an adult would live in, like a giant Wendy house. It had a front garden that was completely overgrown, but with flowers, not brambles nor the kind of weeds that signify neglect. Like the Three Bears' house, like the Seven Dwarves' house, it seemed that no one was home.

'I hardly dare breathe in case this shatters,' I said. I held Ana's hand and tried to catch the whispered laughter, dark on the softened wind.

'Serbia has many fairy tales,' she replied. 'Now we have one.'

Late afternoon, the evening began to draw in. We left the village and carrier bags decorated the trees like jellyfish – flowing, strange tentacle air that sang rustles through the wind. Torn ponytails of plastic stories, stories, stories . . . Our Serbian fairy tale. 'What is that drumming sound?' I asked. 'It's been following us for ages.'

The music was intense and distant. We followed it as if it were luring us in to a woodland ball from which we would never return. We paused for soup and bread under a stuffed two-headed eagle. The music continued. Puffs of potential parties blew in gentle shockwaves. Frothy promises of misadventure.

Rhythms. We followed.

'I think we should find crazy party with boys jumping over fire,' Ana stated. 'This seems correct outcome.' But the reality was even stranger. Bright lights and then an empty sports complex, floodlit, and the music, not drums of parties but Cher singing 'The Shoop Shoop Song' from the film *Mermaids*. It seemed like we'd stumbled on the aftermath of an American football game, but there was no one left. The lights and music had decided to have a party of their own now there was no one there to see them behaving so unnaturally; so alive.

Everything felt alive here despite our being alone.

We were confused with burned-out expectations glowing neon in the too bright light.

We decided to go to the pebbly beach at the edge of the water and walk around the lake-river.

The pedalos waited in silence as we walked past concrete bunkers, empty bars … We kept going till we heard another tune, a song so old it broke its heart all over the lake, bled minor 1930s chords in trickles that floated a slick of melancholic treacle. We called out to the early moonlight and laughed.

There was an old man sat behind a bleared clear curtain of fattened cling film. He beckoned at us wistfully, with wafts of smoke from falling ash, his other hand curved around the beer he wanted us to join him for.

We smiled but did not stop. He was real, I'm sure, yet seemed a ghost.

We walked through torrents that day. Darkness. Deep rain. Tenderising the streets. The stupid ballet pumps I'd worn were full of puddles. We talked and talked that way you can only talk when the world is so strange you and the person you are with are in a dream together. We had got inside each other's heads. This water, this rain and this island. Drowning in concrete and confessions. The sad, sad songs and old men and drenched swans. The little wooden houses.

That day on Ada island was the closest I had ever felt to being asleep when I was awake.

Real-world dream pockets.

When I said I'd been to Belgrade, my friends only thought of long-gone war.

Sometimes I wonder how one city can swirl around you like a far-flung quilt of many others. Undisturbed, we had walked through folds of places, hiding in a different layer, sweating secrets of this city.

Over the years, I have tried to figure out what happened that day. There are various ingredients I've debated that simmered into this potent brew: the excitement of being in a new country; being outside so long in torrential rain – an unfamiliar yet familiar territory of experience as we normally stay indoors in such dreadful weather; the uncanny power of that; the joy of discovery within a new friendship; the fact we had an early afternoon beer while staring at the swans; the music that swam through the air before we knew where it came from; the way we talked – two eccentric writers with such different backgrounds but minds that, fifteen years on, are still in sync for humour and strangeness; the lack of knowing what was to come next; the atmospheric build-up with the earlier visit to the abandoned amphitheatre; the getting lost (though I now know this is just standard when with Ana). Yes, it could have been a combination of all these things.

Certainly, there is something unique in the shared experience of atmosphere here; normally it's something we experience alone, but I'm pretty sure Ana and I had the same feelings of place that day. Still, I cannot shake the sense that we crossed through some sort of dimension barrier and were in a different realm and, like Pamuk's description of *hüzün*, I find myself trying to make sense of it with a list, knowing full well that I cannot capture it. Atmospheres do not like the cage bars of words.

Writers often work best first thing in the morning or in the depths of night. There is a precious moment when our brains are so close to sleep that the atmosphere of the dream realm is easier to enter – when the thin layer of consciousness which veils it is more permeable. Yet outside, in the middle of the day, in company, this borderland should be impossible to visit. I sometimes wonder whether it is partly why poets such as Coleridge liked to experiment with drugs – they were searching for that way in; the entrance to the place where ever-elusive inspiration can be scooped up with a spoon. Yet on that day, there we were, no mind-altering substances bar a single glass of beer.

Was it this day, this company, or this city?

I have never quite found that atmosphere in Belgrade again, whether with Ana or other Serbian friends, yet still it is very much of the city – not a random chance that could have happened anywhere in the right circumstances. Belgrade is a strange place that does not behave like others.

There is that multi-city feel – the streets that feel like other cities yet clearly are not. The fact that it is not beautiful, yet can capture you like a city that is. The vast expanse of water that on a hot day cools you with smell rather than a palpable drop in temperature as you approach. The diversity of neighbourhoods squished together – old village-like Zemun, almost a distinct town on the Danube banks, though not far from the brutal growth that is Novi Beograd; New Belgrade and the Sava.

Trolley buses are like creatures and I can never quite figure out how the old fortress gazes over the city yet is hard to spot from most places. The buses would crawl around a map like caterpillars, rewriting it with the whims of the day. This map would have layers.

History is in layers here – of conflict if you read the books, Ottoman conquest and Balkan wars – yet it is a friendly, laid-back place of which you would not guess this. When I joke with Ana about how the band Depeche Mode are still huge here, the industrial and goth scene does make sense. There is a strange, dark undercurrent that seems to need to push its way up. Erupt, maybe. I remember telling Ana about a Georgian device to trick your car's alert when your seatbelt isn't fastened, so it stops beeping; she replied, 'Ha, in Belgrade we would just smash it.'

Old water, collective memory held in an atmosphere. City as collective, not the people. Belgrade is not so fond of the collective, Ana says, post-Tito rebellion – hedonistic communism. This city rebels. Maybe that's why its streets change so much: it is restless, shrugging off memory like discarded sweatshirts, crumpled in corners, getting damp, trickling dust. Rivers.

There are no internationally famous buildings. The fort, which I know by no other name, is old. The monuments are the forgotten concrete mushrooms, the weird statues. But that is to fall into tempting communist clichés. Once, at Tito's museum, I spent hours admiring homemade batons sent to him as gifts, obsessions with endless relay races. Other gifts – miniature orthopaedic gear, official gifts of the most literal didactic strangeness from official organisations.

Kitsch. Yet anything but. We fetishise the fun side of memories that are dark. Dream noir. Undercurrents – watery; there was an island where people were sent to their death.

I remember eating sesame-strewn pizza on a boat with laughter loud as bees.

When I was dancing in the indie disco as a teenager, Ana remembers the windows of her bedroom blowing in from NATO bombs. The parallel late 1990s. Two friends, so much in common except the experience of youth. Of war. Bombs and fear and consequent hedonism. (Georgian friends talk of this – *oh, but the best parties were during the (civil) war . . .*) But this is oblivion. Friends lost – heroin, idiocy, gangsters – opportunity lost, parties obliterating an uncertain future. The atmosphere – the best party – layering one to destroy another; to become an atmosphere blanket, heightening some senses to dull others.

I wonder how past war, the memory of war, not active bombing and fighting, affects the atmosphere of a city. A hangover undercurrent, an inherent nervousness, a collective PTSD of place. Or a bravado, a sense of invincibility. War as a once strange dream with real consequences.

It is all a mixture. This city is pieced together. Grown together in all these fragments, the atmosphere is so layered, the stitches, the holes, the mending and darning and new patches and old, old bits of fabric from great-great-grandmothers, the buried bits from ancient earth – they are all welded together with metallic thread.

So we cannot simply experience it through our senses and our own memories. It is too complex and living. It is too itself to be made individually just for us. Visitors are water droplets on the surface, soaking in and being absorbed till washed out or not . . . It is all so temporary in the city's eyes.

It makes its own tender map.

It is dreaming in impossibly varied shades of noir.

A recipe for Belgrade:

> The last summer I went there, the contemporary art museum was open for the first time in over a decade of visits. It could have been always there. But was not.

> That summer I took a bursting, boiling bus to a music festival up in the hills with Natalija and Mila and viewed paintings hung inappropriately in a vast abandoned brick factory. The building was the protagonist here. The art a momentary irritation.

> There was a salsa night the night after the tribute to Depeche Mode. This makes sense.

> Shops that are never open with headless mannequins. A display cabinet, free-standing in the street, showcased its wares of a dead fox and some gloves. They were not for sale.

Bars that don't have signposts through unlabelled doors through abandoned shopping centres. There is a design district now.

Always eating shopska salad: tomatoes, cucumber and mysterious cheese.

I once bought the best children's shoes for grown-ups from an old man. I should have bought two pairs.

I left the city once and met some stray dogs and people dressed as Romans. My friend's kid was not alarmed. He now only feels at home surrounded by concrete, despite loving creatures and the sea.

Gypsy flea market under the bridge. The small boy with the plastic gun smiled at me. There was a very mean-looking baby. Unsurprising when they bulldoze them occasionally.

Mila painted her bedroom in Zemun with portraits of her imaginary friend. He was called Joe. This made sense.

A strange number of weddings take place on boats.

One evening in a bar called Idiot, two gangster boys talked of philosophy and Peter Pan – lost boys – too perfect for fiction. One offered the other to me as a gift. When I declined, he said, 'What do you mean you don't want him – he is like Greek god.' He was actually quite attractive.

There are the bombed buildings on postcards decorated with targets, giving them the strange air of mod accessories – a brazen souvenir for tourists from the West: this is what you did. Send it to your friends.

*

Old water, wide hidden water, imaginary water in a city that I know to be real. Istanbul, Belgrade, Venice. These three cities are all real. Linked by the presence of water, their locations where Europe meets the East. Yet their atmospheres do not flow into each other – the rivers, canals, lagoons and seas do not meet, but go their own winding ways, gently brushing past each other, protected by their own invisible atmosphere shields.

They are layered for me with my memories, yet I am well aware how insignificant these memories are in the scale of each city. I am one of millions of residents and visitors. These are ancient cities – hundreds and hundreds of years of history. The atmosphere of a place has to be strong to stand alone, to surprise when there are all these layers that I don't know if they contribute to; or whether these distract us from the true feeling of the place.

I have drifted through these cities. I found ways – anonymous streets held me, took me from one place to another, showed me hidden treasures, the surprises of shops and cobbles, winding passages and dead ends. But I never felt lost in them. There was the obvious help of maps, paper in my case, but the streets always led to somewhere – with a marker that somehow got me back to where I needed to be. I was exploring, but while open to the drift, the experience of the city, I knew I could find my way. The cities are shape-shifters yet my being there was solid. They changed around me, but I somehow knew where I was. Not home, but an in-between, a liminal home keeping me company. Being truly lost is something else entirely. It is an atmosphere all of its own.

Lost and Found

Getting lost, directions, forest, mountains, city streets – it is always somehow associated with the wilds; natural or manmade, there is a maximalism to places where we are lost. One doesn't get lost in a village, a cottage, a small town or gentle fields. Getting lost, to lose oneself, loss ... These are things of scale, tumultuous, vast – there must be a vastness, surely, if one is so entangled in a place or a feeling with no way out? Yet as an atmosphere, things become subtler, more complex again: time gets involved, a place transformed second by second, familiarity, other people, weather, signposts. In ourselves – feelings – one day immense, another a smaller scale. Deep grief is the most lost I have ever felt; it is always inside, a place of loss, where I could get lost, but it shrinks and burrows with time. The privacy of getting lost (it is personal usually) – that is a different scale ...

I have been lost on walks, geographically lost. I have certainly lost myself: there are three years in my late twenties, where due to various factors of family, health, heartache and loss of home I do not recognise myself. I put up an annoying façade that was more sociable and cheerful than I naturally was. Didn't think of consequences, as my intentions – or the intentions of my true self – were always good, and so the character I was playing must have been making this clear, no? Detachment from self as loss. I have loss of place, childhood home. I have been intensely heartbroken. I have lost all of my family. Vast grief when my beloved cat Dylan died. During Covid-19 I was briefly homeless – something I never could have imagined.

I have been lost too with joy; I have been lost in story worlds of my creating – one of the most glorious losts you can feel – an intense pleasure like no other. Lost in imagination, in optimism and daydreaming. Lost with friends in crazy creative collaboration; in the intense realm of the best female friendships. I have been lost in love in a good way that blurred that loss with the cliché of having found something more akin to home. I have been lost in memory – good and bad, the poignancy of nostalgia. I have been lost in cities and forest momentarily, as I chose to experience the place differently, not to worry in those moments, to believe that all will be well.

All of these experiences entailed being lost. And when I think back to them, they all have an atmosphere.

When I was a child I would go on walks where I knew where I was going, but would suddenly detour. I liked the thrill. The almost being lost. The atmosphere of the unexpected. It wasn't sinister. Any fear I had was of being stolen, a fear of the human, not the magical – the 'stranger danger' of 1980s school warnings. The places themselves didn't scare me at all. My little bit of being lost built my strength, my independence, my love of nature and stories; it fed my imagination and therefore me; it provided complete solace rather than making me scared. I didn't crave my return, or even being discovered after a moment; I just enjoyed exploring where I was.

This thrill of the almost lost took me away from the familiar in my home and the places in the village I associated with school and being unhappy. If I was a little bit lost I was an explorer. New places almost functioned like imaginary friends. I would talk to trees, plants and wildlife as I met them. *Who are you?* I would ask. In my forties I still find myself occasionally doing this.

I wonder if this is partly why I embraced the gentle getting lost that being in an unfamiliar country brings ... One of the reasons why we love travel – a safe disorientation from the familiar. But disorientation is not the same as being lost.

Gentle geographically lost as adventure: a conscious wanting to be in the unknown, in somewhere new.

Complete geographically lost as terror: the implications of if we are never found.

What does it mean to be truly geographically lost? Panic is the hardest of physical and mental things to ignore – it dominates, floods, the system. When in panic mode, it is hard to notice anything else. True panic can eclipse everything, is so preoccupying we are less likely to notice things, although for some it can sharply focus through sheer necessity – the survival instinct. Either way, it cannot but have a profound effect on how we experience place. At the same time, while it changes us, it does not materially change our surroundings at all. It is pure sensory filter. It is all human. The place has not decided to warn us, it can't know that we don't know our way; and if we did know our way, the place itself would be exactly the same. It is not threat as in forest fire on its way, impending earthquake, tsunami, things with natural clues, where the land could be feeding us signs. This is a threat in our minds, a knowledge of what might be, rather than is the case of what is about to happen. It is also totally individual – the place itself is not changing, we are changing within it.

Being lost transforms atmosphere powerfully – a place can go from one of ease and beauty to terror at the switching on of panic at being lost. Though whether this is the actual atmosphere is up for debate. It is atmosphere in terms of how we feel place in that moment, but it is a sledgehammer of a force, a trauma that eclipses the subtleties and layers of experience – it could be seen as a temporary screen created by us, rather than anything to do with the true feeling of the place. Technically, one could argue it's not an atmosphere at all, or at least a sub or invasive species of this . . .

Yet there is something in this that is atmosphere and the true panic rarely lasts for long – our bodies can't sustain it.

Being lost geographically is seen as negative. However, that is to suppose that to be geographically lost means just one thing – that something has gone terribly wrong and we are now in a fight for survival. That's why panic sets in and why the acute problem is not solved until we are found or we find somewhere we know. It seems matters are terrifyingly out of our control. Yet if we broaden the definition to other kinds of lost, then the advantages flood in –

imagination, finding ourselves, experimentation and exploration. The discovery of something fresh by being somewhere new can open up or rekindle our lives. Being lost cannot of itself be the problem, but rather a way of escape from what is the problem, especially if we are escaping something in our lives.

Of course running away, especially when this involves young people, can be a much more serious issue, putting individuals in danger, usually in urban rather than rural environments. People tend to run towards other people, strangers rather than trees. Is there something optimistic in the urge: that no matter how dire things are, no matter the risks of inevitably being lost – especially if you need to find somewhere unfamiliar where no one will try to find you – there is hope amidst despair that a new life might flourish, a life that is better than the one you know? Being lost is make or break – it could lead to a downward spiral from which there feels like no return, or it could lead, albeit after a struggle, to a different kind of fight for survival, to a life, a place, an atmosphere, which is everything you did not have before and wanted to achieve. Sometimes it's hard to achieve when you feel trapped. I understand that one more than you could know.

I used to run away as a small child, but only for hours at a time – to see if I would be discovered, to temporarily escape into a world without parents. The childhood urge to run away is instinctive. Our first forays into discovering a world on our own terms. Yes, there is the attention-seeking aspect, but it seems more than this. It is a testing of ourselves in the world. Will the unknown, without the safety of our parents, accept us; will we find something new, an atmosphere, a changed way of being in places? As an adult, I am not sure it is so different when we travel – we want to discover the world for ourselves, to absorb its variety, to overthrow learned fears, to challenge or change ourselves and our lives back home.

There is another side.

Found. To find something. To find oneself. I was lost. I was found. To run away isn't always to become lost. It can be a way of finding somewhere, of being found, not by oneself, but by an atmosphere.

But what if to be found is not to embrace security but to be rid of it? What if the true joy of finding is in losing the life that was dragging you down?

Until the age of forty, Isabella Bird led the life that was expected of a middle-class Victorian clergyman's daughter. She studied, sometimes even wrote on suitable subjects such as hymnology and metaphysical poetry; she helped and supported her family. She was also a woman plagued with ill health since childhood, in chronic pain most of her life; she even had an operation to remove a growth from her spine, a terrifying prospect at any time, let alone in the first half of the nineteenth century. Unsurprisingly, considering this, Isabella also suffered from the ubiquitous Victorian female ailment 'nervous depression' – she lacked energy, felt constantly down, was anxious . . . Eventually, in 1854, a doctor prescribed a journey abroad, preferably a long sea voyage, as a cure. It was a classic prescription for 'highly strung' Victorian ladies, but it worked for Isabella. She talks of how when she landed her pain disappeared.

A change is as good as a break. A change of scenery does you good. These are well-known sayings. And the travel remedy was a common one, especially in the nineteenth century. Seaside holidays, spa resorts, sea voyages . . . Yet many of the places people visited for this cure were often touristy, full of other afflicted English people; a designed, curated curative space, rather than a real change. I wonder if the reason why the change worked so well for Isabella was that she didn't do this. She travelled for a cure, for her health, but rather than a spa or a seaside hotel, a suitable European cultural tour, she journeyed to the other side of the world, and from this moment her life transformed.

A change of scenery. The word 'scenery' suggests that somehow this is a surface move, a view; that by travelling to a new place, rather than inhabit it, we are but skating over; that a scene is being moved before our eyes as if we are but passive passengers (indeed, there is an element of this to the sea journey, the cruise). Yet the power in a change of scenery, the medicine, the drug as it were, cannot be surface or we could conjure it by simply changing what is before our eyes. A magical view! A conjurer's illusion! The power of the change is not in the scenery so much as what is behind the scenes, below the surface; or rather, the world is not surface, not 2D: the power of the change is all around us. In how it works. Beyond 3D, even. The cure is in a new atmosphere.

Travel. A new adventure. It is something we associate more with the word 'lost' than 'found'. Going to new climes, leaving our old world behind, we are searching, but that searching process is more likely to lead us off course, is it not? Yet what if finding something isn't an ending, or an object, or a miracle cure but how we feel as we are doing it? What if how it feels to discover new things and places and interacting in them is a constant finding; that we are not lost until we find something, but are immersed in a kind of constant finding, being found, every day as we travel? And our companion through all of this, the magic breath bringing it all to life, helping the transformation, is atmosphere.

A doctor once said of Isabella Bird that she was 'one of those subjects who are dependent to the last degree upon their environment to bring out their possibilities. It is not a question of dual personality, it is the varied response of a single personality under varied condition ...'. A response, a dialogue, a collaboration with the world.

A grown-up version of childhood running-away play. We can do it for real now.

Isabella's first trip was to America and relatively uneventful. But in 1872, after a period of ill health that had seen her unable to lift her head properly without support, Isabella took the decision that would change her life and set sail for the antipodes. Her plan was then to voyage on to California, but due to travel complications she ended up disembarking halfway across the Pacific in Hawaii, then the Sandwich Isles, and on a whim of adventure decided to stay for what turned into months and her successful debut book.

It was the first trip of many. After months in Hawaii, Isabella eventually moved on to America, exploring the Rocky Mountains in Colorado, hanging out with a legendary outlaw, Mountain Jim, and herding wild cattle. She rode astride in a special outfit she'd found in Hawaii with trousers built in, which finally enabled her to sit on a horse without the pain she associated with the side-saddle back home. She returned, published a best-selling book and went off again – to Japan at a time when it was virtually unvisited by the West. Whereas an Edinburgh parlour left her prostrate in pain, she now rode deep into the interior and to the wild far north, survived damp, flea-infested inns. Later, to what was then Malaya, then Tibet, Kashmir, China . . . A woman who prior to the age of forty was an invalid, was galloping across the world.

It is naive to think that her level of chronic pain could have evaporated; her spinal issues were very real. But as someone with a chronic pain condition, I can see how if it does not evaporate then it can lessen when in a place and leading a life that you want to lead. On one of my trips to Georgia, a country where I spent many months over many years, we went to stay by the sea near Batumi. I had been horribly ill, chronic health problems flaring up again, but here I was doing things that would normally trigger it – getting too hot, not sleeping enough, drinking alcohol, adventuring with no thought to rest or washing or comfort. Yet my body let me be. It liked this place. The feelings of Georgia always did that, danced around with my body and brain so that it behaved differently to when back at home, where it would misbehave and banish me to bed and painkillers. To missing out. To losing the life I should have been leading. *Dependent on our environment to bring out our possibilities* . . . If we find the place that is right for us, which could be many places, not just one, not just a home in the traditional sense, a place of roots, then if it finds us too, if we open ourselves up to it and let it in, can it heal us in a different way? Not a literal cure, but a life that is so enriching and fascinating, that what we have found gives us a new energy – lethargy be gone, Victorian lady stereotype of wasting away on a sofa, be gone. The atmosphere enters us as it naturally does, responds as we respond to it, and we are found by a new life we didn't even realise we were searching for.

I wonder whether if we are sleepwalking through a life with an atmosphere that is all wrong, travel can wake up the world for us? See it as it really is? Whether this is the real skill. That when we ignore atmosphere or treat it as background, we miss the world as it actually is. And this extraordinary world that we live in, with all its variety and consequent atmospheres, is there waiting to be found in its spectacular ordinariness. Real is ordinary. Ordinary is as it is. And as it is, if we notice, can be more extraordinary than our imaginations, can wake us up to live a life more exciting or right for us that we would have thought.

Isabella said that she felt reborn as she embarked in Hawaii and began to explore. She had a feeling of youth she had almost forgotten. Travel as continual adolescence – development, exploration, optimism; the world being experienced for the first time. This is implicitly hopeful. I can see it in the feelings I had, especially in Georgia, but there is a downside. It is hard to live life as a nomad with the funds to be on a perpetual holiday of sorts, rather than settling, working ... Isabella herself wrote from Hawaii, 'I always feel dil (dull and inactive) when I am stationary. The loneliness is dreadful often. When I am travelling I don't feel it, but that is why I can never stay anywhere.'

I travelled and travelled. At the time it was exciting, but now as I look back it seems a little relentless, the constant motion, the searching. My parents sold my childhood home and I put my earnings into travel rather than savings or mortgage accounts. So nowhere was home, and everywhere was potentially home. I was looking for places, for a country where I could experience the intense immersion I had as a child. But I also wanted to find a place where I felt at home, because it is easier to travel with a home to go back too.

The loneliness of constantly travelling – no roots, no ties. Then the loneliness of not travelling, passing time in an enforced environment that does not suit. But not for long.

A fluid life. A life lived in thrall to atmosphere will never be dull, will mean never missing the wonder of what is around you, but it might mean missing the more human side of ordinary. The other communication. The building of a life and family.

It can be lonely to have travelled while all those around you stayed in place.

Isabella Bird was not alone in finding that her health improved when travelling. It is interesting how many of the great female early travel writers had chronic health problems, or family issues and commitments that had tied them into a way of life frustratingly not them. I understand the depths of those feelings. So much of my twenties were spent ill, not building the career and relationships and life that my contemporaries were. Stuck living with family after my first taste of freedom at university. But whenever I felt a little better I flew. University ill, better travel, then ill, then travel . . . I flew and flew and while sometimes it was impossible if my health flared while abroad, there was a golden balance where if I was just about OK, then the distraction and magic atmosphere of adventure made those worries, the life I hadn't built, fall away.

Yet we have to be careful – a travel cure like a nature cure can be helpful, but to presume a cure could belittle very real physical suffering. Women's physical and mental health is still treated flippantly by many today. The amount of times it was suggested to me in the first years of my illness that I was making things up, until I met an amazing female doctor, a top professor, who explained the very real physical mechanisms of my condition so I learned more in thirty minutes than in the previous ten years. Real illness needs real treatment and sometimes that is medication, hospitals. With acute illness, there is no way travelling would help. The health spas in their dreariness did not always work. But still there is a power in travel. If the right place is found, where your life suddenly feels like it should do, when you've been trapped and miserable, then this is a very potent medicine indeed. If atmosphere is a real not conceptual thing, then at its most affecting it is transformative.

Take the doctor's prescription and transform it into your own. I am sure that none of the doctors' advice envisaged the levels of exertion and adventure many female travellers embarked upon. The power lay in the choosing the flavour of the prescription, picking the atmosphere of travel that suited them, having ownership of their adventure cure, which place they collaborated with and how.

Like Isabella Bird, Edith Durham struggled with her health and was prescribed travel, or rather interestingly, a 'complete change of place' as a potential cure. So off she sailed in middle age, down the Dalmatian Coast and on to Montenegro, her first taste of the Balkans, the countries that would define her life. A change of place. If atmosphere is the personality of the world, the feelings of a place, then in some ways Edith Durham was *prescribed* atmosphere and in being so, she found a life of extraordinary adventure and purpose. She was politically involved in supporting the Balkan countries, but her adventures entailed a life so different to her one at home it could barely be imagined. Yes, there is a frustration in how in some ways she still needed 'permission' to travel – her instructions from doctors being a passport to independence, rather than a choice made alone. Yet she ignored the cruise and change of scenery for something much more adventurous that she probably would never have been given permission for. Possibly her most famous work is *High Albania*, where she trekked with locals, the only female, into the high remote villages rife with blood feuds and barely visited by foreigners, especially not women.

Edith's descriptions of her journey are quite extraordinary – the unwillingness to give up, the vigour with which she lived in the Balkans compared to how she had been back in Britain. I was thinking of Edith as I flicked through one of my favourite anthologies, *The Virago Book of Women Travellers*. Not all of them were fleeing ill health, some were also pre-Victorian, while others lived well into the twentieth century. Edith herself travelled in the early 1900s. I think of Edith and picture a woman at home, think of what they might have read, the novelists as well as the writings by male travellers. Where did they get their inspiration to go where they did? The bravery in a time when most female literature was very much of the home, or romantic rather than adventurous. The introduction to the Virago anthology quotes *A Literature of Their Own* by feminist writer Elaine Showalter: 'Denied participation in public life, women were forced to cultivate their feelings and to overvalue romance [. . .] Emotions rushed in to fill the vacuum of experience.' There is undeniable truth in this. Certainly Emily Brontë and Isabella Bird are very different reads . . .

Thinking of maps of tenderness and Scudéry's salon choosing the emotional journey of her protagonist as the thing to map, and young girls embroidering their homes or ambitions, it is interesting that even in mapping the emotions came to the fore. But what if rather than a fiction, rather than a replacement of experience of the world, mapping somewhere with emotion is a way in to this greater understanding, an understanding that arguably has more depth of experience than a stereotypically male traveller ticking off a list of places they've been, what they have seen, but maybe not felt? Conquering over collaborating, listening, emotions are a different way of experiencing the world . . . So, yes, female writers explored romance, maps of tenderness explored romance, but in many ways the new depth of experience in female travel writers, with its less conquering approach, is equally tender . . . However, to set this up as binary – as internal romantic imaginings or domestic experience versus a truer kind of experience via the lived world – is wrong. It is not that straightforward (not, of course, that Showalter is saying it is: I am quoting a quote out of context in an introduction). It is a case of private versus public more than lesser versus more.

If we think of place as full of emotion, if we see that it possesses a kind of equivalent, communicated to us via atmosphere, then travel writing could be the romance literature of place. There is nothing wrong with that. It does not mean weak or soppy – that is to fall into the clichés with which women are so often belittled. Bravery as an extraordinary story as opposed to detached conquering. (One of my heroines, Dervla Murphy, comes to mind – I can picture her no-nonsense instincts bristling at being described in terms of romance, but a literary romance with the world, good and bad . . .?) Description and adventure as bringing freedom – getting stuck in a gorge, being in danger, exploration, forging friendships – all moments full of emotion.

Women's love lives are often described in the language of travel – amorous adventures – and Scudéry's map quite literally does this. We can map the amorous adventure of her protagonist. Women travellers made literal maps of emotion, some in literal pursuit of amorous adventure, such as the nineteenth-century aristocrat Jane Digby, who had various husbands strewn along the way of her endless travels, to the cliché of holiday romances today; while others fell in love with the places they visited. Travel writing combines the interior world of romance with the exterior of the world. Isabella Bird's early books are in the form of letters to her beloved sister Henrietta, and even when describing minute factual detail, these letters have the feel of a love letter, in the sense of the truth of real love – loving someone, despite their flaws. It's just that for Isabella, for me in Georgia, for many women who have roamed the world, the beloved is a somewhere, not a someone. A dialogue with place. They have found love in the most unexpected of places. It might be a place of ease or full of danger. For early travellers, it was probably a place that women weren't supposed to go. Yet it was there for the taking the whole time. They just had to listen.

I drift back to the Virago anthology and read a quote from Lawrence Durrell describing the great writer on the East that is Freya Stark: 'A great traveller is a kind of introspective; as she covers ground outwardly, so she advances inwardly.'

He could have been describing what a true map of tenderness for this world really is.

I Once was Held in Perfect Calm – Japan

I thought it was going to be my last great adventure before settling in to a job and more traditional grown-up life, but it turned out to be more like the beginning. It was 2001 and I had travelled to Japan for a couple of months to stay with friends I'd made in Bath. I flew there from Vancouver, having spent the previous couple of months in Ottawa, Montreal, San Francisco and LA – drifting from city to city where I knew people I could stay with.

My signage problem became clear the second I arrived at Narita International Airport. The alphabet hit me with such powerful visual intensity I was momentarily halted. I'd thought it would be a straightforward journey to catch the train to Ikebukuro station in the centre of Tokyo, where my friend was meeting me. I managed it fine in the end, but looking at departure screens and seeing this beautiful foreign alphabet, as meaningful as abstract patterns to me, quickly shifted my brain in to what would be the reality of this trip and finding my way. Language, in the form of reading, was no longer going to be my tool of navigation, but a personal internal monologue as I found my way around this new country. Getting lost was going to be inevitable and my relationship to that feeling, the meaning or implication of day-to-day being lost, was going to have to change. I had to let go of my mind and accept the intuition of my body. I was going to have to embrace the consequences of 'getting it wrong', of losing my way.

I had been in Japan a few weeks when I decided to go to the mountain. It was December, though not cold, days with weak sunlight stopping the grey becoming too harsh – a gauze rather than blanket of grey with sun flickers filtering through. Other moments, when the rain fell so heavily, to go outside was to move through liquid layers of sky. I had been to some beautiful mountain areas during my stay – blissful days on trains to shrines and festivals, endless little mountains swathed with trees. But I was always in mountain towns and villages – I wanted to be on one of these magical wooded mountains themselves.

I hopped on a local train. I had discovered that while the *shinkansen*, the bullet intercity trains, were very expensive, the local commuter trains were cheap and reached further than I'd imagined. This one went to Mount Takao. Or so I hoped. I had perfected a new attitude to train catching that had morphed into a temporary hobby. I would arrive at the station and get on a train that I hoped was the right one and then see where it went. If it went to the right place – great, but if not, well, then I would still have an adventure and I could always manage to get back to Tokyo. Tokyo was the only city that was nearly always signed in English as well as Japanese on trains.

However, this day I got it right and the train arrived at Mount Takao. Street stalls and trees and a station for some kind of railway up the mountain. I hopped on and disembarked high up and bizarrely straightforwardly at my destination. I cannot remember what I found up there – so many trees and shrines in those days that I don't trust my memory to find the right scene. There was probably a shrine I visited, taking my shoes off to stand on freezing floors and absorb the beauty, the calm despite other people. But I do remember what happened next.

I decided to go for a walk. There were lots of footpaths, which reminded me of country walks back home in Somerset. There were also signs, which, though I couldn't read them, were reassuring in that if they pointed somewhere, then it would be hard to get completely lost – I would end up in a place where a person might at least be expected to find themselves. This felt like it was pleasingly in keeping with my new embracing of unexpected destinations. Signs meant something and there were people around.

But then I made my mistake. Following the main paths started to feel a little too predictable and when I saw an unmarked track that was clearly still a path, and which looked much more interesting with its tunnel of trees and twisting bends, my magic sense of instinct kicked in and I couldn't resist taking it.

At first it was OK – the path was clear and while I saw no one, it wasn't like it was slowly disappearing into the dense undergrowth. I kept going. I could still see the route but the undergrowth did get thicker, jungle-like with plants I didn't recognise, and cool winter air – were there winter jungles? I began to feel a little uneasy, my initial adventure excitement slowing a little. I came to a fork and hesitated – the sensible thing to do would be to turn around; so far, I had only followed one path so I was not lost, I just had to return the way I came. But that seemed defeatist and went against all my walking preferences for not retracing my steps and instead discovering new ways. After all, this was an official route– how wrong could I go? I took one prong of the fork.

Time begins to blur here. I followed the path, but suddenly there were more forks and I tried to turn around but had been so caught up in imaginings that I had not paid my usual attention to landmarks and which way I'd gone. My normal homing-pigeon talent for finding my way once I've walked somewhere before (friends joke it's my superpower) failed me. I could not be sure which way I'd been. I wove my way round the trees, then reaching a point that was overgrown, had to admit that very unusually for me, I was completely lost.

In that moment the atmosphere of the forest on the mountain changed. Same place, a consecutive moment in time, but very different feeling. I was no longer embracing getting lost in my game of not guaranteeing my Japanese destination, but actually up a mountain in the middle of the forest mid-afternoon in December, when days are short. I had been stupid in a way I am not normally, having grown up in the countryside. I knew how bad being lost up a mountain could be, even with the shelter of trees.

Up until this point I had been enchanted. The crisp air mixed with the heady forest smells, the delicate shape of different leaves – filigree veins and elfin points, the exoticism of monkeys in December! A sense of maybe snow. Japan in general filled me with utter calm; even when in Tokyo, its efficiency made me relaxed despite the crowds. But now the path that had meant gentle adventure, a little magical detour, had a slight sense of menace. My adrenalin or a natural warning I had ignored till now? I paused and looked around. Forests are one of the easiest places to get lost – places start to resemble each other and it's hard to trust your memory. Everything could be deceptive. The once friendly trees no longer welcomed me but merged together into a montage in which I could not tell one from another. I tried heading back the way I came but the paths seemed to have shifted and in reverse I had no idea whether I was going back or along a new route.

And then I saw water. A gentle stream, flowing downhill. It had started to get dark and the only signposts I had seen for a while were of pictures of wild boar, which looked distinctly like warnings, not directions. The stream appeared as a noise first, subtly different to the wind in the branches; my ears pricked and I sniffed – faint wateriness, that cool edge the smell of water gives the air even on a winter's day. It was near. I looked around me and at the path – it was keeping level, twisting, but water flows and if it was going down then I could follow, hopefully to the bottom of the mountain. It would at least be better to be heading to the foot of the mountain than wandering round and round, with no notion of how high up I was any more, the woods obscuring my view.

I kept going and there, near to the path, was the stream, and next to the stream another path of sorts – not as wide as the one I was on, but passable. I took a calculated risk and followed the water.

It felt like hours passed as I followed the stream. The path was narrow and at moments almost disappeared. At one point I reached a small waterfall and had to clamber down its side. I saw monkeys. I had left the path and knew that my decision was irreversible – I had to stick to it. But I was also reassured – amidst the panic I knew that as long as I was heading downhill I was going in the right direction and if I was stuck, come darkness at least I would have trees for shelter and the lower I was, the less cold it would be. I kept going and then suddenly a clearing and voices. I rushed towards it and burst out of the trees with relief, only to my astonishment to find myself at the station for the little monorail or funicular that had taken me up to the top. I had arrived at the bottom in the one place at the mountain's foot that I knew.

My relief was intense and in my euphoria, on the discovery of a chairlift, I hopped on and went up the mountain again. Despite the lack of seatbelt I swung my feet – I felt invincible! Staring at the forest canopy below the place was transformed – it seemed surreal that moments ago I had been deep in the forest. It was an abstract place beneath my wide open sky domain. It couldn't hurt me. I had figured out the way, or it had helped me. The stream ... When I reached the top I stared out from a viewing platform, before hopping back on the chairlift and down to the base again. I bought a steamed rice bun on a stick, warm and delicious, and instantly found a train heading back to Tokyo.

Natural Histories, Habitations and Hauntings

Nashville

'Everybody's gonna tell y'all the South's not a place, it's
a state of mind. I think more than a state of mind, the
South is an atmosphere.'
    Jim Waters in 'Searching for the Wrong Eyed Jesus',
                                    Arena documentary

I wasn't sure I wanted to write about Nashville. Of all the places
I've visited it holds the most difficult memories for me. Most of
my time there was spent with a complicated friend. The city was
atmospheric but not profoundly unique the way some cities are,
but when we drove from Nashville to Memphis, then down into
Mississippi, an atmosphere that had long lived in my imagination
became real and transformed the city imaginatively.

I had preconceptions of the South that I had found only slightly
in Nashville. America of songs and stories. The real country music
was there, the true inheritor of the essence of folk culture we have
lost to an extent in the UK, but overgrown heat and doomed love,
strangeness, darkness, wooded mountains to the north, swamps as
you get deeper, damper, trees drenched in Spanish moss, the hum of
insects, snapping turtles, snakes, alligators, murder and faded beauty
. . .

In 2007, on an overly optimistic or emotionally masochistic
spiral, I was visiting my friend in Nashville again, who for years had
gone out of his way to hurt me. For all the personal stress, I couldn't
stay away. The city was hiding something from me, an undercurrent
I couldn't explain, yet as I travelled I was still searching. Partly for
the home I thought I might find through love, but more so that I
just didn't believe the atmosphere of the South could elude me.

There were hints that were too alive, both in reality and also in my imagination, to be tainted in the way places so often are by emotional trauma.

As we arrived in Memphis I felt like I had stumbled on a dream – been transported like Dorothy to Oz. A gleaming metal factory or refinery rose from the suburbs like the Emerald City, but silver, industrial, carving out a low space in this part of the South that was flat and warm and humming. Old rail tracks wove past wooden crossings. The houses were low-rise, falling down in places, but even in the centre of town – in the fancy Peabody Hotel, where we stayed as a treat and drank cocktails while watching the daily duck parade into the fountain (the ducks live in a penthouse on the roof and come down twice a day in the lift), embracing being tourists, going to the Stax records museum – even on the dustiest of streets, I had the feeling that everywhere was overgrown. That even if brown, this countryside, this place, deep down, in its heart, its atmosphere, was green.

As we slowly wound our way out of town the heat grew, though it was February. We drove deeper, down to Oxford with its perfect small-town America feel. We ate Mexican food and drank iced tea full of sugar – sweet tea, as it is known. But this was only a pause on a day of driving. The landscape became deep and dense – I could picture opening the window and trailing my hand through Spanish moss, a soft, draped equivalent of running a stick through railings; it caressing my skin, the sweet smell lingering on my fingers like icing sugar.

We paused again and realised we were at a Civil War site. I could not sense the spectral playback of its memories of death and violence. I was too taken over by the swampy trees, rising out of a pond like a miniature mangrove, hiding creatures, whispering despite the non-existent winter breeze.

It was February, but it felt like summer. Like it was always summer. Seasons too much of a distraction from its core identity; its atmosphere was too strong to be swayed from itself. Yet in Nashville I remember snow.

It was growing.

The atmosphere of the South is a living thing. A creature, an ancient being, so old and strange that human concerns do not bother it. Modern America, post-colonial America, is but a strange smidge of its history.

Yes, I sensed a deep creature, not the horrors of its human past. They are integral to its identity, cannot and should not be forgotten, yet atmospherically I couldn't shake the fact that I did not sense humans at all. Only the music made sense.

We drove back to Nashville via the scenic route, the Natchez Trace – an old road. We stopped at a diner and ate coconut pie, meringue whipped up like a sixties hairdo. We had just eaten what is known as meat and three, though being vegetarian I had just had the three part. Macaroni and cheese counts as a vegetable, don't you know.

It was winter. I know it was winter. But all I see in my head is green.

I cannot write about the South in a normal way.

It has to be its feelings.

It has to be its verdant song.

Prehistoric light ripples, guitars softly strumming, a feeling, dark water, a ghost stares gently, notes are more than notes, music is more than music, the houses float, dripping, kudzu (that strange vine that creeps and covers), banjo strumming, the railway is disused by the old trucks and the boat that doesn't float, still waters are not still waters, rust, fiddles, a small child runs along a road that is no longer a road for most, tell me about what's in your heart.

The immensity of it. Not overwhelming, it is too complete to need that flooding show. Feel but not infiltrate. It is beyond what we feel.

Abandoned bookcases on the side of the road. Junkyard road. Lost school buses have found a home. Cicadas sing and sing. Legs rubbed raw.

They are all at the mercy of the feeling.

The only way it expresses itself in a manner we can try to understand is through the music. There is a reason for the music. The dark strangeness. A different being to mainstream country music, the mass media, it growls and coos and dreams. It bleeds without a goth in sight. Blue.

Murder is at ease here, but it has nothing to do with anything the landscape has done. It is a shortcut to try to explain that darkness in human terms when it is not human.

Love songs are never happy. The landscapes seep in.

Slip into swampy water and just feel the prayer.

Drinking bourbon whisky. The clichés are not clichés but a shorthand for trying to express the depths of the feeling. How strongly the landscape feels. It is drunk and heartbreaking and violent, or it is not, but in its thrall, humans are almost powerless to do anything else to express it.

True country music is a conversation with atmosphere, with the landscape, talking back, asking if this is what they should do. Life, poverty . . . There is so much more poverty in the South. I had never seen anything like it.

The atmosphere is not concerned with material things. Swamps and heat. It is not its role to create jobs.

It breeds stillness. Inaction, yet in thought over-action. The wind passing the car blows my hair and licks my hand and I cannot picture walking, but thinking. I am so full of thinking, words do not have the energy to escape my mouth.

Except in song. People here have the urge to sing their stories.

True folk.

'Wayfaring Stranger'.

The trees breathe differently.

Songs spill from their fingertips. Branches, people . . . Songs spill and catch in branches, flutter in the breeze like a wish tied there. Please. Please . . .

Banjo.

Mother-of-pearl stars on the fret-board. In the woods the crows are calling. Cottonmouths.

Spit the stars out like teeth. Bloody. Stories are everything and everything is stories. How the world works. I wonder if it is clearer here. For the land. Not for the human world.

Coaxed to speak in tongues, the small child cried. They would have been better singing the language of trees.

Spanish moss streamers, torn ragged bunting for a festivity none of us will see.

Jesus or hell.

Traffic lights sway neon in the daytime.

You know you're alive when you feel. Sadness is often the strongest.

Feeling.

The South is alive as it feels. It is a feeling and it feels.

Shotgun kindness.

The Southern gothic makes sense, but this is not Southern gothic, it is Southern song.

It is not analysed, it is not a genre, it is not something you can copy if you don't feel it, it is not an essay in a text book, it is not a voyeuristic glance at lives that have gone wrong; there are no ruined plantation houses, though there are ruined plantation houses and they seem more real overgrown. It is not a haunting, the song, but there is a haunting in the atmosphere.

Can you haunt yourself? Still there?

Sweet scent of Spanish moss. Grapefruit sugar musk. Swaying.

Let me hide up there awhile.

It's a real place.

A lot of the songs travelled from over here. I once heard a version of 'Matty Groves', that old English folk song made famous by Fairport Convention, where after the murder of the wife's lover, he cuts his head off and kicks it against the wall like a football.

The South changed it. This is the true version here.

Hear.

The stop sign had bullet marks.

Then they went to church.

They sing.

Hear.

The lull of insects are percussion for the song thoughts of the creeping green. The kudzu is the speed of incredibly slow lava and as a growing blanket makes sculptures out of lost vehicles: dinosaurs and castles, Rapunzel towers from telegraph poles.

The railway rattles through.

Heat brews and rain swamps when it falls, destroys.

Good makes no sense without evil.

If you sit in a bar it is never silent. Music fills the air. I went to a party and the boys had brought their fiddles.

There is song. There is love. There is a presence. Things happen there.

There is an immensity that loves. There is an immensity that doesn't know you're there.

But it breathes in green. It flows. Liquid leaf.

It does not speak in tongues, though some people speak in tongues. It is indifferent to such human attempts at communicating on a different level.

But it listens to the songs maybe. Or we can hope it might.

Tattoos covering love gone wrong. The green and light tattoos the water, permanent and impermanent.

Prehistoric light ripples.

It is not a hint of creatures but we know they live there. Prehistoric-like – water scales and glass eyes, gold as suns.

I am in love with the disquiet. The green dust. I am in love with the swampy trees. The growing. Cut it back and it just creeps on. Regardless.

The one power.

I don't bring you flowers. Hothouse without the glass.

Hellfire blaring from the radio. Better to let it sing than talk.

Trembling.

There is a better place.

Make a mobile from old bottles, CDs and crunched crisp packets.

People are hungry for God but this place needs no god – it is its own almighty.

There is a place.

It sucks you in and it is impossible to explain how the kindness counteracts the darkness and how you can want to be somewhere where so much is wrong.

But it's in the music. Everyday beauty. The harmony. The verdant song.

A Gentle Haunting

The day we drove back to Nashville along the Natchez Trace, if we had headed in the other direction, kept going deeper into Mississippi, we would have ended up in the place that breathes. A wide river would have flowed and if we had wandered off the trail, deep into the green, lapped our feet with river water, we might have found the building shells and lost hamlets, abandoned churches, graveyards thick with wild wisteria, clematis, magnolia visible from miles. We might have found the grand Southern live oaks, dressed up in the dusty tinsel that is Spanish moss, the feather boas of sweet smelling fancy dress of childhood dreams.

We would have found the place of a truly atmospheric piece of prose: the great Southern writer Eudora Welty's 1944 mesmerising essay with photos, 'Some Notes on River Country'. In the essay, Welty describes the area around Rodney's Landing, a small yet distinct area of deep Mississippi. Welty starts the essay by describing the journey towards her end destination, past ruined mansions, through the troubled human history of this area. It is the home of the Native American Natchez people, massacred by the French or sent into slavery. It is an area once famous for its cotton. Welty explores this history when she then progresses as if she herself were a ghost drifting through the area's more recent past – showboats and poverty, both the joy and the harsh lives of those who dwelled here. The legacy that fills so much of the South.

There is an inbuilt haunting of this past that should be acknowledged and never forgotten, yet the first part of Welty's essay doesn't feel atmospherically ghostly but a journey through and beyond the history. She mentions the history, but it is not the true subject of her essay. That is the feelings of the land, the places her photos capture.

As she arrives at her destination, Rodney's Landing, the description and photos of which form the bulk of the essay, the atmosphere that Welty conjures is of a haunting presence that does not come from the memories of any horror, nor the memories of the people who later lived in the houses and went to the churches, the people buried in the cemeteries, but from the natural world in this specific small place, through the birds and most significantly the plants. She introduces us to the past, the ruins, endless small churches, graveyards and absent river steamers, but then leads us into a deep localised discussion of the landscape, which makes the human history seem a mere moment in this ancient land's history. From recent history, through earlier human history to a time conjured by fossils of mastodons in the ground. She is acknowledging all the detritus, the legacy we leave behind, the nurturing or the destruction, but then she lets the landscape tell us who it really is:

> A place that ever was lived in is like a fire that never goes out. It flares up, it smolders for a time, it is fanned or smothered by circumstance, but its being is intact, forever fluttering within it, the result of some original ignition. Sometimes it gives out glory, sometimes its little light must be sought out to be seen, small and tender as a candle flame, but as certain.

A personality of landscape beyond humans: an atmosphere. Tender light in the dark.

A microcosm in this place of human ruins and verdant growth, rebuilding. Mississippi's natural history – the landscape gone back to nature, as an entity in itself.

As well as the factual history of the South, there is the imaginative metaphorical one of the Southern gothic, full of a haunting that is violent, gothic in the sense of vampires, murder ... But this is possible because of a sense of the South as a populated place in the present – it doesn't work for a landscape where we have mostly moved on. When I think of the feeling of the South, the haunting I sense is different; the lush green is not an uncanny juxtaposition to the human darkness, not there to conjure dread. There is an alternative to Southern gothic when humans are taken out of the picture, and it is a gentle haunting.

The natural world is full of life. Plants, animals, the air all have a presence. Humans and their history can sometimes distract from the place and what it can tell us. If a place, with history horrific or not, is abandoned by humans, their traces, though there, fade and let the feeling of the natural world shine through. Think of Chernobyl or military zones – places we have left slowly returning to nature, just moving on as themselves, without us. Atmosphere developing organically, growing like the vines that twist over the abandoned buildings, ruined verandas as much a frame as trees. Welty tells us:

> I have never seen, in this small section of old Mississippi River country and its little chain of lost towns between Vicksburg and Natchez, anything so mundane as ghosts, but I have felt many times there a sense of place as powerful as if it were visible and walking and could touch me.

This special kind of haunting is not dead as it has always been there; it is alive, it is beyond ghosts: it existed in the past, but through new growth, continues. The place, through its plants, will always regenerate, especially when the human element, the constructed element, has fallen into disrepair.

In fact, there is nothing gothic about Welty's essay and its hauntings, even though its photos are full of the ruins, the ghost town, cemeteries and swampy trees. The only time the word 'Gothic' is mentioned is in the more European architectural tradition, when she is talking about the shapes formed by that which had been overgrown:

> There is something Gothic about the vines, in their structure in the trees – there are arches, flying buttresses, towers of vines, with trumpet flowers swinging in them for bells and staining their walls. And there is something of a warmer grandeur in their very abundance – stairways and terraces and whole hanging gardens of green and flowering vines, with a Babylonian babel of hundreds of creature voices that make up the silence of Rodney's Landing.

The human place is silent, the true place is alive with verdant song. It is hard to be gothic when warm and growing. The place is building its own town, full of who it is when we humans have gone away. It wants towers too, steals our tropes of architecture, but in doing so, takes the gothic away from this place so often defined by a different gothic. The Southern gothic is often verdant and beautiful, but it is mixed with a sense of dread. This is different. There is a soft darkness in the loss, but the overwhelming feeling Welty gives us of this place, so gently haunted, is of release; is of the place sighing, the human memories have been let go.

This landscape is alive. The ghosts that Welty's essay conjures are ghosts as independent beings, not human memories. They are another aspect of presence in this place, a clue to the sentience of the landscape. This is atmosphere of landscape with a past, but in this moment – how it has continued living, evolving. How it was there before us and will be after we have gone. Indeed, for Welty this was a sentient landscape. When describing the beautiful old live oaks, draped with Spanish moss, she writes:

> Their great girth and their great spread give far more feeling of history than any house or ruin left by man. Vast, very dark, proportioned as beautifully as a church, they stand majestically in the wild or line old sites ... It would be hard to think of the things that happened here without the presence of these live oaks,

so old, so expansive, so wonderful, that they might be
sentient beings.

The human history is dominated by the natural history, and it is the
natural history that holds the feeling of this place. Welty concludes:

> Whatever is significant and whatever is tragic in its
> story lives as long as the place does, though they are
> unseen, and the new life will be built upon these things
> – regardless of commerce and the way of rivers and
> roads, and other vagrancies.

The world is haunted but not dead. Place is where our history, our
stories, are held but set free, where layered, in collaboration with
nature, evolve to live a different life, overgrown with atmosphere.

The Imagination of the Overgrown

There is something unique in the personality of cities and streets that have become overgrown. Something about what that unleashes. It is not so much a negation of city atmosphere as a transformation – a way in to a different side of it – the side you see when the urban foxes roam at night, a side that is hinted at when cities quieten down and wildlife returns, when we notice the birds, when we think of all this hidden life that is there and could just become richer – more verdant literally and metaphorically. The South fed my love of overgrown cities. Buildings dripping with vines and trees. Concrete smeared with moss and lichen. Roads made grassy footpaths.

But this is not just a whim of imagination. There are moments when whole cities transform this way. And they are often after the most tragic of circumstance – war, natural disaster, a global pandemic ... Yet there are also moments of gentler human intervention – guerilla gardening, urban beekeeping, exploring our gardens and creating small patches as wildlife havens. There are the less visited parks and green spaces, urban nature reserves ('reserve' is in itself an interesting indicative term – an acknowledgement that nature in the city is to be protected). They indicate a yearning for greenery in the city. The sense that even the most urban of us understand that it adds something – that it gives us something the city might be overwhelming, too harsh without. That it transforms the atmosphere of city dwellers' lives in a way that is good; in a way that is arguably critical. Parks are often described as the *lifeblood* of cities – not their life, not their blood, a straightforward physiognomic metaphor, but a hybrid that is an essential force.

Yet the sense of this coming out of tragedy is an interesting one. I remember when I first read Rose Macaulay's *The World My Wilderness*. I adored the story – Barbary, the rebellious seventeen-year-old girl, sent to London to live with her father post-World War II after years of living a slightly feral life with the Maquis, resistance fighters in rural France, her activities barely monitored by her bohemian and slightly indifferent mother. Among the relatively undescriptive clean prose of the story, there are descriptive interludes of post-war London. Descriptions that led to my discovery of something I had never realised about London after the Blitz: that before the rubble was cleared and rebuilt, the city went dramatically back to nature, and in doing so, its atmosphere of businesses and banks and busy streets transformed dramatically, to one with a hint of secrets simmering beneath the surface. Secrets that talk of a place rather than what happens in it, as Macaulay describes:

> The maze of little streets threading through the wilderness, the broken walls, the great pits with their dense forests of bracken and bramble, golden ragwort and coltsfoot, fennel and foxglove and vetch, all the wild rambling shrubs that spring from ruin, the vaults and cellars and deep caves, the wrecked guild halls that had belonged to saddlers, merchant tailors, haberdashers, waxchandlers, barbers, brewers, coopers and coachmakers, all the ancient city fraternities, the broken office stairways that spiraled steeply past empty doorways and rubbled closets into the sky, empty shells of churches with their towers still strangely spiring above the wilderness, their empty window arches where green boughs pushed in, their broken pavement floors – St. Vedast's, St. Alban's, St. Anne's and St. Agnes'. St. Giles Cripplegate, its tower high above the rest, the ghost of churches burnt in an earlier fire, St. Olave's and St. John Zachary's, haunting the green-flowered churchyards that bore their names, the ghosts of taverns where merchants and clerks had drunk, of

restaurants where they had eaten – all this scarred and haunted green and stone and brambled wilderness lying under the August sun, a-hum with insects and astir with secret darting, burrowing life, received the returned traveller into its dwellings with a wrecked, indifferent calm. Here, its cliffs and chasms and caves seemed to say, is your home; here you belong; you cannot get away, you do not wish to get away, for this is the maquis that lies about the margins of the wrecked world, and here your feet are set; here you find the irremediable barbarism that comes up from the depth of the earth, and that you have known elsewhere. 'Where are the roots that clutch, what branches grow, out of this stony rubbish? Son of man, you cannot say or guess . . .' But you can say, you can guess, that it is you yourself, your own roots, that clutch the stony rubbish, the branches of your own being that grow from it and from nowhere else.

One long paragraph, minimal number of sentences – a sudden flow of the natural world, growing, too powerful to be constrained by full stops, buildings coming to life with new adjectives – *spiring, brambled* – shortly followed with a return to the plot, which makes no value judgement, that shows both sides, the good and bad of the overgrown ruins. But this paragraph held me spellbound as a teenager, and reading it now, it seems to say so much about the true spirit of a place. What happens when we leave it alone and it can be itself. London with the creature of the South crept in. What happens to us . . . The description builds and builds, at one point drifting into speech marks, the quote within making it feel as if the place itself is talking. It is alive, not just with plants and animals, but with the feeling of place as it knows you, your secrets, your deep caves. Human life is listed as a memory, a series of lost identities of human work, ghosts of toil as the churches are ghosts; buildings have the power to haunt, they are gone, dead, yet what has replaced them is *a-hum, astir* and *darting* with life – we are on the *margins of the wrecked world* now and it is not dead but profound and bursting with life; that if we just see it, listen and connect, we can grow roots, be part of the living not the dead of the ruins, we can grow branches from the stony rubbish and flourish.

There is something revealing, not concealing, about the atmosphere of the overgrown city. Like an intense multisensory experience, it is transformative. It might cover up the surface of what we know, but in doing so we are liberated to see beneath the surface, to feel the city, the earth on which it was built. The air is suddenly alive with a feeling of secrets, of a different, older, deeper knowledge. A sense that a deeper being of place will always be there, whatever happens to it; whatever we do to or with it.

As the last page of Macaulay's book says:

> So men's will to recovery strove against the drifting wilderness to halt and tame it; but the wilderness might slip from their hands, from their spades and trowels and measuring rods, slip darkly away from them, seeking the primeval chaos and old night which had been before Londinium was, which would be when cities were ghosts haunting the ancestral dreams of memory.

Yet for something hinting at such a primeval force, or maybe precisely because they do this, overgrown cities, as a real 'concrete' thing, have largely been written out of history. In fact, my ironic use of the word 'concrete' here is telling in itself: we see reality as manmade and solid, when in truth it is pliable and soft; it changes yet its essence is universal – so real that changing doesn't affect it, the layers are part of it, a building up of atmosphere and memory and transformation. It is still the same place. The surface is what appears different. Wastelands are often overgrown. In the aftermath of natural disasters places are left to 'go wild' till we intervene and rebuild, but the place is still there. We have just lost control. Not imposed upon it, so perhaps this is why as humans with a need for control, for history to be human, we fail to mention it. I studied World War II at school, London is my capital city, yet it took reading a wonderful novel for me to discover that for years London, specifically and interesting the area we know as the City, was overgrown – a wilderness.

The City – a city within a city – the mysteriousness of this as an area name has always intrigued me, as if it has an essence of its own; that it should be a heart of London, a location of urban essence. Yet today it is one of the least green areas in the capital. I used to live nearby in the East End, what is now the super hipster Shoreditch, and I mourned the lack of greenery. (Some love the atmosphere of this neighbourhood – the human buzz, the sense of stuff going on – but it was not for me.) I became confused yet fascinated by how I always got lost in the City; its endless façades seemed impersonal, the streets a maze I could never make out.

Looking back, I wonder if I sensed something in its atmosphere – a hidden memory, repressed now, of what it once briefly was, of what makes a place alive to us. How a lack of greenery and a lived-in human experience can block an atmosphere, screen it off, so that all we feel is what the human world wants us to – a corporate version of place, a sanitised history, a place where secrets are left to lie.

Yet I am also struck by how strongly I felt that the City's secrets were there when the humans left at night – that there was a truer atmosphere, the feelings of the place struggling to show themselves. Humans are so much part of an urban atmosphere – the buzz of a trendy area, bars, cafes – but that doesn't mean that the non-human isn't there. History, memory . . . Layers of history in different building styles. The secret life of urban nature – how it would come back if the place, the city, was left to its own devices without us, if destruction occurred on a scale so immense that we could not quickly fix it, get it back under our control. Is even the buzz – the alive energy of a thriving area – really under our control as much as the human atmosphere of more 'boring' suburbs? More staid human urban creation?

However, we have to be careful not to fetishise. Nature is both creative and destructive in urban spaces, unless controlled – ruins do not get rebuilt if left to nature's devices. In *The World My Wilderness*, the voyeuristic aspect of the ruined city is pointed out – for Barbary it is a realm of adventure, but there are well-to-do tourists, unaffected by the tragedy of lost homes and businesses, who 'liked the bomb ruins, and liked to take mementos of them back to Bournemouth, where they lived. Sometimes Americans would go by, and they liked the bomb ruins still more, not finding in Britain as many as they had been left to expect, and wanting to convince their friends back in Maine or Philadelphia that they had really seen the scars of war.'

This quote seems prophetic to me of a very particular kind of urban exploration: the very male approach to psychogeography, which actually goes against the emotional quest of the true term and which is a conquering version of urban exploration, detached and ego-driven; when for the thrill of it, middle-class men explore ruins in neighbourhoods they would never live in, rather than inhabit them emotionally, think deeply about them.

I once watched Julien Temple's documentary *Requiem for Detroit?*, almost a film essay on atmosphere, and the haunting images of vast swathes of a city ruined by economic downturn, not war, mesmerised me. There was a strange beauty; I could see the appeal. But I could also see the (mostly) men who would go there and get a thrill, as if they were caving – tourists, voyeurs of other people's destruction. The remaining communities were determined to stay strong: there was a house decorated with teddy bears, a surreal monument of sorts that was deeply moving; community programmes; people who had stayed for decades, for it was home. Yet the hipster crowd would take photos only of the empty shells of industry, the decay, the dystopian beauty that they had dared to visit. I understood the appeal, yet it makes me very uncomfortable. I was once shown the most beautiful coffee table book of photos of flood-damaged interiors in post-Katrina New Orleans, *After the Flood* by photographer Robert Polidori. It was visually beautiful but I couldn't shake the discomfort that I shouldn't be finding it so – that in some ways it shouldn't exist. Polidori saw himself as a psychological voyeur and admitted he felt uncomfortable with making beautiful images out of a disaster. The people are absent, their belongings remain. These were in many ways no different from looking at photos of crime scenes – only, in this instance, people died due to bad engineering, poverty and racial inequality. There is a moral conflict that is not present in ancient ruins destroyed by time or a love for wilder places; this is arguably not the true atmosphere of the city breaking free, but a requiem to an atmosphere of one of America's liveliest cities destroyed, along with the lives of its people. In some ways, the work should be classified as war photography, not a coffee table book. The true places have arguably gone – are shells, ghosts. And the atmosphere of being there, rather than looking at an image, would have been wildly different – context, smell, lack of human sound, knowledge. Atmosphere of place cannot be captured in image alone – atmosphere of an actual place cannot be covered up. It can confuse, juxtapose conflicting sensory experiences of good and bad, but it cannot be anything but itself.

Nevertheless, if we can block out the context, as a coffee table book it is undeniably beautiful. But beautiful for someone who was never there, in the artificial, disconnected image only. The filter, the frame. Maybe Macaulay wasn't so much prophetic, when talking of her bomb-ruin tourists, as describing an intrinsic human urge: both the voyeuristic urge to look upon destruction and also to see an appeal, a beauty, to recognise that something more is going on – that there is an attractive power in human creations that have failed and been left to the whims of the natural world, however uncomfortable and clearly wrong this can be, as in the case of the aftermath of Katrina. Barbary makes postcards of her drawings of the ruins to sell. In Belgrade fifteen years ago you could still buy postcards of bombed-out buildings with anti-NATO targets overlaid. We want to avoid disaster, but a visit, a sip of its atmosphere, is an urge of which we cannot let go.

Constructions and Manipulations

LA – Autopia of the Non-Place

The feelings of the city were confused. It was loosely aware of other cities. The personalities they had formed through their buildings, streets, history, the humans, the animals, the air, the air blue but not clear, the fumes, the sea, the land, the what-was-the-land. The city.

I know it cannot have visited other cities. Cities don't move, they sprawl. This one sprawled ... But there were versions of its smaller self once – loose memories, distant and asphalted – that sometimes it sensed.

Soft city trembles.

Trembling city.

Disjointed, like the earthquakes, the tectonic plates beneath its concrete feet, it was confused.

It was very much itself. Yet if it was asked to describe itself it would not know how to do so.

Infinite jigsaw of mini places.

Ornate grey ribbons of roads.

For all the buildings.

Spreading slowly like lava. Viscous and warm. Orange seems the right colour.

Sun. Oranges grow nearby. Orange County is nearby. Echoes of names.

Strange angels.

When I think back to LA, my memories are arranged in locations. Not in the normal sense, but rather a series of settings – rooms in people's houses, a bar, a car . . . The city itself was elusive to me – hovering as a concept, more than my twenty-something European brain could comprehend back then.

We arrived. LAX airport, November, but it was hot – more summer than falling leaves and bonfires. The air was wreathed with a different kind of smoke, the infamous smog resting a haze and blurring the air even further, the atmosphere a manmade filter.

We were met by friends of the friend I was travelling with. A gang of tall young men, all skinny jeaned and sharp shoed – limousine shoes, we christened them, though I don't know why. We got in their car and that is where the blurring started. The disconnection. Normally when I arrive in a new city, the drive from the airport is full of the buzz of my new location. I gaze out the window and the city assaults my senses with its particular feel. Its dramatic welcome of *you are somewhere new*. When I think back to LA I can remember nothing of note till we arrived at the friend's house.

The house I remember. Single storey, back yard. I can picture the rooms, but have no sense of the neighbourhood, other than I'd been told it was a bit out of the way. Encino in the valley. The house had an atmosphere, as all houses do, but it wasn't connected to where it lay. It was pleasant and generic. I was aware I was in an American house, but beyond that, I could have been anywhere.

I was there a few days. I could not tell you which one was which. When the different places occurred.

We drove to a few locations. The slightly more bohemian house of another friend in Silver Lake. Another in Echo Park. We drove to a nightclub to see a friend's band play. We drove to a restaurant and ate pasta when my demand that I needed to be fed, that I could not live off smog and booze alone, was finally listened to.

I can remember plastic tables and chairs. I can remember wall hangings and wicker. I can remember a long bar and leather chairs – extraordinarily long shots of spirits, token mixers. I can remember dark. I remember greyed sun. Warm and gauzy.

I remember gun-shaped fingers pointed at the friend of a friend by a crazy guy in quite a well-known band. We were in the car, even though this was a neighbourhood we could have probably walked in. I think the friend of a friend ended up in jail then homeless. I remember our friend's gig, a cult figure of the early nineties indie scene back home. I remember driving back to Encino in a seventies black Mercedes – a gangster car from old movies.

But most of all I remember the feeling of nothing. Of sitting in a car and feeling nothing but the movement of endless roads. Forty-five minutes to drive most places. Wheels spinning on tarmac from one isolated point to another.

It was deeply weird to know I was somewhere, somewhere famous, and to have no sense of where this place was.

I have never felt so foreign in my life. That December I went to Japan and it had nothing on LA for feeling alien.

I thought a lot about this, back at a friend's in San Francisco, then Vancouver, Japan, back home. I couldn't shake the feeling that I had not been to LA at all. I had not been to the tourist spots, the Hollywood sign, the hills. I wondered about these signifiers. If there was another reason they were given such weight – they gave identity when there was not one. I was theoretically there, but that I had also not been there: I'd been in a series of strange bubbles that were their own places, that were not LA. Or perhaps LA wasn't a city at all. A network of roads. Then bubbles.

Places existing, joined by asphalt tentacles, wreathed in the ether of smog.

I tried to picture the desert and mountains. The beautiful hills and canyons I'd seen on telly. Mountain lions roaming. Forest fires creeping in. Joni Mitchell and Neil Young singing – voices dancing through longing sun. *California, California* . . .

I never saw the sea.

LA was like one giant airport. A non-place; a threshold. Cars as shuttles, taking me from one place to another. Terminals. Outposts in a sea of wheels.

It is as much a city of cars as buildings. It was built for them – designed around them as much as people. A utopian vision of independent transport. The American Dream of individualism and personal control.

Autopia!

There is both a 1971 essay by architectural thinker Reyner Banham and a Disneyland ride (1955) by that name. Banham's essay puts not the history or downtown or Hollywood at the centre of LA's identity, but its freeway system. Rather than viewing LA's being designed around cars as one of its great flaws, which environmentally it is, he sees the freeway as being the lifeblood of the city, a place unto itself where LA residents feel an almost mystical way of being. He argues we do not reach our destination at a front door, but rather when we drive down the slipway off a freeway exit, it is like a driveway. This makes me think of portals, the idea that I left the freeway and then arrived at neighbourhood as house makes sense to me.

Freeway as state of mind, as way of life. Banham argues that psychologically all other LAs are but tributaries. Freeway as epic river. Rivers bring life. Yet the horror stories, traffic jams and deaths . . . For him, they are myths to put off non-locals.

This strange atmosphere or lack of. I wonder if it is because the city is under the control of this manmade network, which, like atmosphere, has taken on a life of its own.

The Disneyland ride had miniature versions of real cars, so

children could drive around like true LA residents. In 1955, it represented the future.

Freeways.

You have the freedom of your car. You have less freedom than in most other cities if you do not. I had no freedom or control. Without my own car I was at the whim of whoever was driving me.

I struggle with how LA was a non-place for me, was so alienating. I have friends who've been to LA since, and for them it was a city that held everything – that brought them to life in new ways. I wonder how much of my experience was made of missing the signs, the signifiers – not strolling Rodeo Drive, Laurel Canyon, Mulholland Drive, Venice Beach . . . Of not seeing *the* sign.

I craved the bohemian sunlit hills, glass houses staring out, vibrant Hispanic neighbourhoods, I craved the bright blue of Hockney swimming pools, the dark atmospheric strangeness that is film noir, a genre so associated with this city that sells itself on sunshine. I tried to picture scenes from old films. *Sunset Boulevard.* The mansion with the boat bed I had always coveted. I wonder if part of the confusion is the combination of place and fictional place, of signifiers taken to the extreme which, combined with the endless freeways, make it hard to find a way in. I felt marooned. Struggling through the smog as if it were itself a signifier of how hard it was to find the real city – the one outside of signs and roads, of images of itself. Of places that weren't nowhere.

Poundbury – The Atmospheric Mystery of Pastiche

There is a new town which, unlike most new towns, is not trying to be modern. It does not encapsulate the architectural thinking of its day – the sun-bright windows and lawns of a garden city, the brutalist concrete of 1960s bravado. No, this town in the depths of Dorset is brand new, yet it wants to be old. It wants to have the memories and stories and history, but it does not. It is not old, it is new, yet longing for the intangible feeling that old places have – it is hungry for their atmosphere. And in trying to be what it is not, it is pastiche. Its atmosphere has not been destroyed by extreme renovation, it just has a confused identity – it doesn't know what it is and in this weird confusion, the feeling it gives off is distinct.

I had been meaning to visit Poundbury for years. It is very near Dorchester where I spend many an hour charity shopping, yet despite my love and frequenting of this part of Dorset I had never got around to going there. I have always been fascinated by towns built from scratch – the utopian idealism of new towns that sometimes works, sometimes crosses over to the dystopian, always looks of its time when its heart was in the future, a modern archaeological curiosity. A town landed, out of context, in place, but out of place.

Poundbury is a new town with a difference, though. The pet project of Prince now King Charles, it sought to showcase modern architecture that those who do not like modern architecture would be pleased with. But rather than a unified design, say just mock-Georgian, Poundbury went all out. Georgian, Victorian, weirdly Dutch or German high-pitched roofs, cottages, a medieval market building, grand and domestic scale, town and village style – they packed it all in.

Started in 1993 by architect Léon Krier on Duchy of Cornwall land, it is still a town in progress. It is designed to appeal to people, to work for people. It is pleasant – I have no aesthetic objections to it as many architectural critics do, finding it kitsch and haphazard in its strange mix. It is these things, but people also like it and it made efforts to include social housing and good facilities, the lack of which were the blight of many earlier twentieth-century housing schemes, and it is much nicer than most modern housing developments of boxy houses with small windows.

But in its inevitable pastiche, it's trying to be something it isn't in terms of age (not function), it is atmospherically fascinating.

The first time I visited I drove out of Dorchester. A large roundabout loomed and it took me a while to realise that this was it, its own strange ring road which the central part of the town existed upon, its own tarmac moat keeping it separate, distinct.

I drove in and parked on the edge of the street. There was plenty of space. I began walking. An Edwardian terrace, a little regency street with iron balconies, then the more formal rows of Georgian-style townhouses. It was nice. And it was completely empty. I walked into a shop and then another, one selling gifts, another slightly designer clothes – not village but town shops. Yet I was the only person in them.

It was uncanny in the true sense of the word – the familiar made unfamiliar. The atmosphere wasn't what it should be for the style of architecture, the kind of shops. It was silent. Despite the parks I have a distinct feeling that I could not hear birdsong, though I admit it is quite possible that I am wrong. But the silence was so strong that sounds are blotted out in my memory. I feel that birds would have thought it best to keep quiet.

I kept walking along the empty streets to the main town square, named after the Queen Mother and boasting a Waitrose and a pub as well as some swish large flats. There were a few people there, but it still felt empty. I couldn't figure it out.

I wandered further.

It was the absence. Paradoxically the atmosphere was so strong because there was nothing that would normally create an urban or village atmosphere there. No people, genuinely old buildings, animals or traffic. There were quite a few parked cars, but the place might as well have been pedestrianised for the negligible amount that were in motion.

It was an atmosphere of the strength of absence. Of the absence of the expected. The uncanny feeling that something was missing, was wrong, but in a pleasant not scary way. I found myself wondering what it would feel like to live there, almost tempted to rent somewhere, to live there just for a short time to find out – to see how this quiet and strangeness would affect me creatively. I think it would be quite nice. Yet I could not live there long term. When I was looking for houses during the pandemic I didn't consider Poundbury. It would be too surreal: it is in the West Country but does not have any of the things I love about the area, the feeling, the atmosphere, the ancient cosiness – it could never feel like home.

Pastiche. The atmosphere trickster. The reason that forged works are often lacking something even though identical in brushstroke. Identical except for what builds an atmosphere. The layers, the subtleties. A town built to identically reproduce another would not have its atmosphere. A clone has exactly the same DNA, but the living creature would have a different personality. Places, like creatures, are built of more than aesthetics. Whether we tear them down or build them anew, we can never recreate an atmosphere.

Tiflis/Tbilisi

Tbilisi is the city that lives in me. That has become so much part of me that I cannot imagine myself without it. Its air has seeped in, speckles of dust from the old balconies have colonised my lungs. Tumultuous and layered, so much history – ancient grandeur, Soviet times where decadence hung on longer than in most places. It was where all the fruit and wine was grown and it had those mountains to keep it safe. It had the Black Sea.

My stowaway city, my friend. It is curious about all the other places I see as I take it with me. Its atmosphere merges with them.

Then after Soviet times, the civil war, bombs ripping this gentle sky. I wonder if it was confused. If the city understood what was happening – why its teenagers were now shooting each other in the streets.

Its walls crumbled, weakened by the strange skin condition of plaster known as bullet holes, it flaked and fell. There was no money to build it up again.

And the balconies. For me, Tbilisi will always be a city of balconies.

When I first went in 2007 I walked the streets, and the balconies, with their carved wood and mottled glass, were like swallows' nests for building hearts – hanging on, a miracle of architectural saliva, just like those made by swallows, showing the personality of the beautiful streets. How what it once was, was still there, clinging on, providing a beautiful space and view for its families, holding small tables of bread and cheese and wine, a curled-up cat and old cushions.

I went back again, for months at a time – in 2008, 2009 and 2010. Then a gap of years, till 2016 when I returned full of anticipation for the city I couldn't believe I'd kept away from for so long.

I used to stay with friends in the old neighbourhood of Sololaki, up near the once defunct now very active funicular railway up to Mtatsminda Park. I would walk for hours. In the years of my first visits, the things that normally held tourists' time were not open – museums, shops that sold more than household supplies . . . I walked and walked and got to know the city by where it took my feet. And all this time I navigated by the balconies.

I gave them names – look there's Salome! Dato! Teenatin! I had a routine of daily hellos – down the street past one building, all glass fronted though half the narrow panes held in white flaked wood were smashed. It would have once been the side of an *ezo* – a courtyard structure of homes with wraparound balconies resembling magical corridors of glinting light and neighbour views. There was the balcony as intricate as torn lace, a discarded wedding veil, while others were strong, simple wooden railings like banisters run away from stairs for a better street view.

They each had their own personality.

I always felt these balconies held the stories of the city. Its inhabitants. All that had happened there. And while I knew they could not last as they were, there was a beauty to them they would not have had if they were pristine. Like a beautiful old person with wrinkled skin, no trauma of plastic surgery, no Botoxing away the lines, they showed their life. They exuded an atmosphere of having lived. Of knowing what it is to survive and yet, still breathing, puffing out feelings, memories, contributing life to their city.

I know that I am not being practical here. I know that people need buildings that won't fall down. Homes that are warm and safe, rather than semi-derelict. I know there is a romantic tinge to my love of the beauty of decay in this city. But it is not voyeuristic, more akin to the Japanese notions of *wabi sabi* and the beauty of decay, and *kintsugi* – those vases made more precious once broken when the cracks are highlighted by gold rather than invisible glue.

I do not want these buildings to fall down, but in terms of how they are being repaired, I worry.

I went back again in 2017. The city had changed, as all cities do. Some of it was good, some of it was strange, some of it broke my building heart.

The streets were alive again, shops everywhere! Museums open! Tourists! An old factory, whose ruins I'd danced in on my birthday in 2016, was a super trendy arts venue and hostel a year later. This is not bad – I want the city to thrive. For people to earn a living.

I walked through Sololaki; it looked pretty much the same, then down towards what is known as the old town and the first jolt – the most lace-like and beautifully glazed balcony of all, surrounded in scaffolding and MDF boards. It felt like a premonition, unsettling though I could not say why.

Then I arrived in the old town.

There were always parts here – Shardeni Street with its cafes, for example – that were in better repair than the rest of the town. But as I continued walking I found myself getting lost – landmark balconies were gone and others so rebuilt, they were unrecognisable.

Loud music was blaring. I noticed a strip club.

I wandered further. The labyrinth of little streets I knew so well confused me. The iron spiral staircase was gone. A balcony I used to say hello to was gone. I wandered higher up towards the fortress. Bright fresh paint and wood.

I turned back and round and up and round – spinning – I was disorientated. This area had been renovated. I knew about that. As the city has become more popular with tourists and more money has come in, as the war of 2008 and the civil wars of early post-Soviet independence drift further into memory, there has been a major move to both renovate the old historic areas, as well as to build new structures on a grand scale. But these buildings had not been renovated so much as rebuilt and with it the voices of the atmosphere, this living atmosphere that talked to me more than any other city, was muffled. The feelings that I knew were smothered.

The best regeneration and renovation should bring buildings back to life. Should try to save what they can, though inevitably some bits that are rotten or destroyed will have to be rebuilt. It can sometimes feel extreme, but a listed buildings system like we have in the UK means that the feeling of a building, its atmosphere and history, its stories, are protected as much as they can be. In Tbilisi, it felt as if these were not the same buildings rebuilt, but new builds, hologram versions of what was once there. Empty shells clothed in the abstract appearance of the old buildings. The atmosphere of this part of the city was gone.

It challenged everything.

It was a brand new neighbourhood of ghosts.

Atmosphere is fluid and evolving. But, like ageing, it is usually recognisable. Cities are constantly in flux, constantly changing – it is in their nature; it is a good, healthy and exciting part of what they are. I am even quite fond of the Soviet suburbs – the contrast of the grey concrete towers and the old centre, the surreal bright candy colours that President Saakashvili was intent on painting some of the concrete towers during his time in power, in a surface renovation that locals hated; they preferred the brutal grey. But normally when I am walking a city, despite its changes, the feeling is the same. Tbilisi, my strongest city atmosphere of all, was making me question the very nature of the atmosphere of cities. How much power we as humans have.

Cities are manmade. Yet while this by definition might make their atmospheres constructed, there is nothing artificial to this. The atmosphere of cities (as a whole as opposed to individually designed structures or areas) is as natural as those of forests and fields – which, of course, are managed by humans too, so as manmade as cities in some ways. But walking through Tbilisi, I wondered at our power of destruction. I had always thought atmosphere survived any onslaught. That it emerges, a little different, but its heart is the same. In general, for Tbilisi this is the case. But walking through the old town that day, it felt like there'd been an atmosphere massacre. It felt as though, in the enthusiasm of renovation and a new vision for the city, its atmosphere hadn't stood a chance. That it had been destroyed and replaced with something so new this hadn't had a chance to develop yet. Haunted by my own memories, not even the ghosts themselves, I was in an unsettling no man's land of atmosphere, yet all around me the buildings were in near perfect repair.

I clambered back up to Sololaki. Past one of my favourite buildings, still crumbling, walls held up by wooden stilts. Its street still cradling the hole an earthquake left years ago. It desperately needed saving and I had always hoped that it would be, but looking at the state of it, I felt an urgency of despair. There was no way the effort would be made for this ordinary building of flats on a rundown, out of the way street. If it got any worse it would not be restored, it would be pulled down. The land filled in and flattened. A modern block (for this street didn't even have the impetus for tourist old-town aesthetics to save it) built in its place. The residents might have safer, warmer homes – and that I did want for them, too. But the building's atmosphere would be lost.

There is a town in Kakheti in eastern Georgia called Sighnaghi. I remember that on my second visit, in 2008, it had recently been renovated as a whole and consequently was being marketed as a destination, with endless surreal TV adverts of brides and of restaurants serving traditional Georgian food and wine. I had gone there with my friends, almost expecting to gatecrash a wedding. But there were no brides and it left me cold. It was too perfect. Its atmosphere, though full of balconies, was toy town. Reading the blurb on a pack of postcards, I discovered Sighnaghi was one of the most ancient and important towns in Georgia. There was a telling mistranslation too – rather than 'renovation', the blurb said 'rehabilitation', as if a town of old crumbling buildings just couldn't be in the modern world. So now it had the atmosphere of a new housing estate rather than an historic and beautiful small town in the hills, locked away as if in an old people's home, out of view in favour of a presentable façade.

Yet there are areas in Tbilisi that are being done up where the feeling is still there, softly nestling in side streets, calmer somehow. In 2016, on the other side of the river (as in so many cities, the river acts as a divide, an atmosphere barrier, leading into another city within the city), I walked to a street my friends had said was just reopening after a big renovation. I was curious – I loved walking this other side of the water, visiting this other atmosphere, equally distinct, less full of ancient history and tourist attractions, but with homes and markets.

Yet it was different. It was pristine, which in itself felt strange, but it had never been an old street of faded beauty. It felt calm and relaxed, like a well-to-do Italian town, prosperous, full of cafes and small birds singing. It has probably changed again – as this side of the city gets trendier, the cafes and bars might be loud and full of tourists – but in that moment it felt peaceful. Like it had been renovated rather than destroyed. Genteel quiet – an almost eerie atmosphere for Tbilisi.

I wandered up the sweet-pea tendrils of side streets with their more humble iron balconies, more Parisian than the Eastern promise of carved wood and glinting glass. The plaster crumbled in places, but gently, as if the walls were softly flaking pastry, solid underneath, not internally shattered, not about to fall down with the weight of it all.

The light was warm and pale. I saw a cat with kittens in a nest of leaves.

One wide street all new and smooth. The older others gently resting, same as ever. Relaxing.

The city was different yet still here.

I like to think that it has welcomed the other. That in its rest, it's holding true through all its changes, that there is a little street, an old factory, a row of lower-rise houses, lived in for generations, a corner shop selling fresh flat bread, bowls of ripe tomatoes and small cucumbers, bunches of coriander; that there is a place of refuge, one that opened its door arms, its street cracks and let the old city in. That they are still here somewhere, the stories, hovering in curly iron, carved wood and pastel-painted stone.

Bucharest

I feel guilty when I think of Bucharest, of how I wanted to love it, of how I loved the people I met, but how the city ... I could not love the city.

I arrived one hot summer. I had been invited to run art workshops with local children and then to create my own work inspired by the city to be shown at a gallery, which, if successful, would be scaled up to take pride of place at a metro station. I was very excited, my travels had told me I loved Eastern Europe and I was greedy for any country I had not been to before. And it was another excuse to take flight, another moment of searching, of leaving behind the fact that

I no longer felt at home in the UK. The anticipation bubbled up as I boarded the plane.

But the reality was different. The workshops went well. My piece, using embroidery, old photos, stitched stories in English and Romanian, was selected, though it never reached its final form, the 2008 banking crisis scuppering the funding. But for all the lovely people and opportunities, I had to accept in the end that I just did not like Bucharest. And the reason that I didn't like it was its atmosphere.

Bucharest is a city of scale. The former palace of the brutal communist dictator Ceaușescu was, on its completion, the second largest building in Europe. It dominates the centre. Wide roads heaving with traffic lead up to where it hovers menacingly like a strange residential mausoleum. It watches over, as if its foundations were a throne, a look out, its windows eyes, its feet having crushed all that once existed below. It is trying to be its own city in rivalry with the actual city. In doing this, I fear it began an obliteration.

My first stay was in a flat near this monstrosity. I could not relax. It felt too near and when I left the flat and ventured into the heat, I did not feel at ease until I had surfaced at the other end of the metro ride and was ensconced in the comfort of doing art with kids near the museums. Nothing bad happened on this journey. Nobody was unpleasant. But the whole time I was walking on the street, I felt a strange threat, unhuman; not that warning we might feel, knowingly walking in a dangerous area at night, but something simmering, architectural. It was not what I believed the true city was, but all the impositions – all the monumental bulldozing and rebuilding that had taken place in the decades of dictatorial rule, of repression and cruelty – felt like it was held here.

I tried to rid myself of this feeling. It was logical in some ways that such a vast building and its surrounding area could trigger such feelings. The violent repression of Bucharest's history was too visible. Now known as Revolution Square, the area does not speak of freedom. The only revolution it brought to my mind was the widely televised execution of Ceaușescu and his wife, the grisly end to one of the more violent revolutions at the fall of the Iron Curtain. A brutal end to a brutal time.

Yet when I walked around Bucharest, the atmosphere that pursued me wasn't a conscious thought of these things, but a constant unease. A feeling of being tricked or watched.

There was a street filled with nothing but wedding-dress shops, the road decayed into giant holes I had to dodge around. Nearby, there was a shell of a building. Silent. No roof or windows or floors. I could see the once interior walls. There was a pattern of retro wallpaper and pastel paint, changing colours as it dripped down through what once were floors. The gentle detail of lives, homes, lost and left here, their innards all on display.

A pair of jeans hung lonely and high – an empty half-body – a domestic flag. I had absolutely no idea how they could have got up there.

The poignancy of this place broke my heart and I could feel the remnants of a gentle, other side to this city.

The days continued, my routine continued; moving temporary flats twice, I could not settle. I could not explain the threat. It was creeping. I would sit in a cafe and find it tricky to stay still. I tried walking, getting to know the city better in my usual way. And while I found much nicer areas, big older houses, trees and roses, I still did not feel at ease.

It was not helped by the stray dogs that roamed and threatened. While I love animals, and don't blame the poor things at all for their behaviour, this was the urban equivalent of stumbling on a hungry pack of wolves. So many people I met had been chased or bitten. I had to turn and change my route many times. I winced if I ever heard a bark above the traffic.

The city grew but still I could not find my place – an atmosphere where even if I did not feel at home, I at least felt at ease.

The closest I came was conversely the day when I stumbled

accidentally into the one area my Romanian friends said I should not have been.

I had got to know a brilliant woman from Belgrade, Natalija, still a close friend today, and she, having a similar strange experience, joined me on a wandering quest to find a different city.

We had a couple of drinks in a not very friendly bar.

Then walking and walking and walking.

We laughed and skipped and peered round corners. We followed the city as if its atmospheres were smells our noses could detect and thus seek out the places where we felt we would rather be. If somewhere felt rather than looked better, we would keep going in that direction. It was an experiment, yet the urge was genuine: one last, 'Come on, Bucharest, we want to like you! Where are you?' – the city's subtler atmospheres drowned out by the brashness of the dominant one, the legacy, the hangover, the atmosphere that just could not be it alone.

Walking for hours, we lost our sense of the city. We had not been paying attention to our route, just the feeling of the place, the urge to rid ourselves of the bad atmosphere.

Bad atmosphere . . . We all know what one is – when somewhere or someone feels wrong. We all know that bodily reaction to a potentially dangerous area, our subtler senses warning us, telling us to be careful. Bad atmospheres can communicate for a reason, warn us, a kind place telling us to watch out. Give us clues we recognise. But this was not that. This was a summer light-filled evening. We felt no human threat. It was the place playing hide and seek, drawing us on regardless of what might or might not be a threat. And at the end of it, if we caught it, we had no idea what we might find. We were moving through atmospheres we did not necessarily like, but the thrill of the chase gave this moment its own atmosphere that transformed things again and again.

We heard music. Drums beating. A tinny cassette player. But music on a street! It was the first time we had heard such a sign of abandon here. We followed and before long we had entered an area totally different in feel. Our atmosphere paused and rested.

Smaller, lower houses. People out on the street, smiling. Music. Kids playing. This place was alive. I see wood and stone and colour. I see a maze of crumbled lanes, not streets, where we had no idea of the way out, but this wasn't threatening – it was as if we could see over the top.

We felt our way. Slowed our pace. When I look back I have no idea how long we spent there, whether it was getting dark when we left, how we got back home.

We felt better.

The next day, when we explained where we'd been, people were worried. A rough gypsy neighbourhood apparently, rife with crime, terrible idea for foreigners, yet in a peculiar way, in how the atmosphere felt, I had felt safer there than at any other time in this city.

Bad atmospheres.

They are everywhere. They dominate when present. But cities are multi-layered and, underneath, a different feeling might breathe in the least expected of places. Be free.

The psychology of place addresses the notion of there being a kind of spectral playback. We are all familiar with it. A house might appear beautiful and perfect, but if we hear a murder has taken place there, we would probably reject it as a potential home. In fact, estate agents are obliged to tell clients if something awful has happened in a building. We are all aware of the idea that battlefields and other places of mass trauma have echoes of this in them. That the events so dark cannot leave, but haunt the place, endlessly on playback to visitors.

I wondered if there was an element to this in Bucharest. While the Iron Curtain divided Eastern Europe from the West, Romania was arguably, along with Albania, the most closed off and repressed of all Eastern Bloc countries. I remember talking to a Serbian friend about this – how Belgrade had no leftover feelings of communist repression and trauma despite its more recent wars. She wondered if it had something to do with Tito being a hedonist and therefore the place being more open. That despite all the awful things he did, the people he persecuted, life in communist Yugoslavia didn't feel the same as in other Eastern Bloc countries. The collective trauma was different, had had more time and space to escape the boundaries of its national borders, had lived again in a different way since with wars that made communist times seem not as bad as they may have been.

If a whole city is traumatised for years, if the buildings that embodied the power that did this are still dominant, I wonder if this does have an effect. Since the nineteenth century, people have sought to try to explain strange feelings in place, such as hauntings, to see if memories of what happened there have had an impact. When the Society for Psychical Research was set up in 1882, one of its earliest beliefs was that certain buildings and materials could record and store events to be played back to psychically gifted individuals. Going back a further fifty years, the polymath and natural theologian Charles Babbage, sometimes said to be the father of the computer, thought that words could leave physical imprints in the air. He was convinced it would be later explained by science, and the properties of molecules. If memories, words, events are held physically in landscape, it is logical that atmosphere could be a way of these playing back – a communication of memory beyond ghosts. Of course, spectral playback is not science but belief, thinking and feeling, yet the concept has stayed in our consciousness. People are unwilling to let go of the idea that somehow what happens in a place leaves a real impression on it. However, it is frustrating – or telling – that these cases nearly always involve dark memories, suggesting a voyeuristic rather than genuine urge to delve into how a place feels.

It can involve the power of suggestion. I once took part in an art project in an old prison and while many had extreme emotional responses to the space, I got preoccupied with the hidden beauty and felt sorry for the building, that it was not the place's fault it was built to house trauma – that all these bad things happened there. I sensed the place behind the trauma, not the trauma behind the place. But still, there was something about Bucharest . . .

Outside of Bucharest, Romania felt very different. I took the train to the hills and the fields of haystacks like cosy monsters were warm and gentle. Flat countryside gave way to hills and mountains, and when I stepped off the train I could finally breathe. Bucharest, unable to stretch this far, had let go of its grip.

One of my favourite series of travel books is Patrick Leigh Fermor's journey through Europe as a young man in the 1930s. Perhaps my favourite of all is the second book in the series, *Between the Woods and the Water*, which sees him travel down through Hungary and then through the decadent wilds of Romania back then.

I first read the book after my time in Bucharest and, as I read, I felt an atmosphere creep in that was a strange artefact of what had been lost. But I was also aware that the descriptions I loved, the feeling I loved, were of when Fermor was roaming Transylvania, the countryside – the area with a distinct identity that I too loved when I travelled there. It was not Bucharest. There were communist leftovers – it certainly wasn't as laid back as it was when he visited. I remember strange queues and illogical ticketing systems. The horror when I asked if I could linger more than ten minutes in the library of a castle, rather than continue on the high-speed official tour. I wonder if Fermor could have visited this castle too, whether it was the location of one of his laid-back parties ...

In the third book in the series, *The Broken Road*, a whole chapter is devoted to Bucharest. Strange – I could not remember reading this! I had been so swept up in the feelings of rural bohemia, the wildness, the comfort, the liberal and intellectual aristocratic homes where Fermor stayed, alternated with sleeping in fields and ditches, the stories of peasants and rich families, that I had forgotten he later revisited Romania and Bucharest was his temporary base.

I reread the chapter curiously. The difference in atmosphere was palpable. As he enters the city, all is ramshackle and falling down – there is a strange heady darkness, 'a fluid region where nothing was static', and it becomes clear he has stumbled into a red light district of sorts. Later, he wanders – is almost confused by the grandeur around the central area, which years later so alienated me. The smart, overly dressed people, the impression of sneering. At first, of all the places in his books, it is the one whose initial feel he seems to like the least. It is strikingly different from the rest of his Romanian experience. Yet later, as he makes friends, he grows to like the city.

But what is most striking to me about Fermor's account is Bucharest's decadence and intellectualism. It was bohemian and vehemently cultured. Of all the places he visited, this was the city of parties. Writing the book, he knew what would happen later; he doesn't name those who remained, while others he catalogues as exiles or the victims of suicide, their world and their city changed beyond recognition once the Iron Curtain fell . . .

I try to picture this version of the city, so decadent and free – dancing, no rules, no illogical queues and ticketing systems . . . (I once went to a music festival in the city with Natalija and it took us ages to work out the system for buying a beer. Three queues. Later, watching the gigs, nobody in the audience moved.) I struggle. Even in the now-dilapidated grand villas, I find it hard to picture this scene.

We may or may not believe in spectral playback. I personally don't. But the tendrils of a city's history, like a deep-rooted perennial weed, an atmosphere tap root, can lie in wait, ready to burst forth in the blissful lull that is the beginning of a new spring.

'A fluid region' – history flowing on, currents sometimes dragging it all back in.

The Beautiful Commodity

It is the late eighteenth century and a slightly eccentric vicar, my many greats grandfather, is walking through the Welsh borders. He has a sketchbook. He pauses, looks around at the view; then, with his hands or an object, he 'frames' what he sees. He continues walking, before sitting on a rock and staring down at the river in the valley below. He takes a deep breath, trying to absorb the feeling of all around him. Framing the landscape once again, he begins to sketch.

This scene might not sound particularly unusual, but for the time, the choice of technique and landscape – this way of seeing it and thereby describing and portraying it, being in it and experiencing it – was. For the vicar was William Gilpin, vicar, writer, artist, early accidental exponent of holidaying in the English countryside, object of ridicule, unlikely setter of trends and promoter of the picturesque.

We hear the word 'picturesque' all the time today; we are used to it meaning pretty and bucolic – a synonym of idyllic, if you will. But the origins of the term are quite different. We use the simile 'as pretty as a picture' often too and this is closer: originally, the picturesque did have an element of this attitude, viewing a scene as if it were a picture. However, the kind of landscape that was viewed and framed was different. This was not always the gentle rural England we now associate with the term 'picturesque', but also craggy, wild landscapes which, before this, had been perceived as unsettling and unappealing, or landscapes of contrast, with beauty from unexpected juxtapositions. It sometimes concerned, although not always, the landscapes of the sublime, of which the Romantics were so fond, with dramatic vistas and ruins designed to provoke overwhelming responses of awe. It was about natural landscapes which, in their wildness, it shouldn't have been possible to contain; however, in the way in which Gilpin sought to experience them, and wished other people to do too, they were just that – held in a frame, potentially even rearranged, controlled by the experience and desires of the viewer. Sketchbook as true container of view.

Was this experience purely visual? Did atmosphere come into it? Did it bring people into closer connection with the land or detach them from it? Certainly, there was an artifice to this way of viewing the landscape. In the late eighteenth century, encouraged by Gilpin and his ideas of the picturesque, a device called a Claude glass became popular. Named after the fashionable seventeenth-century landscape painter Claude Lorrain, the Claude glass was a viewing device made from a small curved grey mirror that helped frame and tint the surrounding scenery, reflecting the landscape as if it were a miniature picture, expanded yet contained. This portable device meant that anyone, when out and about in the landscape, could pause and frame the vista, capturing it in a picturesque manner. Pre-photography, the actual view in a Claude glass was of course temporary, yet it could be used as a device for framing a view when sketching outside. Recording through art. Creating memory souvenirs of the places you have been.

Claude glasses were a novelty, a fashion (Gilpin supposedly even had one fitted in his carriage, framing the landscape even more than a window naturally does), yet while they encouraged people to appreciate the landscape, in some ways they also detached them from a true experience of it. To use one, you needed to have your back to the view you were seeking to capture. It was a filter. A distancer. In this respect, Claude glasses remind me of smart phones today – the need to constantly frame and capture, to add a filter on our experience of place. (How many of us find it difficult just to go for a walk without thinking about what it looks like in photos, potentially for social media?) The mirrors framed experience for images, images you would then perhaps capture in a sketch in order to show your friends where you had been. What you were doing. A kind of eighteenth-century, small-scale social media: frame, capture, share. Prove where you were; catalogue rather than simply *be* there.

The viewer. The gaze. These are art history terms and Gilpin was an artist. His paintings adorned my childhood walls. They never struck me as devoid of feeling – they were gentle, actually, not really wild at all. His sketches of trees show a sensitivity that contradicts his written words, which describe a way of being in place that is anything but multisensory. Indeed, in his *Forest Scenery*, whose volumes record an epic quest to describe all the forests of Great Britain, Gilpin describes the picturesque eye as something which 'merely examines Nature as a beautiful object'. Examining, not experiencing, Claude glass as telescope meets microscope, views as specimens of distance, not in dialogue with anything beyond the surface. Nature as surface. Yet I think it is a little unfair to presume Gilpin experienced nature in such a detached manner. His way of talking about place can be off-putting – landscape as object, the possession of a view acting as souvenir – but he was also addressing a particular audience, describing Nature (telling that he gives it a capital 'N') for the picturesque eye; he never claims nature does not exist outside of it. Who is to say how he truly felt in the landscape in the moment or what he was trying to capture? He was endlessly satirised at the time, but if you read his work, he appears deeply sincere. He loved the landscape. In a refreshingly democratic way, he wanted everyone to have access to viewing it with an artist's eye – to experience its wonder as he did.

Nevertheless, if you approach the landscape as merely presenting you with a picturesque view, you miss the details. We might laugh at how Gilpin sincerely talks about how birds are in some respects picturesque with their beautiful plumage, while arguing they cannot really be considered as such because they are too diminutive to have an effect in a painting. Yet he is concerned with beauty – and beauty is a feeling; a quest for beauty is a quest for a feeling in a place.

*

In the late 1700s and into the 1800s, the picturesque changed how people experienced the landscape and the kind of places they found appealing. Before this, the aesthetics of the Classical movement had prescribed that places should be ordered; and certainly garden design was a very formal affair. The outdoors was desirable when humanised, but wandering around the countryside was not seen as a desirable activity for the well-to-do – indeed, what benefit could one possibly derive from doing that? But the picturesque transformed this attitude, encouraging people to venture into the countryside and see it in a new way.

Rather than traditional geometric order, picturesque places (as defined by Gilpin and his peers) had a preferred series of elements – rocks at a certain angle, a tasteful ruin maybe, all elements that would make for an appealing landscape painting. There was an artificiality to this, but rather than deadening an intuitive response to the landscape, it opened up a way of seeing that allowed landscape to be experienced in new ways. The picturesque movement might have been a trend of sorts, but it was also thoughtful and creative, making people question how they saw the world around them.

The picturesque influenced garden design too. While in many ways as controlled as formal gardens of the past, the picturesque transformed people's relationship to the intimate natural places that were important to them. These spaces were no longer enclosed – exterior rooms designed to protect people from the wild – but stretching landscapes, reaching out into the wider countryside. Gardens were designed to look natural, though they were profoundly manmade – churches moved for spoiling the view, fake ruins built, ha-has rather than walls so as not to interrupt the panorama, and, as Tom Stoppard notes in his play *Arcadia*, which deals with this subject, tastefully arranged sheep.

The picturesque also led to the first guide books and encouraged early travel writing. It gave women a chance to experience wilder landscapes without taking risks (although, of course, rural working women would already know these landscapes from their day-to-day lives – as with so many historical fashions, this was a largely upper-class affair). It encouraged people to engage with the land in new ways; to walk them willingly.

People have always walked, both from necessity and for pleasure. However, in terms of modern Western culture, the idea of landscape as offering an experience in itself – as a destination, as something to be viewed like a spectacle, with the landscape 'curated' for mass tourism – this was new at the time of Gilpin. And it was as radical for him as it would be for a Romantic poet such as Coleridge.

The picturesque spanned both the Classical and Romantic movements. It was more controlled and less obsessed with individual imaginative inspiration than the latter. Interestingly, although Romanticism and the picturesque are often lumped together, in many ways their approaches to experiencing place were diametric opposites, with an emotional response being key to the Romantics, while the picturesque sought to frame, analyse and catalogue the land. Similarly, Gilpin and Coleridge were two people who experienced the world in different ways, and whose communion with atmosphere was different – subjective, as in its fluid personal nature it always is. The atmosphere felt when striding the Quantock Hills in wild weather, possibly while on drugs, was most probably very unlike that experienced when pottering around the Wye Valley, sketching – but they are both still atmospheres.

For all their differences, Gilpin and the Romantics had some places in common. They appreciated ruins and commercialised the appeal of these, with Tintern Abbey being the prime example. It could be argued that the Romantics, in their poetic quest for the sublime, did much the same thing as the picturesque movement when it came to commodifying the landscape. They saw emotion as an authentic way into aesthetic experience – and appreciated the value of challenging emotions – but this still privileges emotion over the reality of the land itself.

Despite all their poetic urges to be in remote places, with Coleridge striding across the Quantocks and Wordsworth 'discovering' the Lake District (a bit too close to rural colonialism for my liking; I prefer to think of little Ann Mercer embroidering her map, a creation just as revolutionary as those by Romantics in the area), there was also a touristic aspect to Romanticism – the trend to experience the sublime. So we now have two versions of landscape tourism: one through ways of seeing in the picturesque, one through ways of feeling in Romanticism. They were both seeking an experience of place, but one that conformed to their own ideas of what this should be. The Romantic movement too liked a landscape to be a certain way – suddenly areas seen as 'wild' (albeit a 'masculine' and vast definition of wildness as opposed to the gentle sort of wildness we can see in our gardens, for example) such as moors and mountains – locations preferred by hardy explorer types today – were to be sought out rather than feared.

In many ways, while the picturesque was miles away from the beloved extremes of Romanticism, it was fundamental to Romanticism's development and appeal in popular culture and, more importantly, the way some people thought about their experience of place. Individuals began to seek out new experiences, new ways of seeing, new atmospheres. As Christopher Hussey said in 1927 (quoted in Giuliana Bruno's *Atlas of Emotion*), the power of the picturesque was 'to enable the imagination to form the habit of feeling through the eye'. Indeed, it is this idea of 'feeling' a landscape that is key – yes, there might have been a prescribed way to do this for the likes of Gilpin and his peers, but consciously feeling a landscape, linking it to imaginative power and creativity for non-artists, remains revolutionary.

Although Gilpin may have been a figure of fun to some, his books sold many copies and people flocked to his beloved Wye Valley, desperate to view a fashionable landscape – the wild, as opposed to the controlled nature of formal gardens and parks, now being the latest thing. But when I think of him I wonder: was this not so much an attempt to control how we see things, but rather at heart a quest through a way of seeing, for atmosphere, for the true feeling of place that the built environment so often covers up? A place is a living narrative we respond to. The picturesque was not trying to take something away from place, but in a bizarrely fashionable and arguably contrived way, honestly trying to add something; to bring something to light; to open access to a deeper place experience.

Writing the City

There is something in the idea of the city as a repository of stories, of secrets; the idea something must be 'written' there, as if it were a giant notebook that we just need to learn how to read. In fact, some have even gone further. Michel de Certeau, in his famous essay 'The Practice of Everyday Life', saw us as *practitioners* of the city. The city is a language that we use, it is something we do; and it is in this sense that I see us as speaking not just reading, as writing not just absorbing, our urban surroundings. It is a process that we create. We take it in; then, as we go, we spill it out of us too – we walk, we interact, we create and the city is kept alive by this. It is kept alive by our movement through it.

The subject of walking and the city has a long and sometimes very fashionable theoretical history. There was, for example, the nineteenth-century concept of the flâneur, traditionally an idle male sauntering the streets on a whim, more often than not in Paris. (The female prostitute was a key character in the trope of the flâneur too. In this context these women were often tellingly known as streetwalkers; they had a strange autonomous presence of their own, and whatever the reality of their safety and wellbeing, they had a form of power in that the city was their domain – it was the men, not their city, who posed a threat to them.) Paris would have been particularly evocative when it was still a medieval city, before Haussmann's complete mid-nineteenth-century redesign, but afterwards it still functioned as *the* place to wander, to experience life on the streets among the shopping arcades of the later nineteenth and early twentieth centuries, and with the mid-century political uprisings, left-wing politics and student riots regarding the streets as their realm.

I learned about these theories when I was an art history student in Edinburgh, a time in my life when I wandered obsessively through that city. Edinburgh is good for this: wide Georgian streets, Victorian tenements, medieval wynds and hidden village areas. Hills, river, sea. I used to walk late on light summer evenings, peering in lit-up windows. I had rituals – along the river through Stockbridge and Dean Village to the modern art gallery, Calton Hill and Arthur's Seat, charity shopping in the posh old-lady suburbs. I walked miles, built the habit I've had ever since of getting to know cities by walking them. It was the hardest thing about my time in some American cities, that inability to walk them. All the cities I love and know well I have walked and walked, mapping my own stories in them with my feet.

Similar to Paris, which was torn down and rebuilt in the nineteenth century, Edinburgh's New Town was a creation of the eighteenth, like my Georgian hometown of Bath. New Town: when we think of new towns we may think of post-World War II and places like Milton Keynes, or, if we look back a little further, garden cities such as Welwyn; or even the utopian workers settlements further north, such as Port Sunlight on the Wirral, designed and built in the nineteenth century to house workers in the belief that health and sobriety, good housing not slums, were central to people's productivity and wellbeing.

I wonder what it was like in Edinburgh, perhaps even more so in Bath, when those Georgian buildings were put up. Bath is endlessly discussed in relation to the Jane Austen era, society and parties, but it is hardly mentioned that it was a new town at that time. Before then, Bath was a medieval city with twisting streets, a ferry along the river to the nearby village of Bathampton, and walls with gates that influence the street names today – Westgate, Southgate . . . The abbey was the focal point. Today, we are so used to regarding Bath and Edinburgh as historic places, we forget that they were once new too. With most cities, change is incremental – a new civic building here, a street or a housing estate there – but almost the whole of Bath and much of Edinburgh were pulled down and begun again in a way that was just as dramatic as the rebuilding of Plymouth or Coventry after the bombings of World War II. What we now see as old, beautiful, stately and civilised was once new, and very likely in part as shocking and controversial as the construction of entire new towns can be today. Things that affect the atmosphere of place, such as a sense of comfort derived from our interest in Georgian buildings (the favourite style of architecture for many of today's citizens), an architecture that is now seen as intrinsically harmonic with its classical forms and easy-on-the-eye proportions and materials, would once have led to a very different atmosphere indeed.

It sounds so obvious to say that if the atmosphere of a city changes both with time and in every moment for each individual – atmosphere being inherently subjective, after all – we could hardly expect Bath or Edinburgh to have felt the same hundreds of years ago as they do now, or for Paris to stay the same after Haussmann tore down the medieval streets to make way for wide boulevards and grid systems (interestingly, these features would make it much harder to facilitate revolution than easily barricaded medieval narrow streets, though conversely they are better suited for mass gatherings such as today's protest marches). Yet it is something we don't really think of. We see our cities as they are now – always old, different obviously; but the old being new and the dramatic change in atmosphere that this leads to is rarely thought of. The constructions of these cities, the plans, the deliberate change in the feel of a city can be as dramatic as a rebuilding of them after a natural disaster or a war. This is not a writing of city space over time, a practising of the urban as it grows with our actions and changes around us. This is domination of urban space, the wiping out of layers of stories in order to start again, to rebuild, to attempt the impossible: to create a blank slate in a place where the ground is riddled with memories.

If we build without considering this, and without thinking of the future, we are in danger of bringing about the sort of dystopian legacy created by some 1960s UK housing estates, or the American Projects. In *The Death and Life of Great American Cities*, Jane Jacobs argues cities need old buildings for true diversity, especially in terms of the range of shops and businesses. She does not explicitly talk of atmosphere, but her next point would affect it: she argues that the quirkier small shops would all vanish if people had to pay the rates for new construction. We can see this now in how new malls are dominated by the big chains. The little book and art shops and community projects are often found in older buildings.

We construct cities, we add to them, we can try to control them, or create new ones, but then we set them free. Yet while we free them, we interact with and enable, add, write, read – and, as de Certeau suggested, *facilitate* them. The language of the city is there for us, but we so often do but a superficial reading of this – scan the streets, speed read, rather than pause, think and read deeply. Language changes, new words are added, fresh phrases, slang – the city changes too, with time, becomes its own unstoppable creation of change. It takes on a life of its own, yet it would not exist without us.

The trope of the flâneur sees the city as something that happens to us. It is active in that the flâneur chooses to walk the city, to follow his whims, which of course are likely to be influenced by the appeal of certain atmospheres; yet it is passive in that the flâneur is a voyeur, a conscious spectator, where there is a distance between the city and himself caused by the substitution of a multisensory, immersive experience for that of the gaze – for the detachment of being both in a place and not, of passing through. Is this sense of distance partly also created by the fact that, other than as characters in books or a cumulative theoretical analysis of the idea, actual records of flâneurs – of individuals rather than the concept, the fashion – are scarce? It is difficult to create an active and involved trope of experience involving a kind of person who existed mostly as a theory – it is easier to imagine watching than being. While usually any presence in a city has an effect on it, contributes consciously or not to its evolving language, there is something interesting in the idea of the flâneur as being male and passing through – both of the city and outside of real experience – when for many women the experience of being on the street is anything but detached, whether through their conscious wanderings and political decisions to actively walk streets or through the unfortunate necessity of being hyper-alert. Women would love to have the option to disappear into the crowd, the natural habitat of the flâneur, but city space for us is so often about being seen, frequently when not wanting to be – the subject of unwanted attention in the street, the intense stress of a night walk home. Being seen should be a positive choice, not a threat. These latter feelings are not the city's fault, but its inhabitants, yet it affects the atmosphere for us.

I remember Edinburgh day and night. Day, I would wander in wonder – follow new streets without knowing where they would take me, take paths down to the water's edge, through alleys: none of this held fear, just the beauty of discovery. Yet it did not feel detached. I was not observing the crowd, the people, the street 'life' as a flâneur would, but a different definition of street life – the life of the city – sentient buildings again, sentient streets … I was absorbing atmospheres with my whole body and the streets were not detached from the people but equally active, vital.

Edinburgh smells of brewing and the winds are strong and intense. Bagpipes, cars, train rumbles. Climbing high up the crags or Arthur's Seat, I would feel as if I could blow away. I was discovering. I was remembering. Apart from when I had a crush on some boy I'd seen around or bumped into a friend, I can't really remember the crowds at all (unless it was festival time, but that transformation is another thing entirely in its scale). But the streets and their spirit come to me now, making my dream Edinburgh one of the strongest dream cities I have. The place stayed with me when I moved away twenty years ago – the Meadows near the university bursting into blossom; scuzzy pavements on the big main road whose name I can't remember but whose feeling I can; bridges, layers making the narrow streets below seem impossible. Sudden burst of sea. Large regency villas I dreamed of living in one day, tucked behind student streets. Without a car, I walked and walked.

Yet come night time, even though Edinburgh is a fairly safe city, I scraped and saved for cabs when single. The city changed. I never felt I got to know it at night. Like a Jekyll and Hyde of a city, what might have been a friendly alter ego felt uncertain; like my city could suddenly change and threaten me. This atmosphere was not in the streets themselves, but in my imagination and in the knowledge that humans write the city, scribble on its pages – they are creative protagonists, and the streets, no matter how kind, cannot control what happens in them.

When women march to reclaim the streets, as they have done as an organised movement since the 1970s, they are not reclaiming them from the city – it feels more to me like they are rescuing a friend from a bad influence, taking back something they know to be friendly and true. And while historically women and the streets have a troubled relationship, especially in relation to the male gaze, the streets of a city can be a great space of freedom for women. I think of revolutionary fashion – from self-expression to Edwardian bicycling outfits – an excuse to wear what in other spaces women wouldn't have dared. A space of freedom, outside of the home – a feeling of city as place of liberation, where change can happen – is an atmosphere. I think of all that a city could be if we harness it. It is the space where we write the city, but in doing so I think we can write ourselves.

Atmospheres of Construction

On an island a short metro hop from the old town of Montreal sits a strange fragmented glass ball of a building. Designed by Buckminster Fuller, it is perhaps the greatest example of his geodesic domes, and it acted as the American Pavilion in the Expo 1967 world's fair. The dome was once full of things – abstract expressionist art, commerce, technology. Another legacy of the world's fair is the extraordinary modular apartment building Habitat 67, horizontal Jenga of concrete, still standing and loved by modern design fans today. But most of the remnants of this extraordinary event are gone. There was once a temporary utopian mini-city, quickly abandoned, yet which strove to create an atmosphere, both constructed and ephemeral, knowing it would soon be lost; that the atmosphere it left would be somewhat different than that which it sought to fleetingly be.

World's fairs are an incongruity: weird, eccentric, retro – despite being futuristic – gatherings of things. Possibly more powerful than other world events for which places are constructed, such as the Olympics, the world's fair model sees each participating country create their own pavilion – a new structure to represent them in that moment, but looking to the future. It is the construction of identity using a building as a metaphor for how they want to be seen in the world. Building as the outfit for a nation – the display – its future goals. Contents as national innards on display.

These buildings are archaeological exhibitions of things that are not yet old but inevitably will be. To use artist Robert Smithson's phrase when describing the entropy of a New Jersey turnpike, they have 'fallen into ruins before they've been built'. They are entropic, leaking metaphorical energy, ideas, at an alarming rate. Full of life and idealism and invention in their moment, as soon as they are over, the space is emptied, the ideas become outdated. Moment as glorious over-the-top ambitious precursor to memory. Atmosphere extreme to extreme, albeit not the atmosphere of where they are trying to represent. Utopian follies.

Yet in this temporary idealistic extravaganza they are supremely constructed. An extreme version of the constructed displays we see every day. Unless we are making a pilgrimage to a site-specific work, we are used to our art, our culture, being displayed for us in a constructed space.

It started with a lost building.

It is 1851 and London is abuzz with a new extravaganza. A building has been erected in the centre of the city that is like nothing seen before: a cathedral-like structure of glass, vast as the capital that surrounds it, it is the Crystal Palace. Thousands of people flock to this palace that resembles a greenhouse. It defies logic that a building such as this can stand; it is a magical city risen within the city and it contains an attempt to represent the world.

Science, industry, art. Britain and its allies. Colonial strength. Places for countries, travel as voyeuristic browsing – a museum with no logic except for its ambition. Later, it was taken down. An ephemeral palace, it was rebuilt in south London, before it burned to the ground in the 1930s. Two ghosts for one building in a city. A place that attempted to contain the whole world, could not hold on. And strangely, or perhaps fatalistically, no one expected it to. Its ambition was too vast, its moment too much of its time.

The event it was built for was called the Great Exhibition – no other name would do. At this stage in world's fair history, there were no individual pavilions: this extraordinary building attempted, from a very Victorian British Empire perspective, to contain, to control the perception of, the whole world.

Now there is a modern sports centre in place of the Crystal Palace. A couple of bits of stone are all that remain of this once beautiful building. I imagine it in flames, melting like strange lava and sliding down the hill towards the city and its first home near Hyde Park. I marvel at how the only other hint of this time is found in the giant model dinosaurs, which look a bit wrong, as when they were erected palaeontology wasn't as advanced as it soon became and nobody really knew what dinosaurs looked like. Fossils. Extinct twice over – extinct representations, as knowledge moved on, of extinct creatures. And now they stand still and surreal in a park with an extinct building, twice over, from an extinct time.

All that is left: stone, ill-conceived dinosaurs and an area named for what no longer lives; and a football team, too, which no one would think to link to its namesake structure.

Nearby I once found what can only be described as a pedalo graveyard.

The Great Exhibition led to a tradition that took place around the world for decades to come. The French were particularly expert in these *expositions universelle*, with America taking up the baton in the twentieth century and coining the term 'world's fairs', but they spread wider: to Canada, Japan, China . . . These strange, temporary utopian exhibitions spread worldwide. They left architectural legacies: while crystal palaces were a trend in the early days, later statement buildings became a key part: the Eiffel Tower, Seattle's Space Needle, Montreal's aforementioned Biosphere, Brussels's Atomium – all these famous landmarks, signifiers of said cities, started life as structures for world's fairs. As did art works: Picasso's *Guernica*, perhaps the most famous modern artwork of all, was created for the Spanish Pavilion in 1937.

But this is not just about their legacy of cultural ghosts, things that remain with no memory of their once home. In terms of atmosphere, specifically the construction of atmosphere, world's fairs, or expos as they are often now known, were very strange indeed.

Imagine this. You are in a famous city. Full of streets that have existed for a number of years. Somewhere recognisable such as Paris or London. Yet for the last few months something weird has been going on – lots of construction and whispers – and now the results are ready to be surveyed. You wander through your city, but then it disappears, as if you have entered a weird different zone or stumbled through a portal; there before you is a street from Cairo, now an entire Irish village. You have conceptually been teleported, travelled to a different part of the world, yet it is not this actual part of the world. For all the smells of exotic food and people transported from far-off countries, you know deep down you are not actually in those places. You are in a reconstruction, where spices merge with the smell of damp, the sky is cloudy and grey when it should be bright Egyptian sun . . .

This is not fantasy. As well as the construction of pavilions – those mini-cities of new builds designed to house national wares – in the earlier days, before it was recognised as deeply troubling, whole villages were reconstructed from around the world and real people were imported as living displays. There really was a reconstruction of a Cairo street in Paris in 1889, complete with shops and cafes, there really was an Irish village built in London in 1908, and, shockingly, native people really were taken from their homes and made to rebuild their villages from non-Western countries, to 'live' as they would at home as living tableaux for ogling visitors. *Tableaux vivants*. A simulation of their everyday life devoid of their land.

Land is a place. You cannot move land. Homeland.

It is hard to say whether people really believed they were recreating the feeling of being in these places – the intention was there, but while you can create buildings that resemble others, even import people as well as food and products, you cannot recreate the atmosphere of one country in another. Your recreation might be multisensory, but you can't edit the senses outside, even if there are camels pottering around. The atmosphere of the country surrounding the reconstruction will always have too strong a presence. Grey sky and cold rain, in attempts at tropical climes.

Bricks and mortar, flesh and blood, but no more of the place than a hologram, atmospherically.

Viewers, in those times before mass air travel, might have felt differently – there were reports of visitors saying they felt they had travelled – but it was a different kind of travelling. It was travel to someone else's idea of how a place is, of how it should be represented, displayed, consumed.

As time passed and the pavilion model became the norm, with more nations contributing to them rather than being displayed by colonial powers, the focus moved away from scenes of people and *tableaux vivants* to those of the future. From the 1930s onwards, architecture leapt away from the classical (possibly due to fascist associations) by first embracing modernism and, later, increasingly surreal space-age structures for their own sake – pavilion as temporary sculpture rather than a more traditionally functioning building.

Pavilions also gave rise to a new pressure. It was not just the hosts who had to think about how they wanted to be represented in terms of building, but all participating countries. World's fairs and great exhibitions had always had a strongly nationalistic element, but now it became a case of temporary building as temporary country – a self-created embassy, somewhere of a place but not in it. Strange that in something so tangible as a building, the intangible should become involved – for what is the nature of Frenchness, Englishness, being Chinese or Spanish ... ? How nations define themselves has little to do with physical architecture, but architecture of the emotions; not fact, but atmosphere. Yet this was to be represented through solid objects in a different country where its atmosphere could never really exist.

It is hard to distil a nation in a building. An impossible task, the buildings start to have a common theme, they become more futuristic – progress! – that is a popular theme. If the past and all it holds are too complicated, if the past of world expositions and colonialism is somewhat fraught, then the future is the place to go, where all countries can compete without losing their identity. Where the atmosphere of homeland isn't essential. This world is one of supreme construction. A mini temporary city, but also a conceptual world. If a place's atmosphere is trying to contain the world's, then it is going to get watered down, distorted. Atmosphere's natural power is taken out.

I think back to Montreal, that geodesic dome that was once the American pavilion. It became the Biosphere, an environmental museum, and it seems logical that these ghosts, these futuristic follies, often become places of display. I sometimes think their atmospheric power would be stronger if they remained empty, if the ghosts were left to breathe, but that would be to relinquish control. World's fairs were all about humankind, rather than the world without humans. It seems quite extraordinary that the theme of the Montreal expo was 'Man and His World'. With sub-categories – always *man and* . . . dominance over the world, control, possession. The world has no autonomy in this vision.

Ironic that an environmental museum ends up in a building from an event that was inherently anti-natural.

But when we want to control the narrative of the world, when we want to treat the world as an encyclopedia (and the age of world expositions was the age of the encyclopedia – a need to categorise everything, make it known), not a fluid place, we lose the vitality, the emotion that makes a place real for those who live in it. Fact in a lived world is different to a list of information, a selection of objects without the stories that give them meaning. A world purely of curated fact can never represent reality.

We are used to viewing art as the realm of emotion. But while many museums are very individual, when art – especially modern art – is displayed, the space is much more of a controlled space, an attempt at neutrality, a supreme construction.

White walls.

This is on purpose, of course. The whole point of the white and neutral gallery space is so as not to distract from the art. The feelings of the place, the memories conjured, should be of the art. But when I think of exhibitions I've loved, I still don't really have a sense of place. And rather than highlighting my art memory, this lack of sense of place slightly depletes it. Glorious paintings become objects in moments in a vacuum, a void of atmosphere where they tried to do their best, but something in their full make-up, a natural kind of context, was missing. A gallery is a supremely constructed atmosphere. The white cube template seeks to make them all the same. It is impossible to travel in them. They are constructed boxes, hermetically sealed from the outside world, as if a form of virtual reality rather than a physical place.

Culture out of context. Away from the artist's studio or landscape where it was created. Another filter added, when in this case it was trying to do the opposite; to remove distractions, to let the work breathe. But I am left cold by the clinical, conscious element of it. I remember being in Iceland on a university trip and we stumbled on an exhibition where the paintings were hung on a cliff face. It was so extraordinary, the context so dramatic, that I sometimes wonder if I imagined it. It was like the work had gone feral – been set free to build its own personality, to grow. Art illustrating landscape. There was a dialogue.

All display spaces are constructed in some way, but the extreme of this in terms of galleries, as opposed to, say, an artist's studio, and how we experience culture is an interesting one. We are moving into a profoundly artificial space to view art, which in being creative is inherently natural and expressive. I wonder if we miss something we don't even understand. That the manipulation, or attempts thereof, inherent in constructed atmospheres mean we can never truly see something without its filter. I wonder what would happen if we set everything free. Not into an 'out of gallery' constructed space, but an inherently spiritual space, designed to overwhelm with atmosphere; beautiful and powerful yet designed, such as a Stanley Spencer or Rothko chapel. What if we were to stumble on art in the real world? Not land art, which is a different thing, nor site-specific art, so much as viewing in a natural environment – a multisensory, natural place, with not a white wall in sight?

Rewind. It is 1900 and Paris again and we are at the *Exposition Universelle*. One of the exhibits is particularly immersive. Rather than an object on display, it is a place one can enter. It is a place where one can travel without leaving Paris – and I don't mean the fake exotic streets and *tableaux vivants*: this is trying to connect with you in a different way, to really simulate travel rather than simply display it for disconnected consumption. This is the Mareorama.

Two scenes move before you – panoramas showing sites from a Mediterranean cruise. After leaving Marseille, the images before you in this enclosed room will take you to Naples, Venice, Constantinople ... The greatest hits of coastal Europe. A summary of views via two paintings, each 750 metres long and 13 metres high! But you will not only watch this visual extravaganza. As you stand on a replica ship's deck, complete with smoke, funnels and steam whistles, and watch the images you feel yourself begin to move as if on the sea, as the floor mechanically sways. You take a deep breath and the smell of salt air, seaweed and tar fill your nostrils. Your ears fill with music, played live nearby.

The Mareorama was multisensory. As if sensing that to truly travel we could not rely on our eyes alone. It might have been constructed, artificial, but rather than a slide show, it sought to recreate the experience of a cruise, the feeling of travelling on the sea to far-off lands, the atmosphere. It didn't bring the world to you, out of place and context, by fetching food or people or buildings; rather, it sought to appeal straight to your imagination, to take you there.

It was popular, people sensing that this was not just the latest technology of the day, but a chance to experience a new place. You might not be literally on a cruise, but you were entering a different reality, a virtual reality before the term had even been coined. It was not alone – in this major era of travel and mechanical advancement, similar constructions were made. As if, at a time when the world was becoming more artificial, there was a sense that a human need still had to be satisfied – the need to escape, even within a crowded room; the need to travel, to feel a place rather than simply see it. The Mareorama and displays like it were trying to construct an atmosphere.

These new immersive displays built with the latest technology on the turn of the eighteenth to nineteenth century trend for panoramas, exhibiting paintings stretched across walls, often displayed in rotundas, immersive manmade views designed to confuse represented scene and reality. Interestingly, Wordsworth hated panoramas – they clashed with the Romantic way of experiencing place, the sublime in nature. For him, panoramas were clinical, artificial . . . A charade that lulls viewers into a stupor rather than feeling alive in a real landscape. It is noteworthy that decades later, the creators realised that making the Mareorama multisensory was key to it being an immersive experience – that it needed more vigour. Yet still it is all about control. And surface. I think of the series of views from an actual cruise, the controlled setting of a health spa, versus the adventures of travel writers.

I think back to Isabella Bird. Women travellers. A change of scenery . . . Surface – a fake cruise, surface like the stream of views, a change but not meaningful in the true sense of place. The emotions, the personality of the place that are so key are gone. It could not heal anyone.

These days, the construction of artificial places has taken leaps that in 1900 were not even imaginable. Computer technology has changed everything: it is no longer a case of our trying to simulate a cruise, to take people to places that exist, it has become a field of the purely constructed, an attempt to transport people to places that do not exist in the physical world.

Virtual reality.

We are becoming more disconnected from the landscape in which we live. Or rather, the metaphorical landscape has changed unrecognisably within my lifetime. In a digital world, endlessly claiming to make us more connected, our experience of true physical connectivity with place is diminishing. Even if we are out in the real world – on a walk, for example – we may find ourselves constantly filtering it through screens: a portable layer of disconnection, as rather than the multisensory experiencing of place, we now frame it in snapshots to share in the virtual world. We find ourselves thinking about how we will frame this 'experience' for the viewing of others and how they will judge us by that. Experience is now a marketable thing – a tool of travel agents and advertisers – a desperation to develop the depth of what is on offer, as if sensing the world has changed. In this world atmosphere, that key to deep connectivity with place is lost.

While there is actual 'virtual reality' in the form of headsets and designed worlds, there is a subtler conceptual virtual reality, a layer that has drifted down like a sheer blanket on our lives; so sheer that despite its obvious presence, many of us live as if we don't know it is there. But like any blanket it deadens our senses: it deadens atmosphere.

Those in the field of actual virtual reality (VR) might beg to differ. They are constantly trying to create virtual worlds that seem real to us. But the key is the word *seem*. In VR, we may feel like we are in a certain place through a trick of the senses, our eyes confusing our limbs so we move as if there. Sound is possible, but without the true experience of touch and smell, without our memories and physical being, VR will never have a true atmosphere.

Close eyes. Open. A room has risen around me. I am on a mezzanine level. Cushions. Chairs. A sense of scale . . . When I last I put on a VR headset, it was curious. Having dismissed it in the early days, I wanted to give the experience a second chance. The visual trick worked: I was conscious that I was in a simulation but I could look around and had the sense of scale of a large room. However, my feet were not there. And while I had lost my spatial awareness in the room where I stood, the illusion was simply shattered by raising my arm and it colliding with a bookshelf in the real world. All I had before me was something playing with my eyes. A conjurer's trick. I could feel an atmosphere, but it was not of the virtual reality; rather, it was of what I could see via the headset, combined with the smells and noises and everything else my body and brain were processing in the small room where I actually stood. The atmosphere was me in that moment in the actual room, with an extra strange layer – an atmosphere filter, rather than creator. Something visually blocking me, intriguing, interesting, but atmospherically obstructive, or not even that, just trying to be something it couldn't; trying to encompass a whole experience, when actually it was just filtering in another layer to the dominant one that was my everyday reality in that moment. Standing in that room.

I am sure the technology will develop further, yet I feel that even with all our senses engaged, with our imaginations stimulated, we will still be but visitors in someone else's game, under the control of their whims, the limits of what they want us to experience. Some form of atmosphere may be possible, but it is a trick, less vivid than the creativity of our dreams. The depths of a dream are more atmospheric, conjure a place that truly feels like we are alive there. They are conscious experiences all in themselves, not a part of someone else's virtual creation.

Harnessing natural power. We are used to thinking of this, especially in these greener days of renewable energy – tides, wind, the sun. It is there in a good way, to harness, to try to backtrack on our mistakes and make as better as we can. From lightning bolts to Frankenstein's monster, creation needs power. Natural power. And we talk about this openly, acknowledge it. Yet when it comes to atmosphere, we may try to harness it, but when we do, we do not explicitly articulate this. We try to control it and call it something else – design, architecture, urban planning. Sometimes we work with it, conjure something beautiful, other times we use it to our advantage in darker ways ...

The urge for artists and thinkers, for humans, to construct new spaces is an old one. As soon as people began to design structures beyond simple shelters, as soon as people began to formally farm, to landscape the natural world, the atmosphere of constructed space was in the background of their minds. Classical proportions, grandeur in a stately home, the cosy cottage, open plan, gardens ... The designing of space is the constructing of place; and, in natural reality, one cannot work in place without atmosphere.

The different styles of constructed space are also of their age – with a different layer of atmosphere, the atmosphere of their time.

Victorian houses are somewhat different to modernist ones, with smaller and darker rooms, clutter versus open-plan layouts and swathes of glass. The modern mainstream of white walls affects atmosphere – I crave colour, but this makes my house feel very different to some. Every choice in every time is another factor in the construction. There is the natural atmosphere, but with each conscious choice we are pasting on another layer – collaborating or imposing on the place. Moreover, the fact that constructed atmospheres are of their age often gives them an ideological or political bent. And this was seen particularly strongly, or perhaps acknowledged most openly, in mid-century Europe.

The Situationists were a group of men (I am not aware of any Situationist women with real agency) who are today largely lauded by the slightly hipster (again, mostly male) psychogeography crowd. Formed in Paris and active and influential mainly in the 1950s through to the 1960s, the group, with key figures such as Guy Debord, sought to approach urban space and how we behaved in it differently.

One of their core ideas was the construction of 'situations' within urban space. A fascinating and, I would argue, somewhat contradictory approach (in terms of atmosphere, at least), whereby 'situations' were deliberately engineered, were consciously sought and orchestrated, yet put the emotional response to place first. Debord, in his report on the construction of situations, described them as 'the concrete construction of temporary settings of life and their transformation into a higher, passionate nature.'

So far as I can picture this – and it fits with the general idea of psychogeography, which the Situationists are often credited with founding – it was a geography of the personal and intangible, the emotional, rather than facts. While it can be hard to visualise exactly what the Situationists meant, heightened by the fact that their situations remained largely conceptual, one of their key ideas was that of the *dérive* or drift, whereby one would walk through the city, following emotional impulses and feelings of place rather than setting out with a purpose or to reach a destination. They even talked of areas of cities as being divided up through changes in feeling, *ambiances*, rather than the traditional delineations of borders. Something we could see as a change in atmosphere.

The Situationists accordingly created maps and designs for whole cities in which emotions were given space alongside more traditional geographic elements. Interestingly for a male-dominated movement, they reprinted Madeleine de Scudéry's *Carte de Tendre* in the journal *Internationale Situationniste*, the map at this point having fallen into relative obscurity. I love the idea of using such a method to influence urban design: cities that take into account women's emotional journeys, how we navigate and experience space, is an idea that is sadly still radical and desperately needed today. However, while the Situationists gave Scudéry's ideas a voice again, this was not with respect to her gendered angle, but more to do with how she talked of the emotion of place. Imagine instead a city plan with the true legacy of Scudéry taken into account: a collaborative plan of women's stories, streets designed with this in mind, safe accessible streets. An emotionally un-alienating city. Long debated in gender and urban-theory academic circles, some city planners are now thinking about this more. Better street lighting, transport, childcare ... But still women's lived experience tends to fall way down the list of priorities in urban planning, as it did back then, in the mid-twentieth century.

In the Situationists' conceptual plans for cities, in which areas were demarcated by the emotions they would trigger, there was the presumption that whatever the Situationists themselves defined as being an area's main feeling would surpass any other natural atmospheres that might occur there. It was all about the dominance of what they wanted people's, or even just their, feelings to be as they moved through these conceptual spaces. Rather than democratising space, getting rid of the bourgeois, making it for everyone, or listening to their emotions in the way that Scudéry sought to map these, there were arguably sinister undertones. If we take this manipulation of emotion in space to its logical conclusion, it could even seem totalitarian – a way of controlling people as they go about their lives in the city.

I struggle to see how this can truly be a natural absorbing of place: while it may suggest an abandonment of self, an opening-up to place, the artificiality of construction remains key to Situationist ideas. Again, we have men trying to control place, albeit it under the guise of emotions – but these emotions belong to them, their minds, what they want a place to do and their political aims, rather than just letting an atmosphere be.

Construction is manipulation; it is about trying to control atmosphere; of noticing it, yet bending it to one's whim. If emotions were purely the guide, that would be one thing – more of a collaboration with place, as I view our dialogue with atmosphere – but the Situationists' insistence on construction, on their idea of *dérive* (while consciously trying to create situations where this could occur), and on manipulating urban space, writing manifestos, and posturing in the Parisian left-wing avant-garde, take the movement away from what it perhaps could have been; from what for me would be a true psychogeography.

If we wish to make our mark on how we move through urban space, there are more interesting ways to do this, especially when working with atmosphere. We could seek to be aware of it, to work with it; we could build around its inherent nature, take into account what would suit it – not raze an area to the ground in order to recreate it around what we felt would be interesting, to achieve our goal.

Nevertheless, there were positive elements to the movement. The obsession with ambiences, as the Situationists called them, led to campaigns to save atmospheric neighbourhoods from destruction. All the same, while I applaud this, there is something uncomfortable here, too: perhaps a kind of voyeuristic aspect to why they wanted those neighbourhoods preserved – that they were not thinking so much about what residents wanted, or the heritage, as what they wanted to achieve for their own project. After all, it would be sad to lose the best settings for their *dérives*, wouldn't it . . . ?

The Situationist movement spread beyond Paris, with key figures working in other European centres, such as Amsterdam. The conceptual planning, rather than physical realisation, continued, ranging from maps and meetings to designs for new spaces. One noteworthy project was the Dutch artist Constant Nieuwenhuys's 'New Babylon'. Originally called 'Deriville' after the Situationists' favoured idea of drift, it was a design for an urban megastructure – city as modular building. Historically, it is put into the bracket of Utopian design – that desire for a new, better way of doing urban space – but in its supreme manipulation of place and emotions, its attempts to control atmosphere, it tips into dystopia for some like me.

New Babylon puts the idea of drift at the centre. People live in a giant modular city, where their daily lives are radically restructured in a way where they can follow their inclinations. It was a political attempt at radically rethinking bourgeois society and the traditional pattern of work and family, but in its pursuit of drift, in its pursuit of individual inclination, of pleasure, it becomes a selfish city, a city devoid of atmosphere, consumed (ironically for a left-wing thinker) with the cult of the individual. It was never built, but it is easy to see how the project could have descended into a kind of dystopian pleasure dome, with people trapped in a megastructure, emptily pursuing their next feeling. It is a space disconnected from place and in this way it reminds me of the architecture of dictatorship – from megastructures such as the empty Ryugyong Hotel in North Korea, the largest hotel in the world, to Turkmenbashi's endless building of five-star marble hotels, also empty, in Turkmenistan. Dictatorships are fond of megastructures and of using architecture as control, with sheer scale imposing their whims on the people, representing a fantasy they want to foist (such as luxury tourism) on an area – the pursuit of an individual's desire completely devoid of benefit to ordinary people.

While New Babylon was never built, it and Situationism's obsession with constructed spaces have had unintended yet very real descendants, in the form of spaces we experience every day. The (again, ironically for a largely left-wing movement) spaces of the capitalist world. These are not designs for the liberation of everyday people but objects of hostile design.

Shopping malls are supremely constructed environments. They are an emblem of Western, especially American, consumerist culture. But the impact of their design on our behaviour is thought more about by architects and businessmen than their convenience to customers. Ever entered one trying to find a specific shop, only to wander, lost and confused, ambling through other shops, trying to navigate windowless corridors, a maze, before maybe reaching your destination? It is a deeply unpleasant experience. But then shopping malls are not designed for a pleasant experience. If they were, they would all be full of light and easily navigable. Rather, they are designed to manipulate our behaviour; to make us spend. If we have to wander the long way round, we might go into other shops that grab our interest; we might *drift* into other shops, follow our inclinations and then buy something unplanned. If we accidentally end up in the food court, we might suddenly realise we're hungry and buy food. *Dérive* becomes a tool of capitalism: manipulate our natural drift and our behaviour is controlled without us realising it. If there are no windows, a sense is there of our being contained– of this space being our whole world, total destination; we do not become distracted by the outside, the other options.

There are other, more pleasant ways shops try to control atmosphere. They know the experience of shopping is multisensory – supermarkets don't attempt to make us lost, but they openly pump out smells of fresh bread, for example, to try to make us hungry. Sweets at the counter are a controversial topic for a reason: store designers know they will make children nag at a moment when parents are tired and just want to get the shopping over with.

The manipulation of our behaviour is not only in favour of commerce and not always as benign as through bread smells. Again, we can look back to the Situationist influence in this darker design route. In his 1953 essay 'Formulary for a New Urbanism', Gilles Ivain, real name Ivan Chtcheglov, called for a city designed around quarters, with each representing a feeling. He said this city could

'Correspond to diverse catalogued feelings that one meets by *chance* in current life.' The reference to cataloguing harks back to world's fairs and the need to turn the world into an encyclopedia, forgetting human dignity along the way. This radical rethink of urban planning is as worrying as those older colonial impulses: it is a potential dystopian attempt at mind control – psychoanalysis in the power of architects. There would be happy and bizarre quarters but also a sinister one. Ivain says that this would pose no real threat and, in a sense resembling exposure therapy in modern therapeutic terms, would make the modern world no longer seem frightening, but rather amusing. But his methods – from loud whistles and sirens, bad lighting at night and harsh light during the day – use design to create an alienating place. While I suspect this is mainly theorising and of course such a place would never be built, it is still hostile design, design as manipulation. We are caught again in an endless drift.

This may sound terrifying – the idea that we are but guinea pigs for experimental architects – but, surprisingly, hostile design is an openly used term, from describing spikes to stop pigeons landing, to park benches that are sloped and divided to prevent homeless people sleeping on them. Designers, architects and town planners are well aware of the effect they can have on behaviour. But does anyone think about how this affects the atmosphere of a place? And how that then affects human behaviours in that space?

This is strangely more obvious when creatively explored: think haunted house or Freud's idea of the uncanny, in which something seems both familiar and creepily unfamiliar – where juxtapositions are used to heighten emotional responses. I remember once being in a field on a lush spring day in Cornwall, but the air stank of a nearby factory I couldn't see. It would be a useful instant device to unsettle a reader in a story. But when things are designed to unsettle or control us in the real world, we are less aware of what is being done to us – we may understand how to analyse a writer's toolkit, but a town planner's? That is somehow more hidden, more distant, imaginatively less atmospheric, when its real atmospheric impact could be greater. And when it is totally artificial there is an inbuilt sense of the uncanny – the natural atmosphere of a place with these designed over-layers. We might not be aware of it, but the depth of the place's feeling has been pasted over with all these intentions, concepts, and when an idea of a place is too constructed and artificial I wonder if a true psychogeography is possible, whether one can ever plan it in. A constructed environment is perhaps too unnatural to ever be a place of pure emotional *dérive*.

You could say that natural managed landscapes, even a footpath, could work this way. The path is controlling the route we take and therefore what we see. However, it is but a line marked in a wider landscape that we can see out of and deviate from. In a virtual world or the real world of a shopping mall, we cannot stray from the path. We cannot see outside to the wider world – we are quite literally contained. The variations are diminished. Atmosphere is stunted and held back.

Home, Art, Land

Childhood Home

Home is more than a place. It is a strange hybrid – a feeling we all can recognise, something that we might have at present or that we have lost. Yet as a feeling it has different levels of complexity, of conflicted meaning. It is both a memory and a living thing. An atmosphere. Like all atmospheres, it cannot be conjured on demand, yet it is always present within us, subtly there: it is an emotional knowledge that never really goes away.

From the age of four, I grew up in a warm and rambling old house in a village near Bath, its Georgian façade put on to keep up with the late eighteenth-century fashions and covering up a much older interior of low ceilings laced with beams. Even the fireplaces were trying to hide the house's true nature – Dad took a sledgehammer to the small sitting room fireplace to reveal another half the length of the room, deep enough to sit in, with a bread oven in one side. The walls were a metre thick.

And as I grew over the years the house grew with me. It was not just a building to me but a character. And when a character is an object of stone, something that would seem inanimate to many, its personality comes out in other ways. It cannot talk, but its atmosphere could evolve and communicate with the family comings and goings, and before us, well, there were hundreds of years of memories that must have each in their own way affected what it felt like to be inside – the sitting room with a family baking bread and, later, an old couple sat before a smaller hearth in a room shrunk by boarding up this hint of its less symmetric past; the day when the new windows went in, creating more light but changing the view, the feel. A perhaps more grand history than I felt – it was once the head weaver's house, I believe. Kids playing, pets, wall colours and furniture changing. All these things built up this intangible archive of lifetimes. They show us that we are only in these places for a short while – we leave traces, carve our initials in stone or trees, renovate, decorate, but none of it is permanent. It is but a layer.

I left my own hints. When we first moved in, I slept up in the attic with my brothers, but when I was a little older and my beloved grandmother was too ill to live with us any longer, my parents took her room and I moved into theirs. The Laura Ashley poppies that smothered the walls seemed to grow. I traced lines around them, added drawings, pet memorials when my goldfish and hamster died. The hidden cupboards filled (first with my wishful-thinking dowry for a longed-for horse that would never come, a hay net, saddle soap bought with pocket money, jumble sale Care Bears hidden from a disapproving mother, semi-precious stones from souvenir shops, bags of marbles and shells; later on with records and charity shop dresses), and the beams became the anchor for mobiles and vines – my own artificial canopy to make it feel like a fairy realm. It was like my bedroom became the soul of the house for me – my own house soul among others, where it communicated just with me. Spring brought roses and clematis up its façade. When I was terribly bullied at primary school and my parents didn't really understand what was going on, my room became my sanctuary, petals knocking like friendly ghost fists on the old, thin glass: I felt like it understood.

I wonder if anyone else felt this. Certainly, when my parents had to sell it after twenty-five years, my once close family seemed to fall apart. As if without the invisible threads of the house connecting us, the bones of beams, this network of individual and communal memory atmosphere, we did not know what we had in common. We were each adrift.

It was 2006. I remember the year well. It is a turning point in my life. Without this sense of the old home as a constant comfort, my travelling took on greater urgency. The stakes were higher, though I did not realise it then. Deep down, I needed to fill the void, to find somewhere that comforted me, held me as this house did. I felt unrooted, tried to see it as a liberation – I could live anywhere now! But in reality, it was more of a searching to get the feeling back again. Those were the years where I was away for months at a time – Georgia, Serbia again and again. We all crave knowing where our home is. I had lost mine.

I remember reading E. M. Forster's novel *Howards End* at school, years before we lost our house, and while there was so much human drama, the story of the house adrift broke my heart; Mrs Wilcox's dying urge for the house to pass onto someone who understood it, that I could appreciate. House as protagonist seemed logical, not strange, to me. The places we live our lives define us, and houses are the receptacles for these lives – where we are contained when not out in the wider world. The private atmospheres of place. It strangely makes me think of the artist Rachel Whiteread's work *House* of 1993, which stood for eleven poignant weeks in East London, before being demolished in early 1994. It caused a tabloid discussion at the time; some saw it as an eyesore, others loved it, but for some reason it filled me with the same poignant feeling I get when I see animals up for rehoming. I found it gentle, only brutal in its sadness, its meaning, rather than its heavy form. The weight was only of its past. The concrete cast of a now demolished interior – the air of memories we can't touch made solid, tangible – a monolith in the place of the atmosphere of all those lives in that place that we have lost, viewed by those who pass by still. A last ghost, an echo, concrete yet ephemeral and fading fast out of view; stories still there, soon to be forgotten, except by its old friend atmosphere.

As I got older and moved away from my childhood home and became an almost compulsive traveller in the years after the house was lost, somehow this 'owning' atmosphere seemed to broaden to encompass the wider West Country for me. My own landscape parent. I could not escape it. It was who I was when far from home. My house had travelled with me and grown; sown dust seeds in my pockets that threaded roots through my body to the land, to pull me back wherever I was in the world.

I dream of this house. No other house I have ever lived in comes back to me, but this house arrives in my dreams as if landing like a spaceship from its own realm. In *The Secret Lives of Buildings*, Edward Hollis talks about the Holy House, based on the house where Mary received the annunciation in Nazareth and rebuilt throughout the world – from Walsingham to Quebec. One of the strange legends of this small humble holy building was its tendency to magically appear as if it had teleported, communicating with the faithful, refusing to give in to its own loss. It did not have a set location, but was miracle made manifest as building, an apparition that came to chosen places, blessing them with its presence. My old house is obviously not holy in the Christian sense of the word, but sacred to me it was and is still. (I worry to this day that it felt abandoned, and I gaze up at my old bedroom window and hope the boy who grew up there after me looked after it.) How it behaves in dreams has the same miraculous feel – it appears in the landscape regardless of what geographical location my dream mind has conjured. As if it knows I need it, it comes to me like a ghost I can inhabit while asleep.

Of course, being a dream, it is never as it was. I rarely find the sanctuary of my old bedroom but instead roam a strange patchwork building with secret rooms and floors that change. It is a Transformer of a building, a strange architectural robot of memories, recognisable as much by atmosphere as identity – a sense that *this is my old house* – rather than looking like it did.

I have never quite understood why it comes back this way. Why it isn't as it was – have the rooms expanded to encompass other thoughts and feelings? Is this inner memory made visible? Is it trying to tell me something? Does it represent a loss or a dream of what I'm searching for? It is unsettling rather than comforting, and my old house, the place where my family were happy and together, where I felt secure and supported, *was* comforting.

Childhood forms us. It influences who we are as adults. Creates us – we do not just grow up, but our minds collaborate in a creative act with the world and experiences it as an artist. We are created and creators. It is logical that such an intense period in our lives would affect how we interact with and experience place as we get older.

And perhaps because childhood is where we are created and learn to create, perhaps because it is a realm inside of us, this is why childhood homes come back in dreams as the embodiment of that realm. I am not the only one who dreams of the house they grew up in. Philosophers and the authors of endless memoirs linger on the childhood home more than on any adult dwelling. In adulthood, it seems where we are in the outside world is more influential – a city or country – but when it comes to interiors, it is the childhood home that lives inside us. My mother endlessly dreamed of the Oxfordshire vicarage where she grew up in the days when vicarages were still often vast Victorian houses, as hers was. She could remember every detail – more so than the house I grew up in, where she lived for nearly thirty years. It pales in atmospheric power compared to her childhood home where she lived for a much shorter time . . . Perhaps we all have a space, a room, good or bad, that is part of who we are.

Home. It is at the core of what we carry through life emotionally, and thus helps form our perception of atmosphere, and our relation to the atmospheres of the world, for the rest of our lives. It appears when we need it and sometimes when we don't understand why. It is an active atmosphere, original yet flexible, mutating inside of us, comforting or disconcerting. It is present in our dreams.

Intimate yet infinite. On a different scale to the exterior landscapes we so often associate with powerful atmospheres, yet its emotional scope, its vastness of legacy, is perhaps greater than any forest or mountain. Like childhood in general, it is a formative atmosphere that we cannot lose; we might ignore it, but it is somewhere inside us nonetheless.

My heart has a little hole and in it my house lives in miniature. A doll's house surrounded by the muscle of blood movement and love. It is about the size of a Monopoly house, but unlike such houses it is full of detail. A poetic primal internal image of place, an image of becoming and a refuge.

Unlike atmospheres we encounter in the world, this one is part of me. Both of my body and beyond it.

At the top of medieval maps the Garden of Eden was portrayed, a perfect place we could but dream of reaching; like heaven, it was both there, yet out of reach. If my map was truly tender, my old house would hover like this, integral to how I see the world, its heart always there above me. It is a character, a protagonist in the atmosphere of my life that I carry with me to experience the atmosphere of all other places I have visited.

Home is the first atmosphere – the background to all of them.

The Poetics of Home

In his famous work *The Poetics of Space*, French philosopher Gaston Bachelard explores the idea of our childhood home and what it means to us. For him, the childhood home is the first world that we inhabit. It therefore cradles us. Bachelard argues that if, as adults, we go back and dream of it, we are again participating in this original warmth. It is a comfort. It reminds us of before we were 'cast out into the world' and we comfort ourselves by reliving 'memories of protection'.

There are problems here, of course. Not everyone has had a protected childhood, a loving cradle of a home, or even a home at all. Working with children, I can see how for some of them the prospect of the childhood home returning would be traumatic, not comforting. Yet there is still something universal here, a memory of when we perhaps didn't question that we were safe, which perhaps in very early childhood we weren't even aware of: first home as extension of womb. Warm, safe, before we are aware, at whatever age, of its potential flaws – the darker side, if we are unfortunate, of reality. We all need some form of shelter; this is a human need, a primal need. For most of us, this is most powerful in the childhood home – that first place of shelter.

For Bachelard, this initial cradle offers the best comforting daydreams. For him, daydreams, the poetic potential of reverie, are more powerful and important than night dreams. Here we have the ability to create poetry, to truly communicate with a sense of something deep and original, to bring something forth, which in night dreams is lost to the unconscious; something he is loath to analyse, believing that psychoanalysis destroys something, tries to make sense in a way that ignores creative power and intimacy.

Bachelard believes that daydreams are inherently creative; they bring forth images, original poetic acts that are primal, that can make sense of the world in a way detached analysis simply can't.

Poetry and creativity in all its forms are how we make real sense of the world. Similarly, the perception of atmosphere is how we really experience the world – we come across it, we help create it, and when daydreaming, we are, perhaps, in a trance-like, dreamlike yet heightened state, most likely to feel its inspiration, and be moved by it.

When exploring atmosphere as a creative force, the idea cannot be ignored of home as being the anchor to it – the place from which our poetic imagination is born and returns. Home as a spark, as a pinch of creative dust, something that we scatter through all our creative endeavours, does make sense. Bachelard's main task, and his main problem, is that he is setting out to find an 'intimate concrete essence' that 'transcends our memories of all the houses in which we have found shelter, above and beyond all the houses we have dreamed we live in', and that would be 'a justification of the uncommon value of all our images of protected intimacy'. It is the idea of the 'intimate concrete essence' that I am interested in here. It sounds to me like this essence has to function as an atmosphere; that what we carry with us must be an atmosphere of this original home, which influences how we experience the world.

When I move into a new house I do not rest until I have made it feel 'me'. I desperately nest. But is it an atmosphere of my childhood home I am searching for, or a new creation; a new creative space of solitude, like a hermit crab moved on? Are the two separable?

There is something distinct in an inside atmosphere. Obviously, it is intrinsically different to being outside but I am purposefully using the terms 'inside' and 'indoors' rather than 'internal' here, as I think all atmosphere has an element of the internal, our internal. However, atmosphere behaves differently indoors. Part of this we can explain away because of how our sensory experience will be different. It will still be multisensory – after all, we do not lose a sense when we walk through a door. But we are shrouded from the natural world when indoors. The protection, which can be a comfort, the intimate shelter that Bachelard refers to, also shuts out fresh air, sounds, smells and sightlines and limits our ability to see into the distance unless gazing through a window. This too can be a comfort; there is an exciting atmosphere of cosiness, almost uncanny, when staring out from a window, in a position of warmth, at a storm. But a window is a barrier, a filtered way of seeing the world, just like the modern filters of viewing through endless screens. So with atmosphere thus changed, more contained, more within our control, how it functions for us is bound to differ. What it means to us and what it conjures will be on a different level; not shallower or deeper, just different.

Here Bachelard's ideas start to gain a new strength. If we look at them in terms of atmosphere, but ignore the outside world – if we equate home as shelter as a different kind of home, a different way of being in the world – then we can see how our childhood homes, how all our experiences of different interior spaces come to life. But one interesting thing here is that while, yes, the creative comfort, the poetic cradle, might take the form of daydreams of our childhood home, while this might be what affects us most deeply, it is not where we were able to exercise choice. As adults in our own homes, or even as soon as we were old enough to assert our taste – to choose a paint colour, or plaster the walls with posters, to create our own sanctuary – we can design our interior spaces. In the world outside, we usually don't have such choice, such control, except in our gardens. Apart from perhaps the exterior of the building (though we choose what to rent or buy) or being constrained by financial limits, we make our homes as we want them. We create their atmospheres much more consciously. Just as with what we wear and how we behave, this is a more conscious creative atmosphere; a collaboration in which we, not the wider world, are the dominant creative force. If this is the case, if every time we move home we bring ourselves, our dreams, our ideas and tastes with us, then we will bring our childhood homes and experiences with us too. If we still dream of our childhood home, this will be significant when in an adult one of our own creation – it will probably bring an atmospheric thread, a spindly root to everywhere we live. Be a constant point on our own tender map.

And in the modern world our interior spaces have expanded in concept. We create them online: chat rooms, websites, homepages – linguistically we are expanding into new spaces, yet this is not only (as we have seen) an attempt to create a sense of cyberspace as place, but also an attempt to control our feelings in them with the language of home – a welcoming language in an alienating (to many) world; today, we contain an unimaginable digital vastness within our own walls, making this an interior, not exterior, space. Yet we lose atmosphere. The digital world offers merely a mirage of home without the depth of intimacy, of feelings, that 'real' places have.

Memory affects atmosphere. Yet it is not as dominant as some might think; to consider atmosphere too much in terms of memory or nostalgia detracts from its vital force. Memory is but a sketch, an illusion, which inevitably affects us emotionally, in that everything we have experienced is put there. It is an archive of atmosphere in our minds, catalogued by a rather disorganised entity who likes to play with the truth. But nonetheless it is ever present in who we are. For Bachelard, localisation is more relevant than the temporal in memory. Yes, memory is of the past, but where these memories are located is where they have their power, especially if we are thinking of intimacy, key to atmosphere and creativity.

Intimacy is interesting. It is subjective and creative – it will never appear the same to two people, much like atmosphere. To describe it as if to visitors reduces its depth, just like trying to describe a near spiritual experience of atmosphere in a forest does. (I am woefully aware of that in the challenge of writing this book.) As Bachelard says: 'All we communicate to others is an orientation towards what is secret without ever being able to tell the secret objectivity.' This is a precious thing, I think.

Childhood home may be a cradle, that first place of poetic reverie, of shelter; but it may be something else, something stranger – a vessel, a dream place that exists to hold us, to hold our thoughts; to change and mutate; to be recognisable only by its atmosphere, its weird sense of place; communicating something, appearing to us with a message that we may not be sure what it is. A message from home, an atmosphere recognised across intimate distance, from somewhere deep inside of us.

I sit and picture my old house. I can feel it – even though I know its literal location, I wonder where it is, like a lost pet. No matter how I might see home now, no matter how my definition of what home can be has broadened out of genuine discovery and necessity, I still return to it. Its atmosphere; its once-upon-a-time shelter that, I think, encapsulates what Bachelard was trying to say.

I feel my old house lives inside of me, but I am not rooted there. I grew up there, but my roots came with me. There are other places in the world where I dangled my roots and little ones took hold and buried in – Tbilisi for one ... There were moments elsewhere – Montreal, Belgrade, Sicily ... I am scattered around the world, but that does not change how I feel about the house I grew up in, or about where I have made my home now. These are all places of home, just of different intensity and significance. They each hold their own atmospheres, their memories, their status as well springs of the imagination, of the poetics of space. They might not be as primitive as my childhood home, but they are primal in the creative thinking they unleashed, how they shaped my experience of the world, my atmosphere within it. They all became part of me to some extent. I can communicate this no better than I can describe the dream of a childhood home, which no one else could ever truly know what it feels like to inhabit atmospherically – to be there. That is the true home of the interior. The atmosphere of the places in our minds. Our childhood home may be queen there, hold the deepest power, but other places inhabit it too, creatively, formatively; stitching together and contributing to the patchwork that influences how we go on to experience new places and atmospheres – how we put the world together from the world we carry within us. Our own embroidered map.

My old house pulses inside me. I take it with me as I stride through my forest, up my high hills and breathe deeply.

Homelessness

After lockdown in 2020, I found myself homeless due to a family crisis – the resultant complications left me bereft of home in a way I could never have imagined when growing up. Family and the parental home represented security, I had thought, but as it disintegrated around me, or rather, was torn away, I began to understand that home is a complex thing: it is a concept that grows out from the childhood home and our childhood thinking, but it is also a living, fluid thing that must evolve with us into adulthood.

When I look at my relentless travelling, my searching, when I think back to that moment on the Maypool, it is all connected. I was looking for something, and as I grew and left and travelled the world, that something was the sense of home. I travelled lots in my early twenties, but it was in my late twenties, those endless trips to Serbia and Georgia, when it grew in intensity. The searching. The needing to feel alive elsewhere, to find something in atmosphere. And with my childhood home gone, my beloved building friend, I left my landscape and began to scatter shallow roots.

As my thirties progressed, my travelling calmed and I settled back in the West Country. Losing my home again was a shock and, in 2020, just as the rest of the world retreated into their homes, I found myself on the road searching for a new one. This time, though, I didn't want to run away – I craved my childhood area. I looked for weeks, sleeping at a friend's house, trying to find somewhere that would accept freelancers with pets, an absurd and degrading experience on the rental market. I wanted it to be near the downs and the forest, my two places of sanctuary.

I had tried living in other parts of the UK, but as soon as I got back to the Somerset–Wiltshire–Dorset borders, my body always sighed with relief. I had never before analysed this feeling with any depth. I never thought about home in relation to it, the idea of place, the feeling of being in landscape. I still very much thought of a building as a true home, even if I did feel 'at home' in this particular part of the country. There was a difference.

But now, as I tried to rebuild a life bereft of the bricks and mortar residence that the family home represented, I began to wonder if home wasn't about the atmosphere held in the bricks and mortar but was, in fact, about the exterior. That 'outside' meant more than 'inside'.

I was raised by a landscape. I was raised by a house in this landscape, but now it is gone, the landscape is my true support. When I look back at my childhood it is the places I remember more than the people, or rather, the good moments were often when I was outside, and alone. The times I spent roaming the fields and woods near my house, pottering round the village, playing in the river, formed me more than advice from adults. Perhaps it was strange I had so much freedom, but without this, I do not think I would feel so connected to the landscapes around me today. From an early age, places were my true companions. They were my friends.

As we move further from childhood we expand beyond the walls of our beginnings. My atmosphere had expanded, and could not settle within a single building. It needed more space. I was back. But it was the West Country's landscape that held me, those downs and woods, where sometimes its buildings had failed. I started to think more about a different definition of home.

Three Women: Alternative Ideas of Home

Picture a house. This house was once bricks, but then it is made of glass, and then the glass grows thin and permeable till the landscape creeps, not in, but opens the house out, till the rooms can breathe and the floors and furniture are at one with the grass and the far-off hills, the drink that is fresh air. Picture a house that is no longer a house, but somehow a home. A home that is all around you. Perhaps home is something that a building is simply a symbol of, its most common materialisation. Perhaps walls actually limit it. As I began to reflect on what had happened, I wondered if my true home might be the places with an atmosphere that makes me feel better – my woods, my grassy downs. That what these feelings in place meant to me, a point on my own map, tenderly redrawn, was a sense of home. I walked towards it.

Of all the writers I know, Nan Shepherd is the one who while not explicitly discussing atmosphere and home, penetrates the heart of this so it bursts forth in a beauty of feeling and love for her home in the Cairngorm Mountains. She walks her home every day.

Her idea of *The Living Mountain*, the title of her wonderful book on the Cairngorms, is not so much about a sentient mountain as the title might suggest, but a seeking; an evolving quest to understand its essential nature in the knowledge that it is 'a process of living'. That to be close to the mountain, and to get to know it, formulates a new sense of home, of being, and an alternative definition of how we might look at place. Even something as solid as a mountain is not permanent. She argues that we can never quite know the mountains – there is 'no getting accustomed to them', however much we may walk in them. There is a sense of astonishment, of process and change in every interaction. This reminds me of atmosphere – that inability to contain it, its evolving nature, its developing personality over time. Yet there is still something of great worth, of key importance, in the quest for being with the unknowable, a process in itself. It can be enriching and extraordinary and, as it gets inside us, it becomes a different sense of home – an evolving way of looking at place and our relationship with it *as* a process, as a changing thing rather than an instantly conjurable static state. Yet while moving, it is recognisable in our core – as feelings are. If we accept that a place is not a static location, then maybe we can inhabit it more deeply; it can become a richer sense of home.

Shepherd walked. Not just a gentle potter, or even a conscious I-am-going-on-an-epic-hike for exercise. She did walk slow and fast, near and far, but for her, walking was as much a part of being alive as sleeping, as being awake, as her writing. To walk the landscape of the Cairngorms was to be herself. They were as much a part of her identity as her taste, her thoughts, her body, her personality. They were not separate to it. Her moving, her walking, through the landscape was an act of being both with the land she loved, and of being herself. She got to know it intimately. From the wild places where one should be careful when straying – the heights, the grand landscape – to the minute details of flora and fauna, the different layers that made up her landscape; the layers, the detail, that we all so often miss.

Shepherd missed nothing. It was a life process, this getting to know the mountains. Her life's work as much as her writing, her novels, her job were. Her tender map was not so much formed by her words, but the memories of her feet, of her body, alive in place. Her moving through, of absorbing, then setting free.

This is an intrinsically creative way of looking at the world, a collaborative way of looking, one we are active in making. A dialogue with place. *The Living Mountain* reads like a love story to me. The tenderness lies in the reciprocal nature of it. An attempt not to capture place, but to highlight the impossibility of doing so.

The mountains that were Nan Shepherd's true home heighten

her sense of being alive, her sense of freedom, her need for height and air and space. Nature as home without walls. *The Living Mountain* is full of wonderful natural history details, the plants and animals, her precise yet magical descriptions of the landscape. But it is her exploration of *how* to be with the land that I find so fascinating. Her multisensory approach to the world. This is writing beyond seeing. This is writing that understands how, if we are to really know a place, we cannot just observe it. We need to smell, to listen ... Nan Shepherd is the only writer I can think of who mentions how touch fills our whole body. I think of walking on my own hills – breath more intense and clear, skylarks hovering, the tiniest detail of flowers, miles and miles of grassy views, chalk rivers of paths. To sleep outside is particularly important for Shepherd. She talks of the moment of waking and how, when almost in a trance, the world is distilled in essence – of the body, hyper-sensory, yet in the mind. A true intense experience of atmosphere. A feeling, an experience that is 'peculiarly precious because it is impossible to coerce'. I get that. It doesn't happen every time I am in my home places, but when it does it is gloriously sweet. The poignancy, the bittersweet only happens later; perhaps that is the exile – the exile from being able to conjure on demand, to access the feeling whenever we want it. Of joy.

Sensory experience is not a cataloguing of sensation, but rather a gateway into the personality of and a communication with the landscape. Shepherd notes a 'violet range of colours can trouble the mind like music'. Yet it is not just the grand views that concern her but also the small details, about which she marvels 'that an enchantment can be made from so small a matter'. The simmering magic of detail, of every little living thing combining to create the magic of atmosphere, the magic that becomes an atmosphere of home. The magic that is so powerful to us, yet has no reference to us as observers. As she wonderfully says: 'this is how the earth must see itself.'

So how do we live with this enchantment? If we strive for it, but it's impossible to coerce? Can we still find it, or is this a hopeless quest in which we will always be at the whim of the natural world?

Why does it happen? It is for Shepherd a creative act, one that underlines for me the importance of atmosphere as key to creativity. It is an essence and essential. That doesn't have to mean it is just one thing. That it is pin-down-able. It is fluid, not static. It is vital and alive, we catch it in glimpses, moments of brightness.

> It is, as with all creation, matter impregnated with mind: but the resultant issue is a living spirit, a glow in the consciousness, that perishes when the glow is dead. It is something snatched from non-being, that shadow that creeps in on us continuously and can be held off by a continuous creative act. So, simply to look on anything, such as a mountain, with the love that penetrates to its essence, is to widen the domain of being in the vastness of non-being. Man has no other reason for his existence.

Many people have an intense sense of place through knowing a landscape intimately. But Shepherd's articulation of what it is like to tie your life to a place, to move through life together – the sense of place as process, offering the opportunity for a different way of being – makes me think of simply being alive as a creative project. It makes me think of outsider artists who create worlds within their worlds, the detritus of life filling spaces till the way they live is the atmosphere they are part of; people who create art because it means something to them, with no thought of commerce. I think of land artists, or city artists that work with process – creating something for the moment, in the place, which photos cannot truly reproduce. A knowledge that there is something in a moment, in a place in a moment, which we can interact with, notice, but never hold captive. We can collaborate, but not dominate.

This creativity is not whimsy. It is not detached from facts. It is part of them. In tangent and intangible. Shepherd is hugely interested in and accepting of science as enriching the way she knows the landscape, perceives the flora and fauna, the make-up of the earth, the flow of river into loch. Yet when it comes to simple geographic analysis, she finds this falls short, just as I did when I initially researched what might create atmosphere. After all, science explains facts, but a geography of emotion? Geography might describe appearances but does not offer an explanation of place – types of rock and plant don't explain what makes a place feel the way it does. While we can learn from knowing about them, as Shepherd says, the geography of the Cairngorms 'is a pallid simulacrum of their reality, which, like everything that matters ultimately to human beings, is a reality of the mind'. If reality of place is a reality of our mind, then how we interact with place, the experience we bring to place, who we are combined with our sensory experience, must be key to a truer sense of reality than the physical landscape building blocks.

I think this goes deeper than that somewhere reminds us of a feeling, perhaps of childhood or a place we know. A true feeling of atmosphere and of belonging to a place is impossible to conjure; it refuses to recreate itself on demand: we cannot think that feeling there, we just joyfully recognise it when it arrives. As Shepherd describes it, like 'the whole wild enchantment, like a world of art is perpetually new when one returns to it.' We are not remembering. We are liberated from Bachelard's shell of childhood comfort. Each time is a new experience. It is not memory as nostalgia, but a living thing we somehow know as being *of us*.

Describing the landscape as 'a world of art' is an interesting comparison and not a simple aside in Shepherd's beautiful and carefully placed words. There are certain works of art we know and love that we ache to see again, realising that each time we will experience an intensity of feeling, but not necessarily the same one as before. There is something deep and subconscious in the communication of art and the co-creativity of viewer or reader, which is close to how we experience atmosphere if we open ourselves up to it; if we consciously engage, as we can do with art, rather than pass through, ignore, miss it (as many sadly do with art), filtering through screens, posing for the perfect selfie – image of self next to art rather than as part of its process, its creative experience. Shepherd mentions the walkers who, rather than pit themselves against the mountain, pit themselves against each other, turning hillwalking into a race, reducing an experience to a game. It reminds me of hipster urban exploration – that need to conquer, to cross off a list rather than experience or fully appreciate what you are doing where you are. It reminds me too of a certain difference in approach from artists who work with the landscape, the macho scarring made by some male American land artists, as opposed to a gentler collaboration by both male and female land artists of another bent; artists who leave their work to grow, to be; artists who channel a natural force, who, consciously or not, work with atmosphere.

The final chapter in *The Living Mountain* is simply called 'Being'. It seems the right title for the conclusion to this book – Being with a capital B: we are not striving to live but Be. Being is perhaps how to feel more comfortable in an unconventional home. It is not about shelter and survival, as a political exile would presuppose. It is what it can mean to be alive. There is a purity of sensory experience on the mountain, a way that beautifully makes atmosphere physical – not detached from, but of both body and mind. In these circumstances, Shepherd says 'the body may be said to think.' We are complete – mind, body, land.

The imprint of a body burns, fireworks ignite a fleeting figure, the silhouette is washed away, melts, disintegrates, yet grows. Mud, snow, sand, flowers. Ana Mendieta is not really considered in the (mostly grandiose male) canon of land artists, but when I think of a true sense of being with the land, when I think of how art can communicate the strength of feeling the land can have and our personal connection to it, how any relationship to atmosphere and being is personal, creative, collaborative, then Mendieta's work sings where others seem but an imposition – a carved mark, a statement of human presence, where atmosphere is something to be created by manmade power, even if it is harnessing nature, as in Walter De Maria's beautiful *Lightning Field*. Mendieta is not trying to control nature, to change the land, to make her mark, even when literally imprinting her body in the ground. She is working with it, revealing, vitally and fleetingly collaborating.

In her *Silueta* series, created over a number of years from 1973, Mendieta left imprints of her body in the ground. In the first piece, she herself was there, on a mountain in Oaxaca, Mexico, outlined in an ancient tomb, her naked body covered in flowers. Later, her physical body disappeared from the series, quite tellingly, as if she had merged into the ground, replaced with silhouettes, imprints, ephemeral marks, vital hints at her presence. She left imprints on the beach to be washed away by the tide, impressions burning brightly with gunpowder set alight till a charred outline remained. Mud, snow, water, fireworks. A true collaboration of body and earth, a moment, only seen by most through photographs, private, communicative, ephemeral, but not passive. There is a vitality, sometimes even a violence to the work. But that violence isn't of her imposing herself on the land, but rather a fleeting moment that will disappear; a flaring up of a life force, a bringing forth of the power, of something normally unseen.

If home can be a way of being with the land rather than a physical building, Mendieta's is a complicated home. Exiled from Cuba as a child, growing up in foster care and orphanages in the USA, she talks a lot about her own struggles with belonging, of feeling exiled from her home. Therefore, there is also that other complicated concept here: homeland, nationhood, borders, thresholds, where do we belong? As Mendieta said, 'Because I have no motherland, I feel the need to join with the earth.'

Joining. Togetherness. Snow melting, waves smoothing sand and rain washing mud away – at one not with the permanence but the shifting nature of the earth – how it cannot be pinned down. Like atmosphere, her work is of the moment, changing how that place felt in that moment. It is not a claiming, it is a being with.

There are other dimensions to her work. The political element, feminism of the seventies and eighties, a movement in which she was involved before her tragic death in 1985, falling (or allegedly pushed by her partner, the artist Carl Andre – the circumstances of her death were never satisfactorily solved) from a high window. But her land art is so rich that it transcends politics. It is much more rewarding to explore the works and how they felt in the place; how a creative act, gentle or full of force, can be a way of creating a home in a place, while thinking about where home might be. And if they do not represent home, do they nevertheless create a relationship that can give us a sense of belonging with the earth?

Mendieta talked of a universal life force. This is not a static thing, but rather something that flows, a 'Universal Energy which runs through everything ... My works are the irrigation veins of the Universal fluid. Through them ascend the ancestral sap ... the unconscious thoughts that animate the world.' Universal yet moving, transient, in flux. Sentient yet unconscious. Mendieta's works could be seen as using atmosphere as their material. Abstracting, disappearing her bodily presence beyond the natural materials she used, erasing them to conjure something more powerful, more ephemeral, yet vitality present, almost painfully alive. She is working collaboratively with the earth itself.

If one is exiled, if one is dislocated from a sense of home, as Mendieta often stated when talking about her Cuban heritage, then being able to access this energy, to communicate with the earth in this intense yet personal way, could give a sense of home. In a world carved up by them, if we see borders rather as thresholds, as places where atmosphere changes, where meaning changes, then Mendieta's work – rather than being constrained by borders, the dislocation of exile – is freed by it. It is no coincidence that her works sometimes existed on the edge, the sea, washing it away, a natural border. It is no coincidence that so much of her work was made in Mexico, nation as threshold between cultures, a now infamous border, but then for Mendieta a place of belonging, a new home with deep roots for her. Many critics are unable to see her work without thinking of her exile, but to see it in purely these terms is to simplify things. While she talked of this, I don't see her work as a constant dislocation, an exile; it is a rehoming, a widening of the definition of home to something that can be tapped into like the sap in a tree.

We cannot control atmosphere, those intense experiences of atmosphere in landscape that Shepherd felt, but we can communicate and collaborate with it. Just like atmosphere, Mendieta's work cannot be stabilised – it burns, it flows, it disintegrates. She is not claiming the land as goddess, like the goddess movement of mainly white middle-class feminists did in the seventies (although she was deeply interested in spiritual beliefs, particularly the Cuban Santería religion). This ephemerality does not make it gentle, like the beautiful fragility of an Andy Goldsworthy artwork, for example, but rather in dealing with the 'material' of atmosphere and its creative urgency, she is using its often overlooked energy, the life force we ignore in our daily lives. In much the same way, the urgency of work like Mendieta's is often overlooked, simplified, seen as self-obsessed or a feminine approach to land art, which sells it short. Hers *is* a feminine approach to land art; as she said herself in an interview with the *Daily Iowan* in 1977: 'men artists working with nature have imposed themselves on it. Definitely my work has that feminine sensibility. I can't think of many men who would use a heart image in a serious way.' Yet the key here is *serious*. This is not feminine as the stereotypes would have it. It is more that it is different in a way that a man might have been unlikely to bring forth. It is work without ego, a disintegration of self till it is part of the land, till it brings home forth.

We each have the ability to find our own personal relationship with the universal. If we ignore borders, if we embrace exile as both a loss and a liberation, we can broaden a sense of home and where we might find it. It is not a house, but an atmosphere and that atmosphere does not have to be the same as our childhood home or where we are exiled from. It can influence it, but where we truly find home might be wildly new. Some would argue we need the familiar to feel at home. Critics of Mendieta's work see her exile, her work as uncanny, manipulating the familiar, sowing a discord of atmosphere to unsettle us. Maybe if you literally stumbled on one of her Siluetas it would unsettle you. But we can feel at home in the unfamiliar. Mendieta is influenced by her exile, yes, but in her gentle imprints, her ephemeral shadows, she is drifting, travelling, moving across landscapes in search of something. This doesn't have to be a constant loss, any more than it was for Nan Shepherd; nor does it have to be a searching for a home that can never be found again: it can be a moving forward, collaborating with our notions of what it means to belong and turning them upside down – a creative act to create art. An art that is a home.

When I was a child I couldn't resist the idea of a different kind of home within my known one, smaller and alive and full of possibilities just for me. I built dens –when a tree fell down I made a den in the hole it left, the roots a ceiling of natural chandeliers. I took a duvet into the greenhouse at the bottom of the garden. I would pretend there had been some strange apocalypse, my family all gone and I lived here now. I would lie and look at the sky through the mossy, cracked glass and feel that this was somehow a different life I had accessed. (Something I remembered when house-hunting in the pandemic, feeling more like a child than I had done for decades.) It is a common fantasy for children: running away from even a loving home suggests a deep need to explore, a realisation that one day it really will be just us and the world. Childhood could be seen as waiting for exile. An exile that can mean freedom.

While I came to this realisation in my forties, a twelve-year-old girl is the writer who best encapsulates this feeling for me. Barbara Newhall Follett never lived, as far as we can surmise, to reach her forties. She walked out of her house one night in her twenties and never returned. Her disappearance remains a mystery that many have sought to solve, but to no avail. There is no trace of her after she left her house, no sightings, no modern technology existed that today would track her down. It could be that she was the victim of a crime, sadly the most likely cause of her vanishing, but I prefer to think of her simply choosing to disappear; to leave her married life of convention and become once more the child who wrote of freedom, the adventurer, the traveller always drawn to the wild.

In *The House Without Windows*, written and published to great acclaim when Newhall Follett was only twelve, the young girl protagonist Eepersip decides to leave her parents and live in the wild. It is a very straightforward decision, although her parents are perfectly nice. There is no regret, more a fear of being recaptured, as her parents and their friends try many times. She lives in a meadow with a herd of deer she tames, then later a chipmunk and a kitten she steals from a neighbour. There is utter joy in how she lives, she is at one with the place and its creatures. Yet there is a restlessness. This place that has become home provides views of sea and mountains and Eepersip cannot resist the urge to wander and try out all these other landscapes as her potential home. There is never a question of her searching for a house. She doesn't even really make dens or shelters, just finds a nice place to sleep. It is devoid of the obvious struggles living wild would have. It all comes naturally to Eepersip.

As the title suggests, for Eepersip the world is her house – the word for our recognised home is there, house, but the definition is radically changed of what a house *is*. No walls, no roof, no windows. Home is an evolving exploration of the natural world. A way of Being. It is freedom.

There are moments of temptation to return to conventional ways of living. Eepersip is briefly intrigued by a cottage she has previously found and dismissed, but decides against it: 'Everything came back to her – those foolish coverings on the floors which they called carpets, at the windows those useless decorations called curtains. To think of it! when there was a carpet so much lovelier of green grass or of white sand – and no windows to be curtained!'

As she continues her journey further, moves to new landscapes, we see the true essence of the house without windows. Eepersip leaves the meadows and seashore to go into the mountains and as she does the writing gets headier and more intense. Snow falls but does not harm her. It is a curiosity. A magical encasement which, rather than making her cold, creates frost feathers – is almost magical. The world is achingly beautiful. Almost too much so. Yet not for Eepersip. She begins to float, to drift, to go a little *fey*, as Nan Shepherd would say of those in love with the mountains as home. She feels queer, 'for she felt the feeling of speaking to her heart'. There is a new communication with the feelings of place in these mountains. It is as if Eepersip has found her true home, her house without windows, and as she does so, this intensity of belonging, of Being, begins to merge her into it. Mentions of fairyland become more frequent. One could say that this is a logical comparison for a twelve-year-old girl to come up with, and maybe it is, but it reminds me of that sense of the places where the veil between this world and another, stranger one – one where I feel atmosphere is a natural inhabitant, temptress, illuminator – is barely there. There is an acknowledgement of what happens when one is fully open to the emotion of a place. Where it becomes you and you become part of it. The novel ends with Eepersip disappearing. Becoming the spirit of nature. Spirit. Spirit of matter – an alchemical change. The house without windows is the world and this world has a spirit, a soul. If we too can find this, then surely it has a better chance of creating a home for us than walls.

I think of Ana Mendieta's Siluetas dissolving into the earth. Her echoes now part of it. Not a marking of ego, but like Eepersip, an urge to disappear into its deeper force – be spirit. A spiritual home is not a building. I think of Ann Mercer's map. Another young girl, embroidering mountains, marking them on her map, a hint in thread of her own house without windows, high-up places we cannot know if she visited; what tender points they might have been.

Many people have tried to see something prophetic in how Barbara Newhall Follett disappeared; there is a hope in the idea that she went to live wild like Eepersip, rather than met a more mundane and tragic end. But to focus on the mystery of Barbara misses the point – yes, she was an extraordinary adventurer, hiking the Appalachians, joining the crew of a ship at fourteen ... But the book has an essence that, while wild, is more contained in meaning.

This essence is of freedom. To be truly at home, we must feel free from whatever constraints are bringing us down. The freedom, without walls, without barricades, to be ourselves. It is a similar freedom to that of the creative mind. To be of the earth, create something with it, as in the work of Ana Mendieta, or to feel that sense of Being that Nan Shepherd talks of. Home is somewhere without boundaries.

In 2020, I eventually found a home and after a struggle it landed like magic – like the Holy House – a magical apparition at a time of need. It was one of the cottages I had seen on my walks in which I had always imagined living. I could get up on the downs from my front door. I could walk a little further along country lanes and I was in my forest. Both mainly owned by my lovely new landlord.

I had had a terrible time trying to find somewhere – nowhere else would have me, despite my savings and freelance contracts – yet this house came to me and I knew as soon as I walked in that it could be home. The cottage was scruffy but lovely. However, as I sit curled up on my sofa and think of it now, that feeling of home is not contained in this building, or even the niceness and familiarity of the village, the kindness and decency of the estate I rent from; rather, it is contained in the atmosphere of where my cottage rests between the two places that I love, the places that hold me. I think my sense of home is now determined by atmosphere beyond walls, or a wider sense of where I am.

Looking around my new house, I reflect on this. I have been obsessively tweaking the interior on my very limited budget, putting my belongings in place, attempting to make this lovely shell a home. And it is becoming so. But as I close the door and walk, and walk and walk, as I think about what happened in recent months – the total loss of family and support, the shock of being homeless as a professional in my forties, that brutal decapitation of security – I begin to feel the balm of the atmosphere of where I now live. The hills. The forest. The two places where I feel better – that are alive to me – where I can Be. I was raised by this landscape and unlike my family, it is still there. I am, I realise, walking home – but it's to a different kind of home.

When I arrive at the top of the steep downs near my house, I do not want to leave. I slow my pace and wander through the twisted ancient trees that cling and survive storms, despite being so high up, used as they are to being windswept. I stand near the old earthwork and stare out, miles across grasslands. I smile at the red kites, hovering, almost at my height now as they scan the ground for voles. But most of all, I feel a strange change in myself. An urge, despite being so high up and exposed, vehemently outdoors, to sit and reverently lay out a tea set as a child might. To sit and think, to potter around, to slow down and almost break up my walk, as if this place has invisible walls that are not walls and I have entered a room; as if it is my second home and once here I need to be in it slowly. I stride here, but once arrived, I need to notice everything. To fill my body. My mind eases. My heart pulses, drifting out into this landscape, yet somehow, rather than losing part of it, my heart is more deeply alive and within me than anywhere else. Pottering around the top of the downs near my house, is an atmosphere unto its own; it surrounds me and is in my core, it is my home, and it is a different way of Being.

I look across my hills. I think of traipsing for miles. How walking and the atmospheres I found over the past couple of years have saved me. As Shepherd says in *The Living Mountain*: 'walking thus, hour after hour, the senses keyed, one walks the flesh transparent.' We know flesh, yet flesh becomes landscape, like Eepersip disappearing, transforming into the spirit of nature, like Siluetas disintegrating into the land. Our bodies are very much there, yet when we are truly Being in a place, we dissolve, boundaries are gone; we are absorbed into atmosphere, we become the threshold: 'The flesh is not annihilated but fulfilled. One is not bodiless, but essential body.' Atmosphere is this essential body of the land. We are part of this. We are essential to the health of the world as it is to us. We are made of the same thing. We are both essence and it is not fixed here. As Shepherd says: 'I am not out of myself, but in myself. I am. To know Being, this is the final grace accorded from the mountain.'

Perhaps the knowledge we are all searching for, the meaning, the essential nature of things, of life – that is not static. That cannot be distilled. This is why atmosphere is vital. At its most powerful, we are home.

Realms within Realms

For hundreds of years in folklore and stories, in theology and psychology, the presence of other places within our places has been discussed. Places where we can reach a different way of being, places that could be beyond our everyday world, that we could find by atmosphere.

As I walked during that first lockdown, my feelings of transcendence in the woods grew. I was in my familiar place, home territory, yet also this new place which I had accessed and which offered both a more intense sense of presence and a greater familiarity as those transcendent feelings grew. At the same time, it was also foreign, in that I had travelled within my home place to this new one.

I was more aware in myself. But I did not feel alone.

Within Celtic Christianity there is the concept of 'thin places', where the space between heaven and earth is thin – easier to feel and therefore holy. Iona is one such place. A holy place is a place where we meet with God, or where God has met someone in a special way. It may be a consecrated space, but it may also be an ordinary location – a spot on a footpath, a garden, a street . . . Celtic Christianity believed strongly that the everyday could be holy, that God was always close by, that 'the edge of glory is found at the level of the ordinary'. The same could be said for our experience of place if we just slow down and notice – the sun shining, new moss on a wall, damp and glistening, the subtle whispers of trees . . .

The edge . . . The hem . . .

There are thin holy places, and there are thin places in folklore. Mounds as gateways to fairy realms, wells, streams; all held sacred by different beliefs, but linked somehow in that they are never far away, yet never quite within reach, fluttering a veil between our reality and what we feel, rather than can prove, to be true. While there are the well-known thin places such as Iona, I think we each have the possibility to discover new ones. We can find our own thin places, our places where we can reach somewhere different – a moment with a divinity, or the past, or a closer communion with nature and the earth.

We all have our thin places, both in the world and in us. Threshold places, Winnicott's third space of play and the realms of imagination and belief, our creativity, the places where atmosphere is most intense, transformational.

Atmosphere is the crack in the wall, the 'place' within a place, the third place, a tender point, a dropped stich in a glittering hem; the place where we can slip through.

Thin places. They cannot be moved, conjured. Nevertheless, while walking consciously, I wondered if there was a recipe, if I could brew some kind of steps towards an alchemic potion to transform place. To reveal what was there.

The true quest of alchemy, its process, is not so much the creation of gold, but rather the extracting of spirit from matter. It presumes that matter has spirit – an intrinsic essence. If atmosphere were seen as some kind of spirit of place, then accessing it is an alchemical quest – a primal, poetic, 'science' experiment to understand the meaning of the world. What if, rather than literally crossing into realms, when we experience place differently, more intensely, it is because we are revealing the world as it actually is? Perhaps a place that feels thin actually is the everyday extraordinary. The alchemy of the natural world. A place where the world reveals its true self.

In his once fashionable but now largely forgotten book *The Savage and Beautiful Country* of 1966, psychologist Alan McGlashan talks of alchemy as spirit of matter. He also talks of the 'translucent nature of all things', an idea that 'transforms the sensible universe and invests all objects with a sharp intensity of being'. If we see the world in this way, everything is understood differently, with an intensity similar to moments like our first experiences of love and death; for McGlashan, it is the nearest our minds can reach into the meaning of meaning. But what exactly does he mean?

It is a strange term, the translucent nature of all things. I reread his pages and I am struck by the choice of the word 'translucent', not 'transparent': this is not so much about an unveiling as a filtering through, a partial reveal that echoes how so much in this world is not perfectly clear, not one thing. In fact, translucency is achieved precisely by it not being one thing but a combination of opposites: remembering and forgetting, thinking and feeling, temporal with the eternal, personal conscious perception with a remote archaic internal knowledge. If we see the world in purely scientific terms we lose a different kind of knowledge; this translucence refers to things being not just what they are materially but, in McGlashan's word, a kind of *membrane*, through which we can sense a different order of experience. That remote knowledge, intrinsic to the world, as well as what we consciously sense. A communication with the land can't just come from what we consciously think we know.

McGlashan mentions fairy tales and folk customs, admits that logically these can seem childish, ridiculous, but to see them in such a way is to miss the point. They are translucent too – a kind of 'earthly wisdom' that never turned its back on the importance of both thinking and feeling. Indeed, they represent a slow synthesis of the two, a form of collective memory, the fruits of which could not be invented by an individual. Folk is by nature a collaborative, evolving knowledge of the people. It is also so often localised that this knowledge becomes part of the place. (Interestingly, Winnicott was also intrigued by folk culture, regarding it as an inherited tradition belonging to the pool of humanity, something universal that speaks through generations even if we are not aware of it. He sees creative living as the interplay between originality and the acceptance of inherited tradition. Another combination of opposites, lying – as cultural, creative, experience does – in the third space, our thin place.) It is pointless to try to rationalise away this knowledge – it is from a paradoxical world of myth and dream. McGlashan does not view these inconsistencies as a problem but, from a psychologist's point of view, as signals to the instructed mind, *bidding it note the crossing of an invisible frontier.*

He quotes Goethe and how he saw 'that fig tree, this little snake, the cocoon on my window sill quietly awaiting its future – all these are momentous signals'. We as humans have a choice to experience the world differently, translucently rather than logically, to see these signals. Atmosphere is our ally here: it is in itself translucent, and if translucence bids us to cross a frontier, atmosphere can help us do this. If we want to reach the true nature of place, to experience it, then we need to leave behind our compulsion to explain it rationally. That is not to say there might not one day be a rational explanation; after all, science evolves all the time. It is more that to dismiss what we do not understand shuts off so much.

Until the eighteenth century, the split between physical and mental was not seen as so great. Indeed, in alchemy there was the concept of the *subtle body* – this could be the thing that turned the baser metal to gold, but most interestingly it could manifest itself equally in the physical and mental realm.

There is not necessarily something lacking in that which we cannot explain. There is a value to simply thinking, being curious, accepting the un-pin-down-able translucent nature of all things.

Moments, thresholds, translucent points of tenderness – like acupressure points on the earth's meridians, on a map otherwise recognisable to us, to others.

Home exists in both physical and mental realms, is a place and a concept. It is the subtle body of place. It grows deeper if it feels thin. It is both the most ordinary of our places, the most everyday; yet also the most meaningful, the deepest, where our depth of experience and feeling can open us up to that which seems magic.

The truest places on a tender map would be translucent. Rather than fixed points, they might subtly shift like poles, geographically fluid. In Chinese medicine, points on our meridians hold pulses. Tender earth heart and lung and blood beats. I picture them fading in and out, bursting brightly at certain moments, at others seeping back into their patch of land. Invisible ink, made visible or not, by transcribing our and the world's subtle body.

West Country Magic/
West Country Gothic

'In England what we call the West Country comprises roughly four counties, Somerset, Dorset, Devonshire and Cornwall, and to its natives no other part of the world can hold a candle to it. Cumberland and Westmoreland and Shropshire may boast mountains and lakes and grander scenery, the flat Fen country wider horizons and more flaming sunsets; Kent has its hops and cherries, Berkshire and Sussex their Downs, little Middlesex the honour of holding London; but the West Country is a kingdom to itself with an indescribable spirit that is all its own.'

Elizabeth Goudge

To find a starting point. Sit down. Think. I was raised by a landscape. It is hard to write about the atmosphere of somewhere you know deeply. It has embedded itself, making it intense yet less near the surface. Part of you. It is moving with you all the time. Tenderising limbs and muscles.

I know where I have to start.

Magic

It seems like an ordinary spring day. Though the glorious kind. Bright fresh sunshine, growth, new life rather than summer heat and the sense that everything is a little over, that late summer almost decay. It is morning and dew has scattered the ground, a liquid light-catcher, glittering, melting with my footsteps. I walk softly, but however softly, my prints are clumsy.

There is no one else here except for the animals. The trees appear to be listening to the feeling that is all around me. I cannot see this feeling, but it is there. It is unnerving to know it is there, yet the feeling in itself is both exciting and comforting. Like there is something special happening and I have stumbled in. It is not repelling me back out again. Even though I am a gatecrasher, an uninvited guest, it is not unwelcoming. It is pleasant, uplifting, to tiptoe through this feeling.

It feels as though the plants and the air, the ground, trees, insects, what I can see and what I can't see, are up to something. The sap is rising, seeds are rising as roots push down. The growth is not just of the living things we acknowledge but of the whole world. The landscape is brewing something, potions that create feelings, a spell, scattered as the seeds were last summer and transforming the atmosphere of this place around me.

The emotion of this place is hopeful and tentative. Yet it will not hold back, it will give everything, and because of this the land will change. The emotion of this place is gentle, yet vital – it is bursting with life, yet it is delicate. It feels new, though its origins are old. There is a sense of an ancient magic and stories – secrets everywhere. If I were to dig, I sense I would find first one then another, a treasure trove, a filigree horde of things that are there yet we rarely notice. They are not to be seen so much as listened to. Stories, incantations on the wind, written in miniature, carved like scrimshaw on to the tiniest piece of bark, held in a seed and released on its blooming.

It is a potent feeling of spring, though it does not only appear then. It usually reveals itself in sunshine. It is not an atmosphere of the grey.

Another time, as I climb the steep hill, the trees form a skeletal tunnel of knotted limbs and sunshine, caught and dropped, left scattered in patterns on the road, till the light is not something of the sky, but one of low down, an escapist light, rebellious and free and up to something. Like the light from windows, which has somehow been caught and, let out, is given new life. Light that has passed through, and learned something; a secret of the light world that we can never know. Other light does not always get the chance to join in.

The feeling is of that magic in that moment. Fleeting, yet old. Deeply old, like the memories of mountains and rivers when they were new and not grown yet. West Country Magic is everywhere in this feeling. It's the feeling as a child of going into an imaginary realm. Another world, hovering nearby, full of something. It is a mystery, yet one that is very present. A mystery communicated through the emotion of the place. It is an atmosphere of secrets made present, without revealing what they are. It is the feeling of imagination as a living thing.

Ta-dah! It is not that kind of magic. It is not the abracadabra of explosions, rabbits in hats and people being sawn in half (though these last two have a surreal darkness that it would perhaps understand). There is no dramatic reveal.

It simmers.

It is an enchantment.

It doesn't do tricks as such, though its effects can play tricks on you. It doesn't *do* magic.

It *is* magic.

There.

In that moment.

In that place.

I do not know why it is so specific to the West Country. I am not sure that matters. It is there nevertheless.

Silverydew

On that holiday in Devon, by the magical pool where I first consciously sensed the other world of atmosphere, another key thing happened. My beloved granny Hazel had given me her copy of a children's book by one of her favourite writers, Elizabeth Goudge. This was the summer I discovered *The Little White Horse*. I adored it then and still do; it has followed me through my life. But the reason I adored it so much wasn't because of what happened within its pages in terms of plot, but how the world she created, based on this Devon where I sat, was alive with a sense of real-world magic – it simmered under the surface of every description. She was a magician of atmosphere – someone who could see differently and reveal the hidden essence of places. Moonacre Manor and its valley, the village of Silverydew – their atmosphere crept inside me and I was hooked on this mixture of what I could discover about my real world, and its hidden undercurrents. As I sat in my bedroom reading *The Little White Horse* over and over, I couldn't shake the feeling that I was unlocking something – that this version of the West Country existed and that these pages were a way in. They were a key to finding my own West Country Magic.

I reread *The Little White Horse* recently, curious to see if this magic still held sway, if this children's book still felt like some kind of key. It did. But it wasn't so much in the magic of its pages – the description of Maria's new bedroom with its door too small for adults and clothes and treats that miraculously appear overnight, the fire that seems to light itself, the 'dog' Wrolf who we are pretty sure is a lion. These seemingly magical things were not where the magic was held; in fact Goudge dispels their magic: yes, Wrolf *is* a lion, we discover; yes, there is a servant small enough to go through the door at night and a window with access from a large tree, and her imaginary friend Robin is a real local boy she meets. Rather, the magic is in the place and how Goudge's descriptive tone, her atmosphere as a writer, makes me feel that they are still magical events, even when she has given me clear real-world explanations of them. For me, this is one of the essences of West Country Magic: that it makes what is clearly everyday seem not quite real, when all my grown-up logic tells me otherwise. It is not magical realism, it is that reality itself has a genuine magic, especially of feeling, without the need for impossible events. West Country Magic is a way of experiencing the world as an imaginative child does, which somehow stays with us when other ways of childhood thinking are lost. The place is key to that. It is alive with it, and this is what Goudge shows us.

Interestingly, while it is fairly clear that Moonacre Valley is in Devon, Goudge never explicitly says it is. We can presume as much, as Maria is driven through Exeter on the way there, and Goudge herself lived in Marlden in South Devon for many years. But while many of her books, such as *Gentian Hill*, clearly state they are Devon based, in *The Little White Horse* Goudge simply refers to the West Country. I do not think this is an accident. By locating it too specifically, that sense of another realm might be tied down too much for its spell to work freely, and more than that, I think she understood how the West Country functions as an imaginary space. It is not just a collection of counties, but an imaginative entity as a whole.

In 1947, just after *The Little White Horse* was published, Elizabeth Goudge published a short essay in *The Horn Book Magazine* titled 'West Country Magic'. It is a simple essay, a short summary of her feelings about the place as an introduction to readers who might not know it. Yet there are telling lines. When thinking back to the idea of West Country as imaginative entity, certain phrases jump out at me. Talking of the different counties, Goudge says, 'Yet though there may be many differences in appearance and habit, and strong clashes of opinion, there is an underlying unity in this kingdom that nothing can shake.' She goes on to wonder why, but comes to no concrete conclusion – perhaps it is a shared distant history or ancient strong faith – but what strikes me more is her choice of words, *underlying*, as if this unity is a strange current, similar to how atmosphere functions; and *kingdom* – as if these counties form a realm of their own, monarchless yet defined by a term we rarely use for the whole country even though it is by name a United Kingdom. The unity here is in something else; it is in a feeling.

A feeling is hard to rationalise, to explain away through history. So Goudge turns to the realm of the inexplicable – to magic – and, in describing her West Country Magic, to a subject that is embedded in atmosphere and equally inexplicable: folk history and fairy realms.

For her, 'there is a magic in all four counties'. Yet she feels most confident in attempting to describe that of Devon, where she lived at the time of writing this essay. She then goes on to try to depict this magic: 'It shines in the exquisite silvery light, it breathes in the soft air, it is in the woods and orchards and the old deep lanes, in the running of the streams and the singing of the birds. It is – except on wild frightening Dartmoor – a very gentle magic . . .' This is a beautiful description, but although I recognise the feeling – the light and air – is it really more silvery and soft? Literally no, but atmospherically yes . . . Goudge is conjuring the emotion rather than what Devon's light or air really is. She has gone multisensory in how the air *feels*. The landscape she describes is not an inanimate one, but alive. It is sentient – *it* breathes in the soft air, not us; it is place as protagonist – a magical entity we can only sense in atmosphere if we pass through its magic.

Most of my family are from Devon – Maddicott is a very old Devonian surname, held by generations of farmers; 'cottage in a meadow' is its literal translation. I grew up in Somerset and now live in the wilds of the west Wiltshire border, a sliver of countryside that is also very much the West Country to me. I moved away for many years, yet I always come back and I feel now, as an adult, I am more or less back to stay. Something draws me here. A feeling of place that I can't get rid of – it is too embedded in me. The wild west . . . the land of pixies and dragons and black dogs, wooded valleys and moors . . . ancient people. Yet wrapping all around the wildness is something that is peculiar to the West Country: its pervading cosiness. Its comfort, even when it feels weird or dark or strange. As Goudge said in her 'West Country Magic' essay, 'this gentle magic is essentially a fairy magic. I have always half believed in fairies, but since I have lived in Devon I have believed in them entirely.'

Fairyland, folktales, thin places, spiritual beliefs – these can be inherently creative in our places. They evolve and belong to all of us. A personal yet universal place of experience. It collaborates with us, we create our experience of it with it; part our inner psychic reality, part experience of the outside world, sensory, lived, ours alone in its subjectivity but there for all of us; a place where we can live creatively.

West Country Magic is so strong to me. It comes from the place I am rooted in, a space between separation and union, born in childhood. The West Country is my 'mother' place, not Motherland in the nationalistic abstract universal sense, but something personal and creative, my own space where I have a deep evolving relationship with the atmosphere that was sown in childhood. The landscape that raised me. I sense West Country Magic, I feel its thin places, as it is *my* thin place, is personal. Yet there is also a universal thin place, to stretch the term from Celtic Christianity, which lies in the folk traditions, the simmering undercurrents; the magic.

Atmosphere joins us to the land. It is a new creative thin place, the true thin place that is potentially around us all the time, just waiting for us to slip through.

Goudge herself was born in Wells in Somerset (her father being vice principal of the Theological College) and settled in Devon as an adult, after years of following her father's career to Ely and Oxford.

Throughout her time in the latter she had a longing to move back
west and I wonder if part of the magic she felt was this calling
fulfilled; that her life might not have been what she planned, but
swathed once more in West Country Magic, she at last could build
a home and write – it was in Devon where many of her best books
were written. Reviewers at the time often referred to Elizabeth's
creation of atmosphere, and I agree with this, yet her work seems
to go deeper. So many writers write 'atmospherically', but Goudge
makes more present, more knowable, those elusive feelings of
place. Listing descriptive quotes alone won't show this – it is in the
flow, just like a river, the feel of the whole of a book, recreating the
atmosphere. It is the feelings of place in the feeling of a book; the
book as a container of spirit, personality, emotion – to be opened,
read and thereby released.

She conjures West Country Magic, sometimes even when
writing of somewhere else, as if its atmosphere has become part of
her – seeps in as she sits at her desk, gazes out at her cottage garden,
thinks of the world around her. It is an atmospheric mist that has got
in her work, as it permeates places – spirit, of Devon, of stories, hers
and those much older . . .

The idea of a spirit of place (and I am consciously saying 'spirit'
rather than 'emotion' here) would not have been alien to Goudge.
She was a woman of profound faith, and we can see this faith
wreathing its way throughout her words on the page, whether in the
magical delight expressed in her descriptions or the more realistic
redemption of those in crisis – a gentle healing in a place that feels
right, a strong sense of home. There is not so much desire as gentle
presence here – a certainty of God and how this is at home with her
magic of place. A spirituality of the written word and her creative
process that her beloved fictional landscapes are part of. It is all
together in her faithful life. It is the glue.

Goudge herself had dark moments – loneliness and severe
depressive episodes. She lived with her invalid mother as her carer
well into middle age, not achieving what was expected of her at that
time, a time when not having a husband and children was stigmatised

in a way I fear it still is now. She had commercial success, she had her faith, but I find her depression interesting in a writer so inherently comforting. I wonder if this comfort is the atmosphere – the West Country Magic getting her through. Yet while a Christian, she is aware this spirit is not purely a Christian entity and there is no clash here. If we go back to pre-Christian beliefs in the UK, it was thought every living thing had a spirit – each individual tree, each animal, each place ... And as Christian beliefs grew, it was not seen as strange to weave those earlier beliefs into a sense of God – all living things were part of God's world, after all – and this was particularly strong in rural communities such as the West Country, where what we would consider folk customs today wove their way into Christian celebrations such as christenings and marriage ceremonies.

Folk knowledge, stories, traditions – they are key to understanding atmosphere, and particularly Goudge's own personal brand of magic. When I think of West Country Magic, I don't think of human history in terms of dramatic events – those key moments that historians thought worthy to note, the great battles or events, recorded due to their effect on political life or the interests of the upper classes. I think of the history that is so often forgotten, as people don't always see it as history – not even local history, though it is very much that – but myth, superstition. I think of the folk beliefs that weave their way through the subconscious of the counties, much as atmosphere does. I think of the stories that sprung up inspired sometimes by what a place feels like, as much as what happened there.

The Lost Coombe

A young woman, perhaps in her teens, is up on the hills, staring out. Heather, gorse and nearby twisting trees. Ponies and sheep graze. The land is the opposite of flat. Ditches sink down as mounds rise up, as if hinting at life underneath.

She walks as the wind whips her hair into dancing ribbons of hay. With her hand, she adjusts the crown she has woven from flowers. There is no one around to laugh at her for doing this, for weaving a crown as a child might. It seems right that the flowers are used in this way.

She walks and the landscape shifts. There is a steep valley and the flowers here are thicker, the grass more lush. Lush, that quintessentially West Country word, yet the abundance is delicate. Light. Not heavy with too much growth, with a tropical urge. The leaves are lace-like and throw shadows.

Though she has a crown she feels more like she is wearing wings made of spring – supple new branches, still green, petals fluttering like feathers, the first hint of summer leaves, attached like a rucksack, a parachute that could help her take off with the right jump. A run-up.

The sun is bright yet silvery, not yellow. She sees a cottage at the foot of the valley, a coombe, and a stream running near. She runs too. Echoes its chatting flow with skips. Her feet are mostly on the ground, but she feels as if she is flying, just a little. That if she wills it, a jump will last just too long to be a simple case of her body and its normal ways.

As a child she used to jump off the garden wall and will herself to fly. She hovered once, she was sure, though nobody else believed it.

She reaches the bottom of the coombe. The cottage sits with its thatched-roof hat and eye windows that glint smiles, and a smothering of roses and clematis. There is honeysuckle wreathed through the hedge and flowers burst like thoughts from the ground around it. They are bright and laughing. Pretty, not beautiful, but worth no less for that. Prettiness is right here. Beauty is too heavy to hold all this dancing light.

The cottage is full of life, but empty of humans. There is no one around, yet bees and butterflies drench the air – hum its song. She walks around the edge but does not go in. It should be left like this. Some things should remain undisturbed.

She continues and pauses as she finds the perfect stick. Long, like a wizard's staff, and decorated with seed-heads like starbursts or lignified snow.

She turns it gently, then holds it high. Skips on. Runs, with her crown and invisible wings and her wizard's staff. Forgets the stress of school and boys and that other world. They are gone with the help of this place. With the powers she hardly knew she was asking for.

She is all new here. She is all her.

She has come home to West Country Magic.

Folktales are site-specific, though there is some universality in terms of which creatures appear. Fairies, black dogs, dragons, giants, mermaids . . . but still each creature is unique to the place where the story happens, often unique to a small village or patch of ground. The folklore of the South West is no different. In Cornwall, it is the giants and mermaids that dominate – they define certain villages, whether the sad love story of the mermaid of Zennor in the far west or the other famous mermaid whose anger caused the formation of the treacherous sandbanks of the Doom Bar round Padstow on the north coast. It can be as specific as a building – the church at Towednack, again in the far west of Cornwall, has a strangely truncated tower due to 'the evil one' always bashing down the day's work at night. These stories are part of the formation of both land and human landscape, pre- and post-Christian world – they are all interconnected. Devon is rife with fairies and pixies, and I have stumbled across many dragons in Somerset. There are tales of lost and doomed love, love across the classes, murder and intrigue, so often sung about in folksongs. Yet beyond these universal themes there is a locality – a *feeling* of place unique to each folktale.

Part of the universality of tales can be explained by how they were transmitted before printing presses and general literacy. Wandering minstrels travelled from village to village singing these tales, these ballads, these narrative poems (the old word for poem after all is song) and in each location we can presume local flavour was added. Then the songs were remembered and retold with their own local embellishments, their personal experiences of place woven in. They would evolve but their core might remain the same. And the creatures – they would have been there as explanation, be it origin myth or real belief about unexplained goings on. And they would have all been connected to the living spirit of place. In the days when each tree held a spirit, when the land was seen as alive and this did not clash with newer Christian beliefs, sacred oaks were still danced around, the Christian devil made its way into darker mythical tales and churches became places of story, as did fairy hills, abandoned forts, trees and rivers and deep remote pools and the ever mystical sea.

I believe these places don't just function as the settings for stories, or rather the stories don't just use the places as locations, but tell us something more. They tell us about the inherent feeling of that place, and also often occur in places where something deeper is seen to be going on. They function like thresholds – containers for spirit, locations where the veil between this world and another, fairy or spiritual, external or internal, is thinner. They *are* atmospheres, just not how we usually think of these, in terms of physical sensory experience. They are more ancient; they are both of physical place and the product of hundreds of years of collective, localised, human minds. They are still fluid, but they have an essential quality too, anchoring them as their atmosphere, place and stories evolve. There's a wonderful passage in Elizabeth Goudge's Somerset-based novel *A City of Bells* where she writes:

> Surely that story she had imagined was a real thing? . . . You could not see it with your bodily eyes, that was all . . . Henrietta realised how the invisible world must be saturated with the stories that men tell both in their minds and by their lives. They must be everywhere, these stories, twisting together, penetrating existence like air breathed into lungs . . .

Folktales and atmosphere are linked in this uniquely strange way. Stories this old and specific yet evolving are alive, are part of a place as much as its landscape – they are intangible and contributory to the atmosphere of place; they communicate with our non-bodily eyes, the inner eye, the subconscious (it is no coincidence psychoanalysis is fascinated by fairy tales); they penetrate us like the air we inhale, that sensory experience of touch which reaches deep inside our bodies with our breath.

Elizabeth Goudge was interested in the idea of other realms, thinly veiled and close by. It is likely that, with her theological background, she knew of the Celtic Christian thin places. We know that she read and loved Alan McGlashan's work on the translucency of things and that she herself as a child felt there were 'hidden things' in the world all around her. McGlashan wrote that, for us as adults, the core of a spiritual quest is to find the secret threshold where the world of the sense and the world of the psyche meet, a threshold that we lose as we grow up. If we can find this threshold then place opens in a deeper way; our experience of the world is enriched and in the magic flows. And the folklore of places holds that flow. An older, truer knowledge. Goudge's books are full of places that feel like those in folklore – the borderlands between the real world and fairy realms that are not separate to, but part of our world. The real world in *The Little White Horse* feels like one giant threshold, hinting that the visible and invisible worlds are one.

For hundreds of years in folk culture, it was widely believed that the fairy realm was real, that it was a realm within our realm which we could be stolen into, likely never to return. It was a real presence and there were certain locations where it was easier to cross over to it than others: the thin places of wells, springs, certain hills and trees, for example (the same sorts of place that often pop up in Goudge's work). But 'learned' culture, rational culture, dismissed these beliefs as ignorant superstition. Then, in the Victorian age, with a growing (albeit sentimentalised) interest in fairies and the publication of volumes of fairy tales from collectors (*Grimm's Fairy Tales* was published in English in 1812), there were signs that this was changing. In 1858, George MacDonald published his fairy fantasy stories, as the traditional tales were joined by popular new works of the imagination. The hold of fairies on the imagination continued into the first part of the twentieth century with Arthur Rackham's illustrated fairy books, and the famous fraud of the Cottingley fairy photographs, taken by two young girls in 1917 and widely believed to be genuine at the time.

All this marked a new interest in the idea of other realms – a curiosity about a non-rational side to the world – which grew in tandem with a burgeoning fascination in folk culture and stories. Collectors travelled the land, gathering folk songs and tales from country people, before, they feared, this knowledge died out. In 1882, the first of ten volumes of what have become known as the Child Ballads was published as *The English and Scottish Popular Ballads*, collected by Francis James Child. Many of these tales include mentions of fairy lovers, such as the famous shape-shifting Tam Lin, and people being stolen into fairy realms. There are also elfin knights and a multitude of ghosts – beings that should be in other realms were very present in this world.

This tradition continued with people such as Cecil Sharp, who in 1903 began collecting hundreds of traditional songs and stories. Interestingly, while he collected them not only in the UK but in fifteen countries around the world, it is the songs from Somerset that were the most significant to him, and which he used most in his teaching. Folk atmosphere and magic seem more natural in the West Country, somehow – an intrinsic part of the land. It could intoxicate the most rational and male of collectors.

The Victorian era and early twentieth century were also a time when Arthurian legends were being revived and reimagined creatively, bringing magic and fairies into a strange kind of history. This history was part myth and part real – impossible to prove, academically, whether Arthur and his knights existed or not, or what part of the stories were true. Many believed them to be real – and again, the West Country and its atmosphere, its believability as a setting for magic or the maybe-real, was key. Camelot . . . these places of imagination haunt my real childhood of road signs and ubiquitous hippies: when you approach Glastonbury it says 'Welcome to the Isle of Avalon'.

Up in the Quantock Hills of Somerset, behind my old office at

Halsway Manor National Centre for Folk Arts, stories wreathe the air. There's an Iron Age hill fort where you can hear the ghosts of Viking parties, and where the Other realm might be close. There are pixie mounds and holy wells. There are other rather startlingly named places: Dead Woman's Ditch. There are two well-known beasts: the wonderfully named dragon, the Gurt Worm of Shervage Wood, and a particularly interesting ghostly black dog. Atmospherically, these stories are transformed when you know the place they are set, and the places themselves have an extra layer of atmosphere when you know the stories that live there.

The top of the hills is heathland; come summer, this is bright with purple and gold – the regal colours of heather and gorse. Ponies graze there – not wild like on the moors, but semi-wild, this being ancient common ground. It is from this heathland that the views are most dramatic: you can see across to Wales, and at certain points both Exmoor and Dartmoor are within the eye's grasp. But atmospherically it is a different part of this landscape that intrigues me. More intimate and much more confusing.

The Quantock Hills are largely smothered with the strangest twisting of trees, but the first time I found this particular wood was by accident. I took a side road out of curiosity, and before I knew it I was climbing through a tree tunnel of extraordinarily shaped dappled light. It was broken up like jewels. Kaleidoscope fractals. As my car climbed, each side of the road appeared to be woven with branches that wriggled. The woods seemed one entity enmeshed, like tangled wires. The canopy was low, so I felt I was inside some kind of giant outdoor room with a ceiling. The trees weren't tall, but I could sense their age – there was something beautiful yet almost disturbingly ancient in the atmosphere. I had never been anywhere like it – magic seemed to hum in the air. My friend thought the trees were witchy, that there had to be a darker magic going on, and I do admit I have nicknamed them the witchy woods when I am explaining where I mean to locals – and they get it instantly – but just like saying all witchcraft is dark, to pigeonhole these woods as a dark place because they are strange and, well, woods, is lazy. Theirs is a strange magic for sure, but I find it gentle – they are quintessentially West Country Magic in atmosphere.

Dark and twisting yet welcoming, old yet deeply alive, full of stories yet moving with creatures – birds and giant red stags. Somehow these sessile oaks feel barer than others, even in full leaf, yet the ground is awash with whortleberries, as if to offer a welcome snack to visitors. I rarely see walkers, unlike up on the heathland, yet it wouldn't surprise me if an old lady pottered out with a basket, foraging through the trees, some slightly unusual pet, tamed wildlife, in tow.

So it seems logical to me that the mythical creatures of the Quantocks are not typical, personality-wise. The Gurt Worm is a dragon, yes, and one that locals are terrified of. The story had villagers down in Crowcombe avoiding the woods for years, the beast having supposedly killed a number of ponies and sheep and later people. The Gurt Worm controls an atmosphere in Shervage Wood, and these woods do feel different as you enter. There is a threshold you simply don't cross, as then you are in his realm. Yet his crimes are hearsay, strangely elusive, and rather than massacring the local villagers, he went for animals first, just looking for food rather than violence.

Fearful they will never be able to harvest the delicious whortleberries growing in the woods to bake in their pies, the locals trick a woodcutter from another village into going up; but it isn't a violent battle that ensues, only a slightly sad and strange encounter. The woodcutter sits down on a log to eat his lunch, not realising that this log is actually the Gurt Worm himself. (It's the Worm's favourite way to disguise himself, another strangely cosy detail about such a fearsome creature – today, children are still told to be wary of sitting on logs in the area.) Then, when the log stirs, the woodcutter chops the dragon in half.

In one modern retelling, the Gurt Worm befriends a blind old lady who accidentally wanders past. She begins to visit daily for chats and bakes him whortleberry pie. A gentle, homely detail that might not exist if he were from a different region.

As is the nature of folktales, there are different versions of the story – some more violent and negative, others more sorrowful, but many of them have in common the idea that the two halves of the dragon fell apart and ran in different directions, his demise uncertain. This is almost a comic image – cosy not scary, yet deeply sad. The dragon does not fight back, and I imagine his blood spilling over the Quantock Hills, his blood sacrifice acting as a kind of protection spell. The Quantock Hills are the smallest and first designated area of outstanding natural beauty (AONB) in England. I like to think the Gurt Worm's protection played a little part in this.

The local black dog is also unusual. Black dogs feature widely in folklore and they are nearly always sinister, dangerous creatures – with the exception of the black dog of the Quantocks, the only beneficent black dog I can find. He appears in various stories: in one, he acts as a guide into the realm of the dead (black dogs often frequent this invisible threshold), but his main claim to fame is that he protects children lost on the hills and guides them home. It doesn't seem unusual that it would be here that a black dog is kind, just as it does not surprise me that the Gurt Worm is eccentric and not especially fierce. In terms of tales functioning as imaginative site-specific atmospheres, this makes sense.

These tales are pure West Country Magic. For all the darkness, woods and dragon slaying and beasts, they are ethereal and kind – a little sad, and there is a frisson of danger in any involving fairies, yet none of them make me fearful as some folktales would. They do not bar us from their places – they are just in the air. Even if the tales themselves are lost, I don't think we'd lose their contribution to the atmosphere. The barrier between our realm and theirs, up on the hills, is thin.

The Magic of Bluebells – Postlebury Wood

Of all the plants, they seem to be gentle yet the most powerful in terms of atmosphere, and of all the places where I feel the translucency of things, places that are thin for me, bluebell woods are first among them. All changes in season create a transformation, often beautiful, but somehow most places seem to hold their atmosphere through these changes. Weather, mood – all can alter a feeling. But bluebells create realms – are somehow magic – bring forth a thin place that at other times of year is not there.

Looking at them, walking through my favourite bluebell wood, I find them difficult to describe. The clichés fall woefully short; are a deception. *Not quite blue – as if sapphires bred amethysts and stories. They are watery – flowing – strange currents more than waves – they pull me in.* To enter a bluebell wood in spring is to cross into a transient domain; a place you have to surrender your mood to. The bluebells have control in rain and sun. *I walk and hold my hands out – my fingers are dry yet the feelings of this place lap through them, liquid yet dry. I am greedy for the feeling it can give me. Open-mouthed I eat the air – gulp it down with sunbeams that fall gold – the translucent, the subtle body . . .*

I remember my granny talking to me about bluebell woods. How they were the most glorious places but to approach them with caution. From her Devon childhood she knew that this was where fairies might steal you away; where if you heard music you should keep clear, because – like the site of a pop-up fairy fair, which you would have little chance of escaping in normal circumstances, yet even more dangerous – if you joined the fairy dance in bluebell woods, then once the dance ended you were gone from this world forever. Bluebell woods were a temporary gateway into the realm of magic and folklore.

The path is dry now, the mud of recent months piled and solidified like fossils of wellies and paw prints. It almost crunches. But the ground either side is moist and glowing. Flicks of green flames herald their bells, which cradle the trees high above them.

I sense creatures though I can't see them.

I sense here.

My granny's stories didn't come from her imagination, but a long history of bluebell lore. There is a strong connection between bluebells and fairies, and bluebell woods were seen as enchanted places – thin places. But it was not just that they were enchanted as a whole, luring you into the fairy realm – there was also a power in the flowers themselves. The bell of their name is not only because they look bell-shaped, but that they were thought to ring, and when they did so, they would call the fairies to a gathering. However, if a human ever heard the flower bells ringing then this was more of a death knell – that person would soon die, sometimes after the visit of a fairy. I am loath to write 'evil fairy' here, as I think their morality is not so black and white. They leave you alone if you do not interfere with them, but if you break their rules or happen upon something of theirs that you shouldn't, then it will end badly. Perhaps this is where part of the frisson of bluebell woods atmosphere comes from – the sense that you might be trespassing on something too beautiful and strange to be part of the permitted human world.

As a child I wanted to dance in their dresses. I had a light on my bedroom wall in the shape of their petals. Nothing else would do when I saw it. I wanted to hold any moment of these flowers I could.

The woods know all this but are indifferent to all but their blooming in the present. The stable fluttering that rings silent.

Folklore often plays with, or makes sense of, deeply seated human fears, and bluebell woods are no exception here – they are a place of enchantment but also primal danger: if a child picks a bluebell in the woods, it was said they would never be seen again. Of course, this could have started as a warning tale, to stop children wandering off or picking flowers that are poisonous, as bluebells are, but given that bluebells only exist for a few weeks a year when woods represent a yearlong hazard for getting lost, it seems odd that they would be the flower of choice for this warning. There is an acknowledgement of the enchantment here, I think; of how seductive the atmosphere of bluebell woods is, as if, once experienced, it is tempting never to come back.

Distant rumble as the wind comes like waves. En masse like the cliché of sea, yet wrong – each plant is discernible, stands alone – a personality – different number of bells and level of droop. The breeze blows and the higher branches flutter shadows, staining some bells a little darker.

It is not sinister, but the strangeness is undeniably there.

West Country Magic.

There are a couple of other tales, which I instinctively feel are later – wear a necklace of bluebells and you will be forced to tell the truth, though of course by that point you might be dead or have vanished. There could be a link here to how fairies notoriously cannot lie. And it's not just their fairy associations, either – in folklore, any flower that hangs its head is bad luck, including snowdrops. Even the daffodil could consequently be ill-omened. The only time it seems it was OK to pick bluebells is when they were part of a folk custom, such as the spring flowers in seasonal festivities. Leftover posies from parades were traditionally placed as offerings for a good harvest in lieu of what would have originally been blood (perhaps human in ancient times) scattered across the fields. But these rituals for good crops could also be seen as the folk remnants of the plants' more practical uses – sticky bluebell sap being an excellent glue, including for book binding, where its poison gave it the added benefit of keeping away book-eating insects; their use by herbalists to cure nightmares (themselves a symptom of fairy enchantment); the starch from their bulbs stiffening the ruffs of Elizabethan England.

Sounds morph stillness. Bumble bees. Distant cars. A shotgun breaking birdsong. The wind again. The scent wafts on a whim . . .

Yet for all this dark folklore, when we get to the nineteenth century, when floriography (also known as 'the language of flowers') became popular, bluebells were given a bit of a makeover and said to symbolise constancy, humility and gratitude. I cannot think of a less appropriate list of supposed meanings. Far from constant, bluebells are temporary, and, as we have seen, bluebell woods are notoriously fickle places in folklore; that abundance and power of atmosphere could never be seen as humble – they are greedy for beauty. And gratitude? Well, perhaps this is a nod to placating older folk powers – be grateful you're alive and not stolen.

Soft words.
Soothing yet possibly fickle.
Gentle.
Both new and old.

The pattern of the bells is more pointillist than a 'wash'.

As far as supposed meanings go, I need to know none of that. Their atmosphere is not affected by it, their magic, their ability to transform, to create a new place within a place. Bluebells grow all around the country, but for me, their strange, dark, ancient comfort – the way they are my thin places – is quintessentially West Country Magic.

As I turn and walk back the other realm seems near.

And to try to describe this? How can we capture a place where the atmosphere is part of its being? Where it is so intrinsic to the experience of place that, without it, images fall flat? Photos capture nothing of the feeling – they're quite pretty, but the atmosphere is lost. Maybe the answer is we don't. That to try to 'capture' a bluebell wood is to go against its magical nature. That some places we just have to be in. Some atmospheres are simply meant to be experienced, in a place, in a certain moment in time. To try to capture West Country Magic in its springtime glory of a bluebell wood is a fool's errand – it misses the point.

How to Enter an Imaginary Realm: West Penwith, Cornwall

As the A30 comes towards its end, past St Michael's Mount – a vision to be reached, hovering in the sea, by causeway, sea tractor – nearby lies Marazion; the zs have been creeping in, exoticising place names away from anywhere else in England. Deep Cornwall here. On and into Penzance – left along the seafront till the promenade turns to fishing boats. On to Mousehole – Mowzle, don't you know – then a right to follow the edge of this world, and you are there.

The light is more ethereal, thin gold, fresh and glimmering. Few trees at first. Old fields. Then on towards Lamorna, and a sudden dip of gentle valley feels like where flower fairies should dwell. You have a choice now: whether to detour down the twisting lane to the sea, past the trees I always like to think of as the lost Ent wives from *Lord of the Rings* – with the atmosphere here, the idea that they are 'normal' trees seems impossible; the whole landscape is alive with something . . .

When I was little there was an advert on the telly for the flower fairy dolls by Hornby, which were briefly popular in the eighties. Unlike the alien representation of womanhood that was Barbie, these dolls were delicate yet resembled normal girls. I remember how their knees creased when I bent them. Other than their outfits and detachable wings, the only thing to suggest they were 'other' was their pointed ears. In the advert, they travelled to the bottom of a garden where all their accessories – the longed-for secret waterfall and a carriage, if I recall – were set up. But to child me, this wasn't just a garden with toys I liked on screen – it was a magical realm; the atmosphere through the telly somehow showed that. And still to this day, as I drive down the dip of the road into Lamorna valley, where the left-hand turn takes you down to the beach past the Ent wives, or continuing on takes you past cottages nestled in like creatures of another time, I feel like this is a shortcut back to that childhood realm of magic – the place where the flower fairies lived, the atmosphere which somehow that advert embedded in my head.

Onwards, twisting up and down round hidden corners to a burst of high-up air and Sennen, Porthcurno – surfers and hidden cables – a communications base deep in caves, burrowing across the Atlantic . . . I visited them once, played on old equipment deep inside the earth where nearby waves crashed in perfect isolation.

The road feels high here. Closer to sky and no trees to hide the rocks and old houses – the strangely desolate bungalows forced to stay on way past the time when they were a good idea. They look out to sea and the sky watches them and their strange melancholia – their blight of grey and lack of age in a place so ancient that giants fought for it, mermaids sing of it still.

Onwards and St Just arrives. The video store still existed when I was last there, though no one these days has a video player. The cafe food is lovely, with no customers. The empty hotel, yet a soft sense of the edge of the world. It is hard to go further than here. There is an old chapel that stands like a benevolent creature, enormous windows staring out and making me wistful for one of the many different lives I could have. Living here in this empty, small town on the edge of the world – it is not idyllic enough for tourists. Even Penzance sneers in rivalry. This is a kind place. I can feel it in a warm pale grey that wreathes the sun and makes me think of distances.

After this is where the true wildness starts. The coast road, now besmirched by TV tourists hunting for Poldark and missing the point – that this is a place which only reveals itself in emptiness. One at a time – that is how it likes to be visited. The old mine ruins clinging on to cliffs – one shouldn't dare to touch – such beauty.

Villages are tucked in the crook of its elbow – down lanes to the right like veins with magical endings – Towednack, where the church tower is short as the devil kept knocking it down. He is real there. I have the chipped tooth to prove it from a childhood holiday where he possessed my brother to push a tyre swing into my face. I loved that holiday . . .

The place names drift for miles around – Nancherrow, Lamorna, St Buryan, Porthcurno, Porthgwarra, Sennen, Pendeen . . . The mines watch as the skin of this tip of the country falters with rocks and walls made of boulders. Ancient barns have bones of boulders like pebbles bewitched to grow large on such cool salted air.

Zennor waits gently for me. Home of artists on the edge in search of the perfect light. The mermaid carved in the church – captured, solid, yet but a hologram of her true self, who carves the waves for lost love. The creatures are real round here. No myths and legends. Giants and mermaids – of the old stone and the treacherous, welcoming sea.

It won't be long now till it ends. Till the road twists towards St Ives and its ruin of tourists and second homes and art as commodity that once was so pure in search of light – curved forms and sky views.

This land is a living thing of stories. To forget them is a loss we cannot hope to mend.

Gothic

The West Country is like a soft coating of moss, lichen, something living and growing that attached to me so long ago in a gentle way that it's easy not to notice the darker undertones. I move through it and it moves with me, on my surface but gently nibbling through, soft-anchored, breathing and precious.

Underlying all the counties of the West Country is an undercurrent – a certain darkness that is not scary or upsetting – it is an invisible trembling that is dark yet comforting.

Yet it is not West Country Magic.

West Country Gothic is hard to explain. Made up of and veiled by contradictions and other atmospheres, it has some of the age of West Country Magic, but the lightness is gone – the dancing spritely character is replaced with something deeper down and subtle. Cosy yet dark. Gentle yet wild. Historically important, but provincial in the eyes of many. Magic yet practical – mystical yet down to earth. Avalon, the ancient kingdom of Wessex ... Farms and orchards, sunny pub gardens. The reality of day-to-day life alongside the imaginary realm of fiction and holidays. Literary, historical – inspiration for poets and dreamers, yet yokels abound, the accent is laughed at – we are dim and born to be made fun of – cider, cheese, straw-chewing slow pace of life.

The West Country is dark, albeit in a nice way. It is not what you might think it is from seaside holidays. It is not what you might think it is from how it is portrayed in popular culture. These two things are the great veil that tricks you into not noticing the darkness, but it is there. It is the old sad folksongs, not the magical beasts, that are West Country Gothic.

It is friendly and gentle, but there is a hidden darkness. There is a Nick Cave song called 'West Country Girl', in which he refers to the birds singing bass – that makes perfect sense to me. The birds know there is something else going on. However, it is the woman who is the subject of this song that captures West Country Gothic the most for me.

Love Letter to White Chalk

Songs of chalk hills, wandering, love lost in the air. The landscape rises as I listen. Listen to the hills and their love, lost, chalk-stretching miles, free, free, free, yet somehow alone. I walk up chalk hills and gaze across the landscape for those toffee miles, elastic and sticky, air moving, silence singing, sounds normally hidden made real by a woman whose music has grown as I have.

Fourteen years old and stuck in the crush, I cracked a rib when I first saw PJ Harvey. She was touring her first album *Dry*, somewhere in Bristol. But there is an album that came out in 2007, and that one, whether intending to or not, sung my West Country out into my bedroom. When I try to explain what I really mean by West Country Gothic, how it is not gothic like the novels say, with ruins and vampires and jagged rocks, how it is definitely not folk horror, but a gentle simmering of darkness, a melancholic gothic, soft and seeping in, then the best I can do is tell people to listen to *White Chalk*.

'Dear Darkness', as the second song is called ... This record is a form of emotional map for me – the atmosphere made real as her emotions of place rise and are interlaced with mine and those that are much older. It is an aural landscape – an atmosphere not created by music, but revealed by it.

West Country Gothic. It moves not rests in waiting – deep trembles – darkness dear – grow softly – thrown gentle moss – a covering – a cough of dandelion seeds, paused, then falling fairies slowly. The trees should be waving but this is not wind; they are still with the appearance of moving. The air is filling like a glass from the bottom up. The invisible layer is coating everything, holding what it wants in place, not changing but illuminating – all the stories that are hidden here. They are old stories and they only know what they tell of. We would need to cross through to the other world that hovers, invisible yet real. I love you all around me. You break my heart every day with old chalk hills and forests that embrace my aching limbs. I am in love with a place that sometimes destroys me – rots away my ability to travel the world for fear of being without it. This is not home as we know it – not home as a house or a place we live, but home as a part of us that we struggle to make sense of ourselves without. Both comfort and discomfort.

I think of my places and their memories and I am pinned down by something I would not be without. The depth is unlike anywhere else. The freedom is a transcendence on the hills, the price for which is my freedom.

White Chalk is a quiet album, but the darkness is deep and gentle and as powerful as a scream. It feels like a love letter to the West Country. PJ Harvey is a West Country girl. Her accent makes me smile – soft and thoughtful and holding a secret strength that is so often overlooked. It is a lovely accent, musical, it whispers and holds stories.

I find this album comforting. It broke my heart in 2007 in a way that was good. My human heart was broken with love, yet *White Chalk* healed it with another kind of breaking that set free a sort of liquid landscape that held me, brought me home after the devastation of Nashville and Armenia and Georgia – travels where all had gone wrong, and in the aftermath I was left alone and ill, back in the West Country.

I walked my own white chalk hills, the ground sticky and full of childhood memories. I closed my eyes and I was lost high up, trying to fly kites, aware of the white horse carved nearby, unaware of future heartbreak, but intensely aware of this landscape and how it drifted south into Dorset, the sea, collecting fossils; it was ancient and strange and there was power I didn't understand and I couldn't let it go. These chalk hills held me and held me back – wouldn't let me go. But I loved them, I love them, and the sea and the forests and mostly just the feeling, the atmosphere of this darkness of my West Country – one that is close to its magic but the darkness, the dear gentle darkness – is something else – is my West Country Gothic that I can't lose, that I can't shake or let go of, even if things go terribly wrong.

It is there for me like the saddest of old folk songs – the musical tradition that PJ Harvey is much closer to than modern bands that claim to be folk. If I listen to Shirley Collins, my folk music heroine, then *White Chalk* is the closest modern inheritor of the gentle darkness and heartbreak that is sung out and, through the stories, mourned and healed in the landscape. It is of the land. It understands the feeling; it is beautiful and devastating and I want more of it. I can picture a young girl wandering the hills and finding these songs in the air and singing them back out and no matter what is going on, their darkness holds her, floats across her shoulders. It might bring tears but they are a release. And then as she looks across and sees the strange twisting trees, the patch of ancient woodland, the squirrel looking quizzically, the deep holloway, the ditches and brambles and all that should be dark in the wrong way – the darkness is of a different kind. It is a darkness that is a kind of light, not light that shines but the remnants of the consuming of light; that is a kind of freedom; that is sentient and understands and has seen it all before.

West Country Gothic is layers and layers of years, hundreds of years, of sadness. The landscape absorbs it and keeps it safe so that it is heard. You could easily miss it. It is less present in the parts of the

West Country where holidays are common, so it is not particularly affected by that. It is more felt in Somerset and Dorset and the Wiltshire border, bits of deep Devon. The Exe valley I so love has both magic and gothic, but my chalk hills near my house and the twisting forests have it most of all. It looks for the right moment and then is there. It is waiting. The Groke in the Moomin stories is a bit West Country Gothic – seems sinister to some but she is a poignant figure, old and furry and a little strange looking; people do not understand that she just wants to take some light. She is a presence which, if you got to know her, is a little dark and strange but comforting. Character as atmosphere – she creeps in and changes things, makes them just a little colder and darker, but she means well, others just don't realise it. Just like sad songs heal sadness more than cheerful ones. Just like *White Chalk* heals me. West Country Gothic is there for those who discover it – who feel differently – who notice. It is one of the truest West Country atmospheres and as far removed from the clichés of cider and Wurzels records as you could possibly get, yet cider and The Wurzels still make sense in its context. They are still trying to draw on something old in the air.

There are so many places with dark names in the West Country. There is a Dead Woman's Field just down the road from where I live and the aforementioned Dead Woman's Ditch. Their stories are forgotten. Nearly always women. But they are not dark places, just places where maybe something happened and in their dark naming there is a comfort. They are lost but not lost – the landscape is holding them. They have become West Country Gothic – they have added a layer, a layer that blends with the darker folk songs and tales, and like a graveyard of strange hope, lies like an invisible mist on the landscape, brushing our cheeks, stroking our hair and letting the atmosphere whispers in. There is a knowledge that there are dark stories, sadness in a place of beauty and freedom and light. West Country Gothic is more acute in sunshine than in rain – grey deadens it. The accident of falling light highlights it – it rests in the dappled pattern of sunlight through trees, through shadows, the red kites sailing high above me, the quivering of skylark wings and the sharp nip of biting insects in early summer.

It is not that *White Chalk* explicitly mentions this, but rather that the songs hold this atmosphere. I sense a strange code – anyone could feel the atmosphere – but for those who know the places these songs are embedded in, there is a correspondence with the landscape that is alive and true. It feels like PJ Harvey is talking to the landscape – songs sometimes have this advantage, as they are usually written in the second person which is rare in literature; but even when talking to a lover, it is as if PJ Harvey is talking to the land – the place and what happened there are so interwoven these cannot be pulled apart. It is perhaps akin to poetry, but this is not poetry of the conventional sort – the lyrics on their own would not work and the connection feels more primal, less conscious; there is no sense of 'and now I am writing a nature poem about the West Country'. It goes deeper than that, and one reason might be the depth there feels in the correspondence – how it is active, not detached or observational, but involved with a landscape whose deep nature is alive, has been brought up to the surface from where it often hides.

A letter acknowledges a recipient, even if it may never be read. It is an active communication rather than a recording. Letters have the power of diaries: they retain the personal, yet open it up to another. They reveal something, and in doing so, invite the recipient to reveal something back. They are a literary microcosm – the world of writer and reader – created on a page. When a letter becomes music, then this becomes more. When we listen we enter this microcosm. And when the subject of the letter is a place, then we enter a hidden side of this place too.

It is a song map of emotion.

She softly sings.

When a place is part of you, its atmosphere can be both more powerful and yet less immediate; it is familiar to you, it is so intrinsic to how you feel as you go about your daily life, that isolating it, explaining it to an 'outsider' can be hard. We don't own places, but sometimes I think they own us – that when we leave, when we discover new atmospheres and places we may even prefer, the atmosphere of where we are from will always be there, deep down, held inside us gently pulsing, influencing everywhere we feel.

The West Country is that place for me.

This landscape raised me.

It is a place of many atmospheres, thousands of puzzle pieces making up this vast swathe of the UK. It is full and complex. I could draw an emotional map to hold what has happened in my life, from childhood joy to adult trauma, and this emotional map would be full of the atmospheres rather than the events. That is how I could express these feelings and their places. Emotion isn't static – it is a form of travel.

The Ancient Forest of Selwood

I hold a map of tenderness inside me, and on my body as it moves, of the West Country. A movement of emotion, activated in place, lines thrilling down veins as I walk. I also hold a very ordinary map. For all the times I have drawn or invented imaginary maps, for all the books I own of wonderful artist maps, for all my travels, the map that holds the most emotion for me is my old, very battered, OS Explorer map: Shepton Mallet & Mendip Hills East, number 142. Number

142 holds my forest, the vast swathes of trees. When I'm stressed or bored or want to escape, I can spend hours poring over it, tracing the green marks of footpaths I've walked, and the unofficial, not-green tracks and lines I have wandered. I look and plan and think where I could go next, how I could get from there to there, what season would be best for experiencing the most foxgloves, bluebells, creatures, wild winds – I love the woods as much in winter when the views are clearer than in their summer tunnels of green. It is not a map of emotion in terms of a grand narrative of life events, but one of emotion in that it maps quite literally the place that speaks to me most atmospherically, whose atmosphere I seek out, the atmosphere that makes all right with the world. It fascinates me that there is a paper record at all – that somewhere which feels so extraordinary is possible to lay out like this. It is a strange souvenir of my experiences.

This area of the West Country – the area that holds both magic and gothic and so much more – was once upon a time the ancient Royal Forest of Selwood. It covered vast swathes of ground, stretched for miles; the small Dorset town of Gillingham announces it on its welcome signpost, slightly surreal when driving through modern housing estates and roundabouts. Unlike the New Forest, still known to many of us as an ancient royal hunting forest, Selwood is relatively unheard of, despite the fact that there is still a forest, stretching for miles. I found an old map in a folklore book the other day and Selwood was clearly marked, stretching across a vast area – now it is nearly erased from maps in name. Yet it is possible to walk for hours without leaving the woods. A friend told me that she'd heard that it was one of the longest, perhaps the longest, swathe of uninterrupted trees on any English map . . .

I looked it up in Gilpin's *Forest Scenery* to see if my somewhat eccentric relative had documented it. He had. But more than his mentioning it, I was amazed to discover was that this whole area, the area where I live that borders three counties, was once a mini-county of its own. Selwoodshire. I live in Selwoodshire. In terms of atmosphere it made complete sense. My borderland home was acknowledged as unified. It had a name.

On the map, the road pushes like a needle through the forest. Pierces the green. This is the border road. Wiltshire to one side, Somerset to the other. The forest is both evergreen and deciduous here. It smothers the land from Stourhead to Longleat, two stately piles one can walk between almost without leaving the trees. On the map there is a sea of green. As large as a small sea.

It is a real forest and yet Selwood seems a concept. A place unknown, a place lost to memory, the names of the forest broken into smaller woods. It has released a hive of smaller wood names: Great Bradley is the largest, then Tadbesom, Penstones, Trout Pond, West End, King's Wood Warren, Shady Hanging, Greenland Bottom, Witham Park, Tanner's, Penny's, Marston, Wallace. Names that must mean something. I can imagine their stories.

Fossilised dreams of a place that was once larger. Selwood. Not as famous as Sherwood, but in its time . . . A secret there for all to discover yet not for most to see.

I discovered the forest one day on a driving detour to Shaftesbury and then spent the next few weeks exploring the woods in depth. There are not many places I know so well now. As I walked, there was a melancholy, a gentleness, devoid of footpath signs, going deeper, my sense of perspective gone, my heart occasionally racing, surrendering to the feeling of the trees. I could feel their age. They leaked a sense of stories.

Come June, the flower fairy Hattifatteners that are foxgloves take over – and it was when I saw this that I realised that drive to Shaftesbury wasn't my first time here. Many years before, I'd gone with my dad on a mystery drive and I remember taking a turn and following lanes at random, then suddenly being surrounded by foxgloves in clearings of trees. I recalled the feeling; the atmosphere came back to me so strongly, it was like the place had finally decided to reveal itself out of frustration that I had not recognised it before.

I later found these woods hold the source of the River Frome.

Source of river. River of trees on my map, blue lines of streams barely visible.

Selwoodshire.

I wonder what a map of this place would look like if I made one myself. Somehow the OS Explorer map both works and does not. I wonder what would happen if I drew on it, added on the stories, the places. It is easy enough to draw on a map. It is one of the appeals – we can change them, they are paper after all. They are naturally expandable, open to each of us to decorate with feelings, with secret discoveries the cartographer never found or thought to mention, updates as our landscape changes, as we do. I look at older maps and the shape of the forest is the same, the colour or paper different, the nearby towns smaller, the roads less clear. I can hardly picture the roads and buildings added later – they seem a stranger addition than if I scribbled my own words, traced thoughts to be revealed only to those who'd understand, bewitched like an ancient grimoire.

Yet I cannot bring myself to draw on my OS map. Both a practical thing (I don't want to cover up a footpath I might one day need to follow), but also the scale is wrong – the thoughts need room to breathe – extensions and pages, secret advent calendar window upon window (I went through a phase of making 'advent calendar' works – old photos and drawings with doors that led to my writings of their secrets – the thoughts of the places), a tunnel burrowing down, disguised by magic, a mine for all the lost stories. The feelings of this place. But if I cannot deface my map I wonder if there were any less literal maps – not the old maps from decades before, easy enough to find online – but an imaginative one; if not a map of tenderness, then a map of a different side of this place. I wanted to know how this obscure place made someone else feel.

I recently stumbled on it: a map in a book that was to go with a poem that shows the area around the Wiltshire, Somerset, Dorset border. The poem is the rather grandiose *Poly-Olbion*, written by Michael Drayton (who was popular in the Elizabethan court but whose services were rejected by James I in 1601, perhaps giving him time away from city life to work on his eccentric epic) from about 1598 and published in 1612. The map is one of many in this volume created by William Hole to accompany the work's strange mix of poetry and topography, myth and geography. Drayton was trying to create a record, a topographical poetic guide to the landscape of Britain that combined scientific knowledge with lashings of Celtic and Arthurian myth, histories and traditions. (The first volume also included writing from John Seldon of a more factual historical nature.) It is a somewhat strange book: at a time when people were striving for the most accurate of geographical records – for example, Christopher Saxton's *Atlas of the Counties of England and Wales* was published in 1579 – this topography is one of arguing rivers and landscapes. Rather than illustrating the places of the poem, or there being a map for each county, there is a map for each song. It is illustration as much as cartography, seeking to capture the feeling of Drayton's poem, his talking of muses, his sense of the feelings of the place.

The poem's imagery is highly anthropomorphised and the maps show this, brimming with personifications of each town and place, rivers that wriggle like snakes and creatures, hills, forests depicted as characters rather than landscape features. Looking at the maps, you expect them to suddenly talk; for the women and creatures, the spirits of the hills and trees to add their piece, to guide you as much as the words. When combined with Drayton's verse – with his subjective take on the landscape and his muses, his guides to the landscape – and with Seldon's prose information, *Poly-Olbion* travels beyond cartography and poetry towards a new form. A collaboration of visuals and words as well as a collaboration of men, on a quest. It is seeking out the British landscape – it might not be a map of emotion in terms of consciously illustrating feelings, but it acknowledges that place has feelings that words alone, that science alone, cannot fully bring to life. Art, poetry and fact – place is a creative collaboration. To truly express it we need more than cartography alone would allow.

Knowing the vast scope of the work (it is 15,000 lines of verse long and seeks to cover the whole of the country!), I was surprised to see my area covered – the places I recognised described in verse, illustrated on a map. The personal locality of it. Drayton's poem reveals his taste in landscape (it is a very subjective work) and it is clear that he would have loved my downs – he is a fan of Salisbury Plain, open and light – and hated my forest; to him, forests in general were gloomy and damp, rotten with fogs and cobwebs and, surreally, caterpillars, to which he had a strange aversion. The words were interesting, but the map of my area held my attention like a jolt of a realisation, a new discovery. Here was my place.

Finding an ancient depiction of somewhere so local to me made me view the map with tenderness. A new map of emotion – mine layered on to a view, an opinion or experience from long ago. I look at the classical mythical figures that mark places: they are no more sinister in the forest than in the towns or the plains, so it does not hold emotions in that way; we cannot tell from the map those elements that the poem makes clear triggered wildly varying emotions in Drayton. These figures wear wondrous hats and they are different – Bath, Bristol, Salisbury are all represented by naked yet classically draped women with headgear made of miniature buildings, while the forests are represented by women with trees either next to them or on their heads. One woman casually leans as if a decadent giant, at home with a forest all hers. But what drew me to it was how Selwood Forest is marked. This elusive place of trees, name long-lost to mark the area, was there: a large woman, larger than the towns, backed with trees and holding a bow and arrow like Diana, goddess of the hunt. It is not a map of tenderness, but somehow her presence, wilder than the towns but just as strong, standing there, bow and arrows in hand, glancing to the side, marking a place that these days is almost a concept, a lost place, present in trees yet forgotten, makes this map tender for me. My place, the place of my map of tenderness, was important, is marked.

Here, there are women as symbols, classical motifs, drawings of rivers as symbols, yet at the same time they hint back to the idea of a literal spirit of place, the ancient idea of the spirit of the river, the goddess of the woods (do not forget that in folk culture trees had spirits) ... I wonder if the places Hole chose to represent were not so much the locations mentioned in the poem, but those places where he felt there might be some spirit – which explains the presence of Selwood. A map of tenderness, not in feelings, but in terms of acknowledgement of the hidden; that we can work creatively together to find something, that landscape is alive even if rivers don't literally argue with each other, as they do here. This urge to anthropomorphise, to include myth alongside historical fact and geography suggests the idea that in place, even in an act of cartography, there is something else going on. We have to acknowledge this. These feelings – such as Drayton's hatred of forests in favour of plains – this is a preference of atmosphere. Here he (somewhat theatrically) strives to show it is alive.

A Ten Mile Walk

There is an artist of the West Country who has taken ordinary maps and made them into something else through his actions – turned them through art, not into maps of tenderness, but echoes of a moment, of experience, documents that can never be anything but an inadequate record of being in a place full of atmosphere. The experience itself is the art. And the art involves travelling.

The map is the starting point and part of the record. But it contains nothing of the art itself. It highlights the inadequacy of physical maps. How authentic maps only live inside us.

Richard Long makes art in the landscape, often in the West Country. His work is usually in situ, sometimes existing only in a brief moment, though I have seen his paintings – mud from the River Avon, which flowed through my childhood village, smeared across the gallery wall. But I am thinking of one specific West Country work – a work whose record is a map with a line drawn on it, but a work whose true being was a walk through the landscape; a moment, one that would have been deeply atmospheric for Long, but which we can never hope to know, though we could try to re-enact it.

In November 1968, Richard Long drew a straight line representing ten miles across a map of Exmoor. He then walked it, without detouring from the line, sometimes intersecting with paths, other times hopping over walls, skirting bogs, wading through uneven territory. Most probably trespassing at times, the art was in the process, the intention. This conscious decision to traverse whatever the landscape brought to him meant a controlled act led to less controlled terrain. No path, the atmosphere of the walk was in thrall to an invisible line, a mark on a map made by him, brought to life by his feet, against the intentions of the cartographers. Against attempts to control how we move through place.

The record of this work is the map with the line called *A Ten Mile Walk England*. It tells us nothing. It is not a map of tenderness, of atmosphere and emotion, yet it is a trace of a moment, a conscious marking of a conscious act that acknowledges our experience of place is fleeting. It anticipates the map of emotion, of his body. Yet I could follow his line. Do the same walk. But it would not be the same piece, in that for me the landscape would be different, the atmosphere would be different. Long did other walks too, sometimes photographing them or making ephemeral works that are the traces of lines in grass he has trodden down, and which won't last except for him. Photos can't capture place as collaborator, this dialogue of his feet with the land.

The work is made individual by process and experience, by how we interact with the place in the moment. With how it felt for Long; how it would feel for us if we did it. And in this way, the line is an impossible map of tenderness – an acceptance that marks can tell us nothing; that the real meaning is in the experience of place. It is not so much a souvenir as a memorial – a nameless plaque for the unknowable – the meaning of which none of us, except for Long, can hope to understand.

Definitions

Multisensory Layers

'The senses don't just make sense of life in bold or subtle acts of clarity, they tear reality apart into vibrant morsels and reassemble them into a meaningful pattern.'

Diane Ackerman, *A Natural History of the Senses*

Our senses are how we experience place. All experience in the world, in the simplest terms, is sensory experience. It would be logical as a start to say that how we experience atmosphere is through our senses.

Our senses are not just individual organs with roles but rather the feeders of our brains. As Diane Ackerman puts it in her wonderful *A Natural History of the Senses*: 'The senses feed shards into the brain like microscopic pieces of a jigsaw puzzle. When enough "pieces" assemble, the brain says *Cow. I see a cow.*'

The brain is so responsive and remembers the shards so well that even when a real cow is not present, but simply a drawing, an outline, it can still recognise a cow. It seems to me that atmosphere is the most subtle way a similar process might work, but also the most powerful and confusing – it changes, it doesn't make provable sense that others can corroborate, like a cow being a cow does.

Atmosphere is not a stand-alone sensory experience like recognising an animal, or even a more evocative one such as a smell triggering a memory, but rather a flood of sensory experience; a tsunami that washes over us physically and mentally in perhaps the most complex puzzle our brains have to try to make sense of. Perhaps that is where the subtlety – the challenge – lies: it is sensory, yet we cannot make sense of it in the way our brain has learned to translate the jigsaw of experience; it is thus both *of* and *outside of* normal sensory experience.

Is the magic ingredient what our brain adds on to the sensory experience? A web of memories and creative interpretations? Feelings beyond the physical? Which, when combined together, don't lead to a definite conclusion, but more of an open-ended feeling – an inkling, a swirling experience that is both of place and outside of it, and both of us and outside of us in that it is happening within a particular location? Perhaps the entirety is both an experience and a location, in terms of the fact that we inhabit it. We don't inhabit looking at a cow, or inhabit hearing the wind by itself, but combine a bovine view over fields with the smell of earth and manure, and a warm wind caressing our body, and the memories of another such place we visited as a child and the ideas it gives us for a story ... well, then this experience is like entering a world within a world. We are both in the place where the atmosphere is being created and, in being part of this creation in a moment in time, we are *inhabiting* the atmosphere itself. By opening ourselves to and absorbing the atmosphere, we are *travelling* through a strange sensory swamp, being wrapped in its tendrils, being taken somewhere partly created by our bodies but which can take us outside of them into a different realm.

Atmosphere, therefore, could be seen in its simplest form as a combination of all our senses with our memories, imagination and our own interpretations. Perhaps a bit of our subconscious thrown in, too. Riddle solved, or is it? In a more profound way, atmosphere could be seen as the most complete, yet complex, the deepest experience we can have, but the hardest to explain. The potential of the complexity makes me wonder if it can be as simple as the combination of human experience and thought. Is it even possible for it to be more than this, without an element of faith or belief in the supernatural? Is there more going on? How do we contend with how individual atmosphere is, yet how universal place can be? What of other factors we cannot sense in the normal way – history, the memories of others, or the constant feeling of the essence of a place even when sensory factors, such as the weather, change? What of our unconscious or subconscious experience? Is it just our experience, or one of the earth's too?

Conscious Pathways

Atmosphere equals senses mixed with memories, subconscious, imagination, subjective interpretation ... ? I knew this wasn't enough, yet when I tried to research a further scientific explanation within the physical world, I struggled to find an answer. I looked at physics and failed. I wondered if I was searching in the wrong place, the structure of the world, held back by my own understanding of perception and what it is. Perhaps I needed to delve deeper into neuroscience than physics, to delve into consciousness itself.

Atmosphere is a conscious experience. I can say that with certainty. However, it is a specific kind of conscious experience, more complicated than most.

When neuroscience examines perception, it looks at not only our sensory experience as the product of five distinct inputs, but seeks to understand why we experience our senses as we do and thus attempts to determine the truth of our understanding of the world around us – searching for a testable theory (or, as is often the case, theories) for why we experience the world as we do and what this means in terms of the actual nature of reality. For example, why a colour is what it is. How we recognise something – why our brains recognise a drawing of a cow is a cow.

When we are unconscious during an anaesthetic, we do not dream or have memories of our experience; our sense of time is gone. To experience the world, and therefore atmosphere, we need to be conscious. It is how we know we're alive. But what is the reality of the world around us?

I am not trying to summarise in a few short paragraphs one of the biggest questions in science: what is consciousness? (Some think it can be simulated, others that it is in everything.) Rather, how the science around consciousness might shed some light on our experience of atmosphere.

Atmosphere is undeniably tied up with perception. It is a perceptive experience. One scientific theory concerns the Neural Correlates of Consciousness (NCC), which puts forward the idea that all conscious experience should have a measurable specific pattern of neural activity. If this is the case, then when we experience certain things, our brain reacts in certain specific ways. This seems highly logical to me. Perception is, after all, a biological experience.

According to this approach, all conscious experience has a measurable pattern of neural activity. Any experience we have is because our brain is sending signals. Everything can be explained away. I find both a comfort and a horror in this.

Conscious experience is all about perception. When we perceive something, usually through our five senses, but interestingly also through our inner, interoceptive senses, organs and our central nervous system controlling our bodily responses and how we feel, messages are sent through our brain and it takes a guess, predicts what it is that we are perceiving – and that is the best stab we have at understanding what reality is. We don't really know what reality is.

In his book *Being You*, neuroscientist Anil Seth talks of the brain as sitting in our heads, in darkness. Perception comes from it to us. Top down. We are the source of how we perceive things, not the world. I feel sorry for all those brains in the dark, as if they are weird pets, kept locked in . . .

However, we are not disembodied brains. Our brains are in our bodies and our bodies are in the world. Atmosphere is a physical thing and it exists in us, but could it not exist in the world outside us? Red might not be red.

The idea of the sky not being blue both fascinates me and breaks my heart. Yet it is blue to us and if there is no way to experience this beyond ourselves, then I will hold on to the magic that is the blue of sky.

However, I wonder if atmosphere is more complicated than this. Whether it can be explained away by neurological responses that would be the same for everyone, when by nature it is so fluid and subjective. Is it a specific form of conscious experience? It is not an emotion, though it triggers an emotional response. Is it too fluid for a straightforward neurological explanation? Requiring imagination, creative interpretation . . .

How can we identify a pathway when atmosphere is inconsistent and changeable in a second? It is not fixed. It varies from person to person. We could maybe measure the feeling most people have if they are somewhere creepy, for example, but that is not the same thing as identifying a unifying pathway for creepy atmospheres. Moreover, another person experiencing the same place might find it funny . . .

Interoceptive perception can explain emotions. Our body responding not to a feeling, but a feeling responding to our body. We become the centre again.

Is atmosphere both standard perception and interoceptive perception? I could see how most of life would be that way. It is impossible to have one without the other. We are our bodies, after all.

But these bodies are in place. We might not be able to prove scientifically that the place is how we perceive it, yet there is still a dialogue. We are picking up on its signals and then processing them. A series of 'best guesses', a 'controlled hallucination', to use Seth's terms. I cannot possibly hope to truly understand as he does, to have a theory I could hope to prove. And yet . . .

Atmosphere could be both pure perception and interoceptive perception, which explains the emotional part. It could be our body's best guess at a situation, perception at its most sophisticated and nuanced, with all our past perceptions feeding in previous results, biological responses. We say we know 'in our gut' if somewhere or someone feels right to us, and atmosphere is undeniably a physical experience, whatever our beliefs might be around the possibility of a more spiritual dimension.

I am not sure we can ever know.

Memories might trigger best guesses, but what about our

creative urges? Inspiration, imagination – they create atmosphere, too, and I do not know how they work in terms of consciousness. They complicate my understanding, my willingness to see atmosphere; not defined neatly, but explained by the same means that help me understand what perception is, and what consciousness might be.

Dreams are conscious experiences, as being asleep is not the same as being knocked out – so does that explain their atmosphere? The atmosphere of a fantastical city, for example, when we are physically asleep in our beds?

Yet virtual reality does not have atmosphere in the same way for me and I am also too conscious of where I really am without the deceiver that is sleep. The relocator that is the dream world.

A fluid thing. A moving thing. A travelling thing. Both inside and outside. A perfect metaphor for the different kinds of perception. Logical, the perfect fit, yet in terms of explanation, tantalisingly, like a scientific thin place, just beyond my grasp.

Wondering about how much we miss, wondering about this transcendent feeling, I decided to pay attention and went for a walk differently round the familiar fields and brook of my then village. I wanted to pay attention not just to what I saw, the odd noise or sudden smell, but everything – to go pure sense – to use my whole body – to think of my skin in contact with the wind as a constant sense of touch. To combine it all in some strange soup of walking experience, to see how much more aware of atmosphere I could consciously be.

I went for a walk to try to trick the transcendent out of the ordinary, the familiar, what was then home.

It was sunny – a mid-April heatwave during the strange time of the first Covid-19 lockdown, whereby even less people than normal were walking around my old village. With no one around, multisensory walking is easier – no chats, no wondering if people will look at me strangely if I close my eyes or whirl my arms around. I wouldn't mind, but their glances, their presence would be a distraction – too much thought when my goal was to let go of thinking, that internal monologue as I move. I wanted to shut it off.

The wind was strong. The smells of the dry, newly ploughed field climbing higher than the dust my old shoes stirred up like mini puffed tornados.

I had read recently about touch. Previously, when thinking of walking and when teaching descriptive writing I'd always mentioned not to forget touch, but thought of it as texture; touch as something related to your hands when you pick something up. However, the skin is our largest organ, so our whole body has the power of the sense of touch. The thought was revelatory for me. So obvious, yet for years it had alluded me.

Now, I raised my arms and felt the wind blow all around me. My armpits cooled with the breeze. My feet were aware of the uneven earth my shoes were cushioning me from. My hair whipped round my face and tickled – it smelt like hay – dry summer baked with fresh air. Its curled strands changed the play of light. The sun warmed my forehead, while my lips were chilled. Movement of wind as touch. Temperature as touch. Surface texture through layers. The feeling of my clothes as I paid attention to how they brushed against different parts of my body. I was walking, not touching any objects, yet my whole body was alive with touch. The world felt different, strangely new.

I took a deep breath and felt the air go up my nose and down into my lungs. I remembered how it feels to drink water. Water touching my throat, a cool sense inside my stomach. Interoceptive? Touch is the only sense that physically travels inside our bodies. Air touches us everywhere, it keeps us alive – breathing is touch.

I kept going. Paid attention, while holding on to my sense of touch, to the plays of light. I saw my shadow walking with me and felt empathy, as if it were truly an appendage of my body, with its slipping over the tumbled dry brown earth, puckered with white stones and the newborn hints of a crop of green.

Birds flew overhead. I listened to the wind and threw my hearing further. The rumbling breath of a tractor. I could almost sense its vibrations through the air.

Further now. Greener fields and the softness of grass – the instability of the moulded shapes of earth below. I was almost in a trance. The world of thought had fallen away and what was left felt unreal in its immediacy and power, yet I knew it to be more real. This is how I exist in the world. This is how I always exist, yet thoughts distract me. My brain normally distracted me from the nature of the place I was in and without my thoughts the atmosphere was bright and pure and strong – primal – of the place.

I dripped down to the river. The air cooled. The light softened into dropped chandeliers of pools – not gold as I'd always thought, but silver. If I really looked it was silver – gold had just been what my brain had deduced as it is a warmer colour ... Perceptive best guess ... The water rose in an above-water pool of scent. I could be both above and in – under the water that ran beside me. I paused and drank it in. Opened my mouth and tasted the air – taste is partly smell – without smell we can't taste and I wanted to see if the air that was touching my mouth and lungs and filling my nose with scent could taste of earth and water too.

I threw out my hearing – birds – some small song and the distant cawing of a rookery; water playing over stones, distant machinery – invisible yet a strange mechanical presence that almost gave a psychosomatic metallic tang to the air.

All senses in action here, I felt overwhelmed. I started to feel wobbly. It was almost too much. Is it possible to be truly aware of all our senses at the same time? Does our mind shut out some of the messages deliberately to keep us functioning? I could not have held a conversation now. I could not walk straight. Yet I felt calmer and less worried than I had in months. Better than any meditation, where I find anxious thoughts rush in, I was free to this strange realm.

If we throw out our senses to the world, it lets us in. We are in touch with hyper-real sense of place, of life.

I felt more alive.

I felt I had unlocked the world – it was not an opaque, unaware 'going through the motions' but rather a 'symphony' of my senses, the puzzle pieces of atmosphere slotting together, harmonising.

Is atmosphere our brain's way of communicating the feelings of a place in a way we can handle? Is the way it is almost beyond words due to the fact that our brains have diluted and blended this hyper-sensory experience into a unique place 'perfume' our brains can compute, experience but not truly understand? The sensory identifier – the personality of place condensed for us to make sense of? Or not to make sense of, but to be in . . . To feel . . . It is a greeting from the world we move through. The world we inhabit.

For I do think we inhabit atmosphere. It is not a simple sensory experience but a place; while it is tempting to say one that is invisible, intangible, that is to deny how the visibility, the tangibility of our experience of being somewhere contributes to it. Everything is part of it. It is hard to describe everything.

When walking this way we are agents of atmosphere. It is a creative act of perception – a creative reading of the place. This trance-like feeling – it reminded me of when I am in the perfect creative state for writing: that strange joy and contentment, that other world where I am existing in a different layer of reality to normal.

Inspiration. Is atmosphere where inspiration lives?

I continued along the path and listened to the bubbling of water over a patch of larger stones, yet my eyes were drawn to how the lace patterns of sun on the footpath were tinted slightly pink. It was as if the sound were illustrating the light, they seemed so illogical yet right together. The light could illustrate the sound of water. A symbiotic illustration.

Sight illustrates sound, illustrates touch, illustrates smell, illustrates taste . . .

Atmosphere is an endless illustration of the components of place, our sensory experience of place. Memories dance in, feelings dance in. Emotions are not left aside here.

I am wholly in this moment. There is no dilution. The atmosphere is both overwhelming and gentle. It is a wonder.

Back home, the feeling lasted until nightfall. Walking would never be the same again.

After my multisensory walk, the feeling and the memory of that hyper-sensory experience stayed. Yet it was different to when an atmosphere overcomes us by surprise. I was trying to delve deeper into it, in that moment on that walk, to see if I could reach a different point of feeling of place at that time. But the experience also raised questions. When atmosphere floods us unaware and we are being less conscious, more passive, is there some force therefore creating this power – the earth, the place communicating with us? And if this is so, then to ignore it . . . I began to think of everywhere I'd been – not just out in the countryside, cities, inside cars, different countries, alone or in crowds. We live in a time when the world is changing so quickly; with the digital revolution changing our inner space as much as the Industrial Revolution changed our landscape in the nineteenth century, we retreat inwards, yet move further from the connection of that inner space to the world around us – walling ourselves in, rather than welcoming the outer world deeper. We live in a time of climate change, of urgent political action. Everything we do takes place in our world, in a place. If atmosphere affects how we behave, there could be an urgency to how we connect with it. It would be collaborative and creative – it could be the force underlying everything – the key to how we live in the world that we all unthinkingly ignore. It could be the key to change.

I think of multisensory, hyper-sensory walking and it suddenly feels inadequate. A luscious experiment, which showed me how we can tune in, but also taught me nothing beyond atmosphere as sensory experience, scientific, rational; yet my creative mind wanted to know more. I felt like it was something else – more multi-faceted. I needed to explore. I needed to set out on an expedition, both of the outer and the inner world. The one does not exist without the other.

If the first explanation of atmosphere looks to science, to consciousness and perception to define it as creative multisensory experience, combined with memories and ideas; then the other extreme is to see atmosphere as pure irrational experience – as evidence of something else, of the divine.

Of Soul-Thought and Joy

It is an unseasonably chilly June day. I am sat in my study, trying to concentrate, staring out at the countryside, staring back at my computer, trying to think, to pull this puzzle together.

I look at Ann Mercer and Dinah Cartwright's maps again. I took photos in the museum and, staring at my phone, I zoom in. It is Ann's I am drawn to suddenly – there is something in the brown stitching of the mountains that is familiar; that triggers a memory of another map. Or maps, perhaps. I had been so caught up in maps of tenderness, how these young girls had stitched the truth of their worlds into being, that I had missed the parallels with better known homemade maps, the ones not so tender but of imaginary worlds I had dismissed. I think of Narnia and C. S. Lewis: when Narnia was created, it wasn't just an adult invention – I knew this. Could the seeds of his more 'literal' map of Narnia have been sown in a way that was more tender than I realised? That held his feelings, his thoughts of how we experience place? Could this in some way hold another key to unlocking the mystery of what atmosphere is?

I find it hard to picture C. S. Lewis as a child. Despite his fame as a writer for young people, he forever seems an older academic, sitting in his Oxford study by an open fire, surrounded by walls of leather-bound books, musing ideas of faith and story. Yet when he was a child, Lewis invented Animal-land – a place so real to him that he felt at this time he lived as much, if not more, in his imagination than in the 'real world'. Animal-land was not a simple invention of moments – an idea picked up for a couple of rushed story paragraphs – but a complex world, a world where animals talked and were dominant, a world I feel was alive in a way that most of us don't see the world can be: a world where nature is as conscious as we are, where a child can easily see this difference of perspective; is open to the idea that we are not as dominant as we wish to believe, or where perhaps because we are different there is a value in imagining the world a different way, without us interfering.

In his autobiography *Surprised by Joy*, he talks of how reading Beatrix Potter's *The Tale of Squirrel Nutkin* was a profound experience for him. We can see an influence here in terms of the sentience of animals and their plight in a human world, but as those of many children are, his thoughts were more philosophical. He said he was troubled by the 'Idea of Autumn' – he felt an intense desire to understand, to possess the feeling, the unpossessable, perhaps what could be construed as the atmosphere of this time of year. He loved other seasons and other Beatrix Potter books, but this 'Idea of Autumn' became like a strange desire, a love for a feeling of a time of year. Although he knew he couldn't possess it, this strange desire still drew him back to the book in an attempt to 'reawaken' this feeling, this experience that to him felt beyond normal experience or ordinary life. He concludes that it can only make sense as a feeling that was in 'another dimension'. A dimension of feeling in an experience of place, which one cannot possess, yet one yearns to recreate . . . His creative endeavour, his idea of the feeling of a place, the roots of Narnia, could have started in the quest for an atmosphere he'd lost. Yet with this quest an acknowledgement that simply going for a walk in any old autumn wouldn't do it. This experience was beyond what our senses could simply conjure. For Lewis, this would lead to a sense of the divine. He called it Joy.

In his autobiography, C. S. Lewis talks of an 'unsatisfied desire which is in itself more desirable than any other satisfaction'. This desire is different to straightforward want, and it is connected to how we experience the world. It is impossible that this desire can consist of purely outward sensory experience, as then it would be obtainable, and Joy cannot be controlled. We can try to summon it, but it has its own will, its own timetable on when and how it will reveal itself.

Joy can appear as the memory of a memory triggered by standing on a country lane and the smell of berries – that seemingly disconnected moment bringing a memory back with exquisite nostalgia, bittersweet and intense. The Joy lies not in the wanting of the memory back but in the brief re-experiencing of it, the intensity that came unwarranted in that moment. The moment itself is Joy, as well as the desire for that intensity of feeling. I would say it is akin to the bliss of intense experiences of positive atmosphere. Sensory experience, memory, creativity – Joy has all the rational hallmarks of atmosphere, but it also has something else. It moves out into the irrational, yet makes the whole world seem full of deeper meaning. And like atmosphere, there is an intense desire to *reawaken* it, but this is outside of our power. Atmosphere and Joy are the most intense and exquisite pleasure life can give, and they are completely beyond our control. We cannot conjure them.

For Lewis, this later became clear as a sense of faith and God. When as an adult he finally accepted a deep Christian faith, this childhood sense of Joy became for him our yearning for a unity with the Absolute. Yet if one struggles to find faith, if a sense of the Absolute is not a God, then for another it could be a sense of something deeper within the world. He regarded his moments of Joy not as a deception or distraction from life, but that 'its visitations were rather the moments of clearest consciousness we had'. This idea of clearest consciousness – of truly being alive and awake rather than distracting oneself from the 'real' world – makes me think of intense experiences of atmosphere. Faith or intense consciousness, a sense of an Absolute – this is something beyond a simple interpretation of sensory experience.

But what if we have no faith? What if a sense of God, or even of an Absolute, a non-Christian idea of the divine, is not something we can experience? How do we then make sense of experience beyond the rational? Yet we do not have to be religious to experience this Joy: for others, this intense feeling of place has in fact been the 'evidence' of something beyond even God.

Richard Jefferies is well known as a nineteenth-century nature writer; however, one of his lesser-known works is a somewhat eccentric autobiography called *The Story of My Heart*. It is a deeply strange book – stream of consciousness at times, barely mentioning events in his life, although he was clear on it being an autobiography. It occasionally rambles into a slightly dubious idolisation of the human body and the Spartan ideal of perfection and discipline, combined with an anti-asceticism. But the parts I find interesting are when he focuses on his feelings of being out in the countryside. When it comes to his ideas on how we as humans play our part in atmosphere creation – through 'soul-thought', as he calls this – and atmosphere's symbiosis between humans and nature, well, then I think there is a rusty key in there somewhere.

The book begins with Jefferies describing a climb up a grassy hill in the Wiltshire wilds. I think of my own hills by my wild Wiltshire house, and I begin to wonder if he will feel what I do. But rather than awaiting what Lewis would call a sense of Joy to come to him, which according to Lewis cannot be guaranteed or controlled, Jefferies is clear that a deep feeling of connection between land and body, of atmosphere, is something he can conjure in the right conditions – and that does not make it less profound. It is just different, perhaps not taken up with his memories, but something more universal – the past spirits, the prehistoric people who would have wandered these hills, perhaps buried in one of the many strange tumuli that scatter these wild Western hills. If he is aware of his body, past bodies, this land, its past, how it is in this moment; if he lets go of anxiety, the worries of life, and frees his mind through walking in a way we might associate today with mindfulness, and allows what he calls 'soul-thought' to take over, then a profound sense of feeling in place is possible. It is another way of looking at atmosphere, and it is one that he sees not so much as being connected to the divine, as beyond this.

This feeling we can find – this access to 'soul-thought' – has other benefits that I can recognise. Jefferies talks of how there is a dust that can settle on the heart, as on a shelf; that his 'heart was dusty, parched for want of the rain of deep feeling' and how he knew that the cure for this was a need, a desire like that for Joy perhaps, a *necessity* he felt for a strong inspiration for 'soul-thought'. This need is both abstract and part of him; it is taken from the abstract of the mind and through the soul, in connection with the land, made real. He uses the word 'soul', though reluctantly says some might prefer the term 'psyche' as he does not mean it religiously; yet still for him soul feels the right word. Soul is not negated for him by lack of Christian faith, but is real, residing in the unexplainable realms of the universe. And in finding it in connection with the land, as opposed to purely within ourselves, we can truly become ourselves – feel ourselves in a way different to normal; perhaps, I think, in the way we feel when experiencing the most intense of good atmospheres. (Bad atmosphere is a different thing, though not so distant to Jefferies' way of seeing the world as it at first seems.) We can overcome that feeling of being stuck in life, brush the dust off of our hearts. He describes:

> Moving up the sweet short turf, at every step my heart seemed to obtain a wider horizon of feeling: with every inhalation of rich pure air, a deeper desire ... By the time I had reached the summit I had entirely forgotten the petty circumstances and the annoyances of existence. I felt myself, myself ...

I was utterly alone with the sun and the earth. Lying down on the grass, I spoke in my soul to the earth, the sun, the air, and the distant sea far beyond sight. I thought of the earth's firmness – I felt it bear me up; through the grassy couch there came an influence as if I could feel the great earth speaking to me. I thought of the wandering air . . . the air touched me and gave me something of itself. I spoke to the sea: though so far, in my mind I saw it . . . I desired to have its strength, its mystery and glory. Then I addressed the sun, desiring the soul equivalent of his light and brilliance, his endurance and unwearied race. I turned to the blue heaven over . . . The rich blue of the unattainable flower of the sky drew my soul towards it, and there it rested, for pure colour is rest of heart. By all these I prayed; I felt an emotion of the soul beyond all definition; prayer is a puny thing to it, and the world is a rude sign to the feeling, but I know no other.

'Prayer' is an inadequate word for Jefferies and he later goes out of his way to set up the idea of the universe as existing beyond religion, more powerful and just as mysterious and unexplainable. Nevertheless, this passage is a prayer through thought and action. It is a prayer in collaboration with the earth, with a sense of place; it is a communication through a feeling, it is a seemingly 'spiritual' conversation with the power and emotion inherent in land, the power the beliefs of so many ancient cultures hold, in the places that speak to us. The land is alive with feeling, which, if Jefferies can access it, transports him to a transcendent place within; an inner place where the soul is nourished, where he can be his true self – not cut off from, but vitally connected to the land.

Soul-thought is a dialogue, interactive, vital and alive.

The Story of My Heart may be a strange book, but if we can feel the land as Jefferies does, perhaps we can get closer to a sense of what atmosphere is. If we combine the science and sensory perception with Joy, desire and memory, and then seek atmosphere out – the potential conversation and collaboration – then perhaps what Jefferies unwittingly does, is show us a map to experiencing place, to sensing its vitality, its importance, in a way that is both personal and political; that seeks out not a hidden essence, but a non-essential, personal, subjective (yet no less true for this) fluid 'essence' – a malleable, alive 'spirit' of place that is there to support each of us in making our best way through the world. In his quest to 'be full of soul-learning', to labour for soul-life and soul-thought and be exalted with more soul-nature, perhaps Jefferies had opened his mind to the power and vitality and breadth of the everyday world, the ordinary, which in our obliviousness to feelings in place, we walk by and ignore each day. As Jefferies says at the end of the first chapter: 'What is there which I have not used to strengthen the same emotion?' I wonder how much we miss . . .

I began to plan, to think deeply and collect together the places in the world where I had connected with this. My brain and body and my experience of the world started to feel like a strange archive I was invisibly laying out across my study. I closed my eyes and pictured the places hovering, how they would be visually if I conjured their atmospheres as a spell and they floated into view like atmosphere ectoplasm. I began to search for my own way in – the biological, my own Joy, my own 'beyond God', a union with the land, rural, urban, good and bad, something new, something deeply old, anything . . . I began my quest to understand atmosphere more deeply.

If I combined these three tiers of experiencing the explainable and the unexplainable, would I ever get closer to understanding, not necessarily what atmosphere actually is, but how its power changes the world? I began to wonder if we all have a responsibility to be aware of it, to open ourselves to it, to let it flow through our bodies and use it to see if we can make a difference. I wanted to understand what I felt, to discover what others felt.

I set out with trepidation on my impossible voyage. This book. How to capture my own soul-thought place dialogue. Hello. My map of tenderness. It is nice to meet you properly.

The Optimism of Inspiration

Hope can express itself through atmosphere. It is part of what fuels us to continue when so much seems bleak: if we can access our own 'flash', as Emily of *New Moon* describes it, this is one of the few things that has the power to get through to us in the darkest times, when we are preoccupied with all that seems hope*less*. It searches in us and helps us find what we need in that moment to come out of ourselves and be reminded of the world. It is more deeply connected to atmosphere than we realise. It also reminds me of another of atmosphere's creative forces, its vital fluid; it reminds me of inspiration.

All creative people know that moment. The moment where the world becomes extra vivid, when the mind is hyper-alert and alive and so within itself the rest of the world disappears. If we are lucky, this may last for hours, but more often than not it is tantalisingly fleeting, we desire it and – as with Joy – are on a constant quest for more. We want and need to reach this place for our work and for ourselves. Work and self become one in it. It is extraordinarily satisfactory. And as a state of mind it has an atmosphere.

Like atmosphere, I think it is often overlooked in favour of what it concretely produces – the creative work rather than the process, the result rather than the moment. But as a state of mind, as an atmosphere of inner and outer worlds colliding, it is necessarily ephemeral. Somehow, the idea of the ephemeral seems loaded with the suggestion that this state is somehow less important than the concrete; that something which, by definition, cannot last, has less 'weight' to it, less worth. But this is a materialistic way of viewing that which belongs essentially to a different value system. Is a beautiful Andy Goldsworthy sculpture intrinsically of less value than another work, because it decays into the land and cannot be displayed in a gallery? Is something that is inherent to inspiration and therefore the creation of all that is more concrete therefore not as worthy as its outcome? What of process art itself? Walks and following pieces from Richard Long to Sophie Calle . . .

I've always been suspicious of valuing outcome over process – the idea that we all must achieve something measurable for it to be worthwhile. So much progress, so much wellbeing, so many unforeseen positive future consequences, is and are immeasurable. The former approach is the scourge of the education system . . .

If you ask an artist what is the worth of those fleeting moments – the flashes that are both atmosphere and moment of being, which lead to inspiration – they will say they are most precious and, as for Emily and her flash, unexplainable.

Inspiration is a result of atmosphere, that complex swirl of how we feel in the world, the meeting of interior mind and external world, the lifted veil into a different way of seeing. It is fleeting. It can never be truly commodified, even though it does sometimes lead to the concrete outcome of work produced. Unlike so much we put value on in the world, this outcome is not without question its greatest worth; there is value too in the moment, the feeling, the power that is arguably impossible to reproduce, yet which filters down through creative work, or scientific discovery and the solution to a problem. Its result is creative thinking, and that is in my opinion one of the most valuable life skills one can have, whatever path one chooses to take – not a saleable commodity, but something that with time can lead to inventions of concrete value or increased job potential. Yet this is not the point. The atmosphere, the process of inspiration, is of value in itself – it is one of atmosphere's precious gifts, the way it lives and breathes with us in the active world.

The abstract expressionist painter Willem de Kooning talked, in an interview with David Sylvester, of certain moments as slipping glimpses. 'I am a slipping glimpser,' he said – a poetic phrase that I can't help but like the sound of. The idea of being a slipping glimpser isn't as flaky as it sounds. There is an element of chance, of lack of control, but it is also about something deeper, something born of thousands of years of art history, of memory and experience, of being in the world and letting the world be; of letting go of trying to pin down content; of letting the work be and develop, giving yourself up to and dedicating wholly to the process of your work. He famously struggled to ever see a painting as finished, but de Kooning was no artistic drifter . . .

Like Jefferies on his Wiltshire hillside, sensing the presence of the history in the tumuli, feeling closer to the earth through its presence, his bodily presence, soul-thought and the depths of the past, de Kooning's glimpses suggest that moments of inspiration are not internal, are not part of the cult of the artist as genius, but connected to something larger. They might show through the outcomes of artistic genius, but the moments, the atmosphere of inspiration itself is tapping into something more universal . . . I think of Mendieta's universal life force, earth energy, fluidity – one can only slip through something so powerful and fluid, it is hard to grasp. Atmosphere is ungraspable, but this doesn't mean that in the process of trying we don't, rather than capture, create with its force something inspired, something wonderful.

For de Kooning, content was but a glimpse, a seeing of something, a tiny flash. It was small in the wider context of the work. The wider context that could be seen as the world of atmosphere the inspiration tapped into. But the slipping glimpses are something different. Compared to his American contemporaries such as, say, Mark Rothko, de Kooning was not an atmospheric artist, he strove for emotional responses, yes, particularly in his later landscapes rather than his famous earlier figurative paintings of women, but he was not trying to say something spiritual, to control an atmospheric reaction in his viewer. But when he talks of his artistic process and slipping into a glimpse, I think what he means is that creative moment of grasping inspiration as atmosphere, a fleeting feeling that we fall into and cannot capture and bottle, but are constantly seeking. It is part of this world, yet clearly something else. As de Kooning put it:

> Y'know the real world, this so-called the real world,
> is just something you put up with, like everybody else.
> I'm in my element when I am a little bit out of this
> world – I'm on the beam. Because when I'm falling,
> I'm doing all right; when I'm slipping, I say, hey, this is
> interesting! It's when I'm standing upright that bothers
> me: I'm not doing good; I'm stiff. As a matter of fact,
> I'm really slipping most of the time, into that glimpse.
> I'm like a slipping glimpser.

The real world to be put up with is a real world devoid of atmosphere, of inspiration.

A slipping glimpser, a seeker of inspiration, of atmosphere. You could compare it to the Romantics climbing mountains, Coleridge experimenting with opium, seeking another world of inspiration (though I think it is a false cliché that an artist needs to get out of their head, to distort sensory experience, in order to find inspiration). But what I think is overlooked is that inspiration isn't a concrete thing, a thing that can be caught and contained and consumed for an end product. It is a vital thing, alive and fluid and uncapturable. Whether Emily's 'flash' or de Kooning's 'glimpse' – it is a lifting of the veil between this and another world. It is arguably a conceptual thin place. It is an atmosphere.

However, it is wrong to claim that this is only available to artists or writers, to people defining themselves as creative. I would argue all people are inherently creative, with the ability to use this in ways seen by society as creative – but fear locks it down at a young age. If atmosphere can lead to inspiration, *is* inspiration in our everyday lives – 'the flash', a 'slipping glimpse', 'Joy' or just a feeling of being more alive in place – then it is where the creativity of everyone can lie; not just that of artists and writers, but where we as humans are inherently creative. If the inspired state of mind can be an atmosphere we can all access, then atmosphere is both inherent in our external and internal worlds; it is there for us, it can democratise inspiration, show us that creativity is for all. It encompasses all our living time: it is the feeling of when we are most alive, as well as the elusive feeling of when we dream. It is everywhere, all around us, and it is for everyone. It is atmosphere, captured as a thread from the world beyond the veil, spun and recast as something human.

If we cast this out in to a world where we are also aware of place, of internal and external atmosphere, collaborating together, connecting us and the world, then the future that can so often seem bleak, is hopeful.

I have a game I like to play when out walking, which calms the most anxious of moods. If I ever feel stressed about the modern world, the intrusive technology, the increased detachment under the guise of being more 'connected', work, money, health, loneliness, I pause my walking and really look. A shaft of sunlight falls gently through the cut-out of sky left by some branches. It is the most beautiful thing. I cannot touch it, but it makes the dew on the ground sparkle and then weaves the leaves of the plants on the ground through light and shade. I can see the sun as if it were made of smoke. My hands would move through it like a ghost. It is overwhelming and magical. And it is *real*.

Abstract stress about whether something has happened that I don't understand in my day-to-day life: *not real*. Or rather feels real but is not real in the way that this wonder and beauty of place is.

Bluebell woods appearing like sudden fairy armies of petals. *Real*.

Rain pouring releasing the warm smells of damp earth. *Real*.

The flight of birds. Light making a lake glitter. A mirage on the road. A reflection of sky in a puddle. The feeling of the wind lifting my arms and making my hair dance and slice the air. The buzz of a foreign city. Its energy. Its smells and heat and people talking and moving and the changing buildings, evolving streets – *all real*.

I wonder how much people notice these things. How much atmosphere is being diluted by the virtual reality of modern existence. Digital space does not have an atmosphere, but rather, a designed look – an image that is defined simply as content. Content that you can describe. And if we are constantly staring at our phones, we can miss the atmospheric signs – a danger on a street, a tree branch about to fall . . . The real world can give us so much. The real world can make anxiety, stress, abstract troubles, seem unreal. A true way into wellbeing – a way of being in place where we are well, where the world is well.

In the first half of the twentieth century, there was a wonderful teacher called R. L. Russell in the small Northern Irish village of Tullycrawley who said the supreme gift of the imagination is to see things as they really are . . . Details, life and its magic, the world and its magic: *real*.

The content of the real world is sometimes indescribable. We just feel it. Its atmosphere surrounds and permeates us. Imagination is part of it. The creative, the strange – how we interpret rather than consume the world. It is real. I am so very grateful for that.

Epilogue

A MANIFESTO FOR
BEING IN PLACE

A fluid. A moving thing. A travelling thing.

Through all this I have been travelling. I have been searching. Through place, through art, through story, feeling. Searching for something that is both lost, yet plainly in view. A place that is lost for many, was lost in my past, yet not hard to find; a place within a place; the feeling of a place which, if we can access it, can transform our lives. A place I once had all around me.

When I sat in the rowing boat on the pool when I was nine, I knew what I felt was important, profoundly so, but somehow as I got older, though I was obsessed with feeling intensely in place, exciting atmospheres, new places, noticing beauty . . . somehow I had also lost the ability to truly *be* in those moments like I had as a child. I experienced atmosphere, but my inhabitation of it had changed, was less immersive, was transient, less conscious.

Would the sky fractal into a kaleidoscope, dragonflies like jewels, a trembling in the air all around me now? Would I feel the hills and water as if they were trying to tell me something, were saying hello? I walked out into my garden just now and tried to conjure it. To will that feeling back, or rather the feeling that is unique to my garden.

It is July and the newly fledged swallows loop the loop through the hazy sky. Bees and hoverflies hum. The grasses I leave to grow tall for beetles and spiders sway and this little world held in by my cottage and the extraordinary old brick wall that surrounds the field, is alive around me. It is so blatantly alive, and not just the birds, the insects.

I am almost there . . .

It is not that it has disappeared, this closeness to atmosphere, only that we have lost the intensity, the urge to seek it out; the consciousness to pay attention to its vitality, to make contact with it. Sometimes what we have lost can be found right before us. Like searching for your glasses or keys held in your hand, it is possible to be unable to find something that is right there. And it is there before us; it is waiting.

It has not lost itself. It is a place that is both in the world and in us. The loss in us, where it has been misplaced, is not a physical place but a mental one.

It is both lost and not lost.

To find something, to find atmosphere, we need to know it has been lost, which most of us do not know, so that we consciously begin the search. The seeking in itself, the travelling with and for it, can enable it to burst forth – like in that moment the other summer, when I was in my forest and suddenly felt it again, the sheer luscious scale of it, the sheer impact of its power, its potential, all around me. I was back in that rowing boat on that pool. My body was not something separate to the forest, but in it, part of the whole scale of the world and our places and how we are in them; what we are in them. We are all part of the world. We are all part of its atmosphere. We just don't always notice, or pay attention, to the wealth, the beauty, the fear and force of what is really there. The phenomenon that we help create. The friendship.

As I sit and write and gaze out of my window at the fields and hills of this wild bit of Wiltshire, I wonder how it could have been lost, and why it is so: were we careless? Is it indifference? A case of it never being pointed out to us when growing up that it is there and we can enter it like an imaginary realm? Generation upon generation of not thinking about it . . . Forgotten in plain sight . . . Or was it ever something wholly acknowledged? Except for the odd moment, like the trend in the eighteenth century for seeking out the sublime, it has been a silent partner in our dialogues around landscape. Always there, yet unacknowledged.

My instinct is this is historically different in some cultures – such as Australian aboriginal culture with its extraordinary song lines, its sense of spirit and story in the land. Those who live more closely with the land. I am aware that I cannot help but see this with Western eyes, with English eyes . . . Yet with these eyes, I think I can say that there is a disconnection with how most people these days relate to place. Even if we love somewhere deeply, we are not wholly aware; we observe rather than immerse; we contemplate rather than communicate – passive not active, not collaborative. We don't know how to *be* in place any more. We stumble – consequently sometimes destructively – through.

And we long for that connection. Nearly every thinker I have stumbled on in the writing of this book looked to an older inherent something in the land.

Yet to think of atmosphere as signifying something ancient, connected to being closer to the land, does not mean we should ignore its fluidity and ubiquity, or see it as something old and unchanging, and miss its potential for the future. Atmosphere is everywhere. Brand new places have an atmosphere. Cities. Factories. Wild moorland, the domesticity of a suburban bedroom. A nightclub or gig venue, a country garden. It is not something only present in beauty, in the 'natural'. It is a deep part of a place, but its evolving nature, its movement, its subjectivity and flexibility mean that to find it we have to be more aware; but we don't need some ancient or spiritual knowledge. We just need to open ourselves to the search.

It is lost but not lost. It is ignored, forgotten or not even that. It is simply not usually acknowledged as being part of a place. Part of what makes the places where we all live our lives, where we feel things, make decisions. It is not factored into the equation of how we feel in our daily lives, yet I would argue it influences everything that we do.

We might make the decision to join a moment, caught up in the energy of its collective atmosphere in the streets. We might choose to do so many things because we fall in love with a place. Hate a place. It might give us the energy to change things or lull us into the status quo. We might feel a connection to a place because of something that happened there. We might associate it with storms, with sun; anxiety or joy.

Functioning like a force, a feeling, changing our decisions every day.

And if this is the case then surely harnessing atmosphere is a powerful tool. A tool we can all learn how to use. We can begin by creating, by noticing our everyday world, full of hope of capturing our own feelings, and like inky creatures, freeing them to live on our own tender map.

Atmosphere is a place's personality. Whether or not we seek a scientific or divine, poetic, closed or open-ended explanation, is up to the individual. And this personality of the world – that is not something to be ignored. We are so often passive to atmosphere, yet the more I thought and read and wrote, the more I realised that atmosphere is the opposite of passive – it is vital and collaborative and deeply important. It affects how we behave, how we feel, the creative inspiration we feel, the decisions we make. Nevertheless, for all these vital things, most of the time we don't think about it. If somewhere is creepy or scary, yes; but less so if we just really like somewhere. We sometimes use it practically – such as when walking into a house and following our gut as to whether we want to live there, or choosing not to walk down a certain street. But it is seen as an aside, or – being 'in our gut' – a feeling that is merely within us. Inside us or outside and ignored, the link is gone in this attitude, the significance; yet if we view the relationship as being more symbiotic, it makes more sense; it is a collaboration and it could be how we can communicate with the world around us, how it moves with us through our lives. This makes it foreground, not background; makes it profound, makes it political.

Dismissing atmosphere as a practical 'in our gut' feeling still opens the way for questions: if it is the product of our subconscious, this doesn't mean it is not vitally communicating with us. It brings up both neuroscience and poetry, psychology and creativity. This vitality is, well, vitally important. From how we behave, to mass atmospheres such as political rallies – political in how we choose to live our lives; political in terms of the climate crisis and how the earth might communicate with us; political in how we treat the natural world, move through countryside, plan our cities, treat our neighbourhoods; political in what we create, what mark we leave physically and mentally, creatively as human beings. It is everywhere and therefore in everything. To dismiss it as background is akin to dismissing the subconscious, to close ourselves off to the depths of the world, its layers which could be as numerous as those of our brains, of consciousness itself.

I began to wonder if we all have a responsibility to be aware of atmosphere, to open ourselves to it, to let it flow through our bodies and use it to see if we can make a difference.

As humans we are all biased towards the things we care about. The best way to create change, to actively change rather than ruminate about something, is to tap into whatever means something to people. And the world means something to all of us – it can't not. All the same, there is a disconnect – individual lives, consumerism and real practical need make us sometimes forget the impact of our behaviour. It's why climate change is denied by some – it doesn't seem real, yet it is as real as the sun shining through branches. If we stop and notice the wider world, if we scale up the noticing of detail, the extraordinary transformative power of the real, of the feelings of place as we move through them, of the world, then just maybe we can find a way in to realising the importance of how we live on this planet. That the impact of our behaviour is real.

Atmosphere in the background, ignored, overlooked, is a missed opportunity. If atmosphere is a creative dialogue, the world communicating with us and a way in to appreciating how it feels to truly be in the world, then being aware of it and how it affects us and our behaviour could be key to our changing for the better. And in this noticing, we could see an enrichment in our own lives – for there is a benefit to all from living in harmony with the world, but also a true pleasure in noticing the beauty, the life, the strangeness. Of leaving behind stressful jobs and worries and noticing the richness around you. When my family collapsed and my work had dried up and the warning signs suggested that things were going to get worse, walking in my woods saved me. Noticing the beauty, a bird, a deer.

But this doesn't just have to be a 'nature cure' (I mean something more reciprocal and dynamic than that) and cities and their lives can have the same benefit as countryside when their details and atmospheres are noticed. If we notice people and places, how a place feels to be in, then we care more and things change, or not, whichever is better. Preserve or revolutionise . . .

Atmosphere is a feeling we can ask, tap into and see how it responds. How our behaviour and changes make the places we inhabit feel. We inhabit atmosphere. We inhabit the world.

Atmosphere is intrinsically political, in that it is naturally engaged with everything in the world. It is there to help us make things better, to live in a world that is open for everyone, with support and meaning. It is also there to communicate with us when things are not going so well. When there is a warning. There is, for example, the natural power of an unseasonable storm, warning of our changing climate. But there are also more human, in-the-moment clues – like how a protest march that risks tipping into a riot will first change in atmosphere, or how a problem with someone can change the atmosphere in a room.

There is a dark side. When I look back to the previously unthinkable storming of the Capitol Hill in Washington DC, I do not think the event would have been possible without the sinister implications of people getting swept up in an atmosphere without noticing it. Going along with the crowd, behaving in ways they never usually would, justifying something clearly wrong. Similarly, mass hysteria, mass suicide and cults would all be impossible without the power of atmosphere, and also impossible if people truly acknowledged why they might be going along with things, following a feeling, charisma, getting caught up in the moment at the end of its terrifying logic.

Regimes control the atmosphere with displays of power: just think of Nazi rallies and the mass hysteria of the cult of personality that Hitler created. Think of military marches in dictatorships today. Think of the fear of surveillance culture, the threat of exile ... The Stasi in East Germany listening in, the ominous presence of distant Siberian gulags under Stalin. There is a presence to these threats. Atmosphere is not immune to human goings on. To the power of suggestion, pomp, pageantry, eerie silence, a feeling of being watched ...

Yet this can also work for good – we might get caught up in a movement for positive change, human rights and making the world a better place. The feeling of others connected to a moment can awaken us to how we have been metaphorically sleepwalking through our own lives. This can be listening to the atmosphere of people coming together; it can also be listening to the feeling of the world.

It is important to keep aware of this – to not let it slip. I remember as a teenager in the early nineties being obsessed with saving the rainforest, endangered animals, the hole in the ozone layer, as so many people were. But then getting caught up in other things, and while we still cared, the environment seemed to slip from common consciousness until a reawakening in the last few years, almost too late. Women in the 1900s and the 1970s did so much for women's rights; then these issues drifted from consciousness once again.

We need to remember. We need to communicate. We need to be in tune with atmosphere. The world, if we listen, is telling us something. We each bring our own rich map of tenderness to it. If we listen to the girls who embroidered mountains, the women who travelled to escape, to learn, the women who put the feelings of their heroines in place at the fore, and if we put the story of place at the fore, then the world might just be a little better.

To work with atmosphere, with this strange, beautiful and undefinable world, is to hope.

Bibliography

Ackerman, Diane, *A Natural History of the Senses* (Vintage, London, 1995).

Alain-Fournier, *Le Grand Meaulnes*, tr. Frank Davison (Penguin, London, 1966).

Bachelard, Gaston, *The Poetics of Space*, tr. M. Jolas (first published by Presses Universitaires de France, 1958; Beacon Press, Boston, 1994).

Banham, Reyner, 'Autopia' in *Los Angeles: The Architecture of Four Ecologies* (Allen Lane, London, 1971).

Barr, Pat, *A Curious Life for a Lady: The Story of Isabella Bird* (Penguin, London, 1985).

Blocker, Jane, *Where is Ana Mendieta?* (Duke University Press, Durham NC, 1999).

Bruno, Giuliana, *Atlas of Emotion: Journeys in Art, Architecture and Film* (Verso, London, 2002).

Calvino, Italo, *Invisible Cities*, tr. William Weaver (first published by Giulio Einaudi, 1972; Vintage Classics, London, 1997).

Debord, Guy, *The Society of the Spectacle*, tr. Donald Nicholson-Smith (first published by Buchet-Chastel, 1967; Zone Books, New York, 1995).

Fermor, Patrick Leigh, *The Broken Road: From the Iron Gates to Mount Athos* (John Murray, London, 2014).

Gilpin, William, *Forest Scenery Vol II* (Fraser & Co., Edinburgh, 1834).

Goudge, Elizabeth, 'West Country Magic', *The Horn Book Magazine* (Boston, 1947).

—, *The Little White Horse* (Knight Books, London, 1969).

—, *A City of Bells* (Hodder & Stoughton, London, 2017).

Greenhalgh, Paul, *Fair World: A History of World's Fairs and Expositions, from London to Shanghai 1851–2010* (Papadakis, Winterbourne, 2011).

Hollis, Edward, *The Secret Life of Buildings* (Portobello Books, London, 2009).

Jacobs, Jane, *The Death and Life of Great American Cities* (Penguin, London, 1994).

Jefferies, Richard, *The Story of My Heart* (first published 1883; Longmans, Green & Co, London, pocket edition, 1907).

Lewis, C. S., *The Magician's Nephew* (first published by Bodley Head, 1955; Harper Collins, London, 2009).

—, *Surprised by Joy* (first published by Geoffrey Bles, 1955; William Collins, London, 2012).

Macaulay, Rose, *The World My Wilderness* (The Book Club Edition, n.d.)

McGlashan, Alan, *The Savage and Beautiful Country* (Chatto & Windus, London, 1966).

Montgomery, L. M., *The Alpine Path: the Story of My Career* (first published 1917; Fitzhenry & Whiteside Ltd, Toronto, 2001).

—, *Anne of Green Gables* (first published by Harrap & Co Ltd, 1925; Puffin, London, 1977).

—, *Emily of New Moon* (first published by Harrap & Co Ltd, 1928; Puffin, London, 1990).

Morris, Jan, *Venice* (Faber & Faber, London, 1960, revised 1993).

Morris, Mary (ed.), *The Virago Book of Women Travellers* (Virago, London, 1996).

Newhall Follett, Barbara, *The House Without Windows* (first published by Alfred A. Knopf, 1927; Hamish Hamilton, London, 2019).

Pamuk, Orhan, *Istanbul: Memories of a City*, tr. Maureen Freely (Faber & Faber, London, 2005).

Rawlins, Christine, *Beyond the Snow: the Life and Faith of Elizabeth Goudge* (WestBow Press, Bloomington IN, 2015).

Seth, Anil, *Being You: a New Science of Consciousness* (Faber & Faber, London, 2021).

BIBLIOGRAPHY

Shepherd, Nan, *The Living Mountain* (first published by Aberdeen University Press, 1977; Canongate, Edinburgh, 2011).

Vidler, Anthony, *The Architectural Uncanny: Essays in the Modern Unhomely* (MIT, Cambridge MA, 1992).

Welty, Eudora, *Some Notes on River Country* (University Press of Mississippi, Jackson MS, 2003).

Winnicott, D. W., *Playing and Reality* (first published 1971; Routledge, London, 2005).

Yard, Sally, *Willem de Kooning: Works, Writing, Interviews* (Ediciones Poligrafa, Barcelona, 2007).

Zacarias, Gabriel and Hemmens, Alastair (eds.), *The Situationist International: A Critical Handbook* (Pluto Press, London, 2020).

Permissions

Text

ix   The author has made every attempt to ascertain and contact the rights holder of *The Savage and Beautiful Country* by Alan McGlashan. Please contact the publishers direct with any comments or corrections: info@septemberpublishing.org.

121   Excerpt from *Some Notes on River Country* by Eudora Welty reprinted by permission of Welty LLC.

126–127   Excerpt from *The World My Wilderness* by Rose Macaulay. Copyright © The Estate of Rose Macaulay 1958. Reproduced with permission of the Licensor through PLSclear.

229   'West Country Magic' by Elizabeth Goudge, published in *The Horn Book Magazine*, reproduced by permission of David Higham Associates.

Picture

9   *Carte de Tendre* (*Map of Tender*) by Madeleine de Scudery, Cornell University – PJ Mode Collection of Persuasive Cartography.

28   Map samplers reproduced by kind permission of the Wells & Mendip Museum.

All other photos supplied by the author.

Acknowledgements

This book has been a long time in the planning and making and I couldn't have done it without the support and advice of my publisher Hannah MacDonald, who believed in it when I was waffling for hours about atmosphere and the landscape personalities of my travels without a clear idea of the end book. Also Sam Boyce for helping when I was stuck, and Charlotte and the wider September Publishing team who are a brilliant bunch. I am extremely grateful to them and to my lovely thoughtful agent, Jon Curzon, who goes above and beyond.

I wrote this book during an extraordinary hard time. I could not have managed without Hannah Little, to whom this book is dedicated, (and her husband Martin and the kids for putting up with me in their home for so long – endless patience!), as well as Chandra Haabjoern and Astrid Johnston. I can never thank you all enough.

Thanks also to other friends and acquaintances old and new who knowing it or not have helped somehow or cheered me up hugely: my poetry partner in crime, Ana Seferovic, Emily Hammond, Alice Stevenson, Jodi Auld, Luminara Star, Lucy Large, Amber Hitchman, Emily Bick, Travis Elborough, the Belgrade magic ladies that are Natalija Simovic and Mila the magnificent (Joe has made their debut!), Maka Bubashvili, Teo Natsvlishvili and all the Tbilisi gang, Hazel Plowman, Crispian Cook, Bridget Telfer, Sebastian Seymour, Sue Bishop, Kate Moore and the lovely ladies in the village, Richard Williams, who kindled my love of urban theory way back in my Edinburgh University days, and Sam Roberts, cat rescuer extraordinaire.